Buffalo Inc.

Buffalo Inc.

American Indians and Economic Development

SEBASTIAN FELIX BRAUN

UNIVERSITY OF OKLAHOMA PRESS : NORMAN

Library of Congress Cataloging-in-Publication Data

Braun, Sebastian.
    Buffalo Inc. : American Indians and economic development / Sebastian
Felix Braun.
        p.   cm.
    Includes bibliographical references and index.
    ISBN 978-0-8061-3904-3 (hardcover : alk. paper)   1. Cheyenne River
Indian Reservation (S.D.)   2. Cheyenne Indians—Economic conditions.
3. Pte Hca Ka, Inc.—Management.   4. Bison farming—South Dakota—
Cheyenne River Indian Reservation—Management.   5. Consumer
cooperatives—South Dakota—Cheyenne River Indian Reservation—
Management.   6. South Dakota—Cheyenne River Indian Reservation—
Economic conditions.   I. Title.
    E99.C53B73   2008
    978.3'5—dc22
                                                                    2007028660

Contents

Illustrations

Photographs

All photographs were taken by the author.

Maps

Tables

Acknowledgments

My thanks are due first and foremost to the people on Cheyenne River Sioux Reservation for their hospitality, their trust, and their friendship. Special thanks to Fred DuBray, Dennis Rousseau, Willetta Ducheneaux, Tim Pickner, Albert Arpan, Chris Arpan, and Michael Collins. Thanks also to James Garrett; Henry Ducheneaux; Christine, John, and Lisa Ducheneaux; Linda LeBeau; Denise LeBeau and the kids; everybody from the LeBeau *tiyospaye* of Blackfoot; Dana and Wynema Dupris; Roger Lawrence; Bevin Circle Eagle and all the wardens from Game, Fish, and Parks; Zach Ducheneaux; Stewart Sarkozy-Banoczy; and everybody else—thank you with all my heart.

Judy Wood from the Lower Brule Community College and all the helpful county seat librarians all over the plains, but especially the one in Timber Lake, deserve my gratitude for all their help. Thanks also to the countless people who discussed buffalo, sheep, horses, cattle, grass, and the plains with me from Indiana to Montana.

Thank you to my family, especially my mother, Dorothee Steinle, who always kept faith in my judgments no matter how scatterbrained they were at the time and who let me go my own way and never tried to change me. Thanks also for her financial support. Growing up with the knowledge that I could always pack up my tent and come home was invaluable, as was the freedom to go to the ends of the world without parental objections.

I need to give thanks to the Swiss National Fund for Science for honoring me with a generous grant that allowed me to conduct the fieldwork for this study. I also need to acknowledge the Josephine De Karman Fellowships Fund for a writing grant and the David C. Skomp Fellowship Fund that made the fieldwork possible with two pre-dissertation grants. Finally, the Indian Studies department at the University of North Dakota helped out with travel money.

Thank you to Raymond J. DeMallie, Richard Wilk, and Henry Glassie at Indiana University. Raymond DeMallie continues to teach me how to be an anthropologist, how to handle knowledge, and how to be *ikce wicasa*, while lending me his support in many ways. Richard Wilk has gone out of his way to lend me continuous support and advice over the years. Henry Glassie introduced me to the writings of James Agee and thus opened a new window on the world (see Glassie 2006:7).

Many thanks are also due to Birgit Hans at the University of North Dakota for making me submit the manuscript and supporting my work on it, as well as Liz Harris Behling for discussions about writing, style, and accuracy.

Thank you to Alessandra Jacobi Tamulevich, Jay Dew, and Emmy Ezzell at the University of Oklahoma Press, the two anonymous reviewers, and Paula Wagoner, whose patience, critical advice, and support made this text much better. Most of the editorial work was done, however, by Claudia Frigo, my assigned copyeditor. All errors and shortcomings are mine alone.

Among the many others who have influenced my thoughts and supported the writing of this text are Ann Reed, who also bore the brunt of my mood swings and mental and physical absences, Candice Lowe, Christina Burke, Douglas Parks, and Matz Bieri. Thank you!

Buffalo Inc.

Introduction

I think back and I cry for the glory of land which now becomes only a
dream.

Buell Anakak from *Magic Maker*

Near Swiftbird, May 21, 2002

It was a warm May day on the Cheyenne River Sioux Reservation. Soon, the summer heat would arrive. On such a nice day, miles and miles of the Missouri River valley are visible from vantage points on the bluffs, the long, yellow grasses waving in the wind. In contrast to the scenes from one of Karl Bodmer's paintings though, there is no longer the meandering river lined with sandbanks and trees or the deer and birds of all colors and sizes. Instead, the cobalt blue waters of Lake Oahe now fill the valley. The lake provides an eerie contrast, a mirror for the endless skies, a reflection that underlines the starkness of the landscape. On this day, the fierce, gusty winds kicked up so much dust, one could hardly see for a mile. This dust came not only from the dried-up pastures but also from the barren lake shore. Years of drought had taken its toll on the lake's water level, and the grasses barely grew.

Sitting in pickup trucks, the wardens from the tribal Game, Fish, and Parks Department (GFPD) and I were not there to admire the scenery. We were there to do what people in Bodmer's time had done—perhaps at that very spot. We were there to hunt buffalo. The herd, led by the older cows, fled on our approach down the bluffs to the lake. We were waiting for them to calm down.

After a while, we made our way along the shoreline and crept around the bison herd. We pushed the animals toward a ravine and forced the stragglers back into the herd. On the opposite side of the herd, others, whom we could not see, crashed through the sparse bushes, intercepted calves and young bulls, and channeled the herd. When we topped the ridgeline, we could follow the movement of the bison uphill with our eyes.

On the higher slopes of a bluff, the designated shooter positioned himself. The buffalo made their way up the ravine—all four hundred of them. I could not help but think of a successful bison drive in the past, almost like the scene unfolding before my eyes.

But these buffalo were not being herded into a corral or toward a cliff. These buffalo were moving toward a shooter in an old blue Chevy pickup with an old-fashioned camping shell; the pushers worked from two white Ford Rangers. In the background, the blue tractor with its front loader out to shovel up the dead animal and carry it back to the slaughtering plant came trudging across the pasture. There was nothing romantic about this hunt. The historical hunts probably were not romantic either: they were sweaty and dangerous. What was taking place now was similar to the past in some ways. It was the same act and the same strategy of taking an animal's life for the welfare of the people; there was the same excitement of the hunt, the same cooperative effort, and the same necessity for the hunt to be successful.

The bison kept walking toward the distant truck, and the truck kept moving closer to intercept the bison, until the animals were in range. One of the young bulls presented himself as a target and was shot. The herd's steady movement was suddenly disrupted. Then, over the radio, came the confirmation, and we could see the blue truck close in on the dead animal. The truck slowly pushed away the dead buffalo's curious peers, claiming what was his.

We converged on the spot where the buffalo lay. He was a young bull, lying on his side, with all four legs stretched out in front of him. A small puddle of blood had formed on his side but was coagulating quickly. Some of the wardens nudged the bull with their boots and made some remarks about his size. The more traditional wardens grew very quiet. However, eventually, we did what was necessary. One of the wardens broke open a cigarette and rubbed some tobacco into the bull's nostrils, and we followed with a prayer.

The tractor pulled up to haul the bull back to the slaughtering facility. The bull was still warm; it had run up an incline just ten minutes ago. Small steam clouds rose from his nostrils even though it was not winter. We hooked him to the front loader with chains, and the tractor lifted him up. Although I was ahead in one of the Rangers, I knew what would happen. Usually on the ride back on the tractor, one could see the dead buffalo exhale one last time, the last breath of air escaping his body. It always seemed to me that finally, the buffalo had acknowledged his sacrifice.

The situation of Native communities in the United States has received a lot of attention over the years. Many people—scholars, activists, elders, visitors, businessmen, charlatans, and others—have contemplated the consequences of historic and contemporary policies, cultural and social organizations, colonization, religions, and a host of other, mostly relevant topics. This book is simply an attempt to bear witness to events that unfolded in one particular community, the Cheyenne River Sioux Reservation in South Dakota from around 1990 to 2006. It gives an account of what can happen when a community decides to take its economic, cultural, and ecological future in its own hands and to control and manage what is sometimes called "development." Specifically, I look at the Cheyenne River Sioux tribe's efforts to build a tribally owned and operated buffalo operation.

On another level, however, that is not what this study is really about. Sidney Mintz notes that his "book on sugar is not really *about* food—it is about the rise of capitalism. Sugar (sucrose) was simply the vehicle that served as an illustrative instance of that process, a long thread in the social and economic fabric of Western history" (2003:4–5). Similarly, this work is not really about buffalo, but they serve as the vehicle to illustrate certain aspects of contemporary Lakota culture and society and to present a model of indigenous people's efforts to gain control over their futures. The bison also serve as a vehicle, therefore, to look into issues of sustainability, economic development, sovereignty, ecology, health, representation of history, and not the least of all, the intersection of all these complex concepts: place. This is not a book about *place* in the strict sense but as Timothy Beatley says (2004:3), "[a]t the heart of this book is the belief that reconnecting to people and landscapes at the local level and having a better understanding of the built and natural surroundings in which we live will result in better, more enjoyable, healthier, and more fulfilling lives. Meaningful lives require unique and particular places."

Although bison have always been present on American Indian reservations, since the early 1990s, reservations in the United States have been taking a more focused approach to buffalo. Communities have consciously established bison herds to restitute economic, ecological, political, cultural, social, and physical health. This sense of restitution originated in the symbolic importance of the animals to the communities, especially on the plains. I look at how these initiatives are playing out roughly ten years after their inception. I do this against the background of the various aspects in which buffalo have come to importance and by focusing on one tribal buffalo-raising operation, *Pte Hca Ka*, Inc., of the Cheyenne River Sioux tribe in South Dakota.

The Cheyenne River Sioux Reservation was the logical focal point for my study for several reasons, some of which became clear to me only during my fieldwork. Pte Hca Ka, Inc., the tribal buffalo operation, had been a model operation for tribal buffalo herds for several years. Fred DuBray, the director of Pte Hca Ka since 1991, who had in essence built the program, was also one of the founders of the InterTribal Bison Cooperative (ITBC), a network of tribal buffalo operations that spans most of the United States. His hopes were not only to build a buffalo operation that would provide desperately needed jobs on the reservation but also to revive, through the buffalo, ecological, dietary, and cultural aspects of the traditional society that had guided the Lakota well before reservation life and would again guide them well in their contemporary situation. When I started my fieldwork, Michael Collins was running a buffalo management program at the tribal college in Eagle Butte, then Si Tanka College. This study program, originally developed by Jim Garrett, stressed not only the business aspects of a buffalo operation but also the past and contemporary importance of the buffalo for Lakota culture and spirituality. In accordance with this approach, which is a philosophy that respects the buffalo as a relative, Pte Hca Ka also operated the world's only mobile buffalo slaughter and processing unit, which was modeled on such units used by reindeer herders in Sweden.

In short, what a visitor could see on Cheyenne River in summer 2000 was the cutting edge of tribal bison operations, a vision to bring traditions, spiritual knowledge, economics, and ecology together and find a unique way to solve some of the problems that reservations face. It made a lot of sense to me, and I wanted to write this story: A story of innovative visions transformed into reality; a story of global resources coming together in one of the poorest regions of the northern plains to help a truly local and holistic restoration project. Above all, I wanted to write about positive results coming from an American Indian reservation. As I will explain, many things have since changed at Pte Hca Ka. Reservations are not cut off from the rest of the country or the world, and many of the same pressures that apply to outside situations are felt on the reservations. But this is still a positive story, and I sincerely hope it will continue to be one well into the future.

I have come to hold a certain approach to development, which departs from the importance of particular cultures as symbolic structures and holds that economics are intimately tied to this globally relative but locally absolute cultural system and to the political system in which all of these ongoing processes take place. In other words, I hold that an answer to the manifold problems on plains reservations—and other areas, whether indigenous or not, that face similar issues—cannot be economic alone but must be holistic, which includes ecological, political, cultural, and spiritual restoration. I began this study in absolute agreement with George Tinker (2004:4):

> As Indian people begin to identify the social dysfunction of Indian communities, it is becoming clearer to us that the healing of Indian communities is Indian business, to be conducted by Indian people and Indian community organizations in a way that is consistent with Indian culture and values.

In this vein, I was attracted to tribal bison herds exactly because the community activists who built them saw the reintroduction of buffalo herds as an attempt to liberate American Indian nations from the spiritual, economic, political, and social bounds that kept them disenfranchised. It is important to understand in this context that the reasons to rely on buffalo as the means to accomplish this were not exclusively economic: buffalo were chosen because they are traditionally seen as relatives of the Lakota and other plains societies, and the fates of people and animals are seen to be intimately linked—not in a romanticized New Age way, but in a real, genocidal politics kind of way.

Here was a chance, then, to provide an account of a project that approached concerns of the well-being of disenfranchised and colonized people from—as I am still convinced any such project should—perhaps first and foremost an approach that was embedded in liberation theology. Because of this emphasis on a holistic approach, which included a specific cultural approach, I maintain that the tribal bison operation that I came to see in the beginning of my fieldwork was an example of successful sustainable development. Some critics think that the term sustainable development "is an oxymoron" (Boff 1997:67; see also Churchill 1997:348; Tinker 2004:6). However, I think it is possible to have truly sustainable development as long as both elements of the term are seen as predominantly cultural. I come back to this point toward the end of this text.

Although the return of the buffalo to the reservation might have started as an act of liberation theology, not all people agreed with this approach. Many residents on plains reservations have no special cultural connection to buffalo anymore, and the symbolic aspects of the project were therefore of little importance to them. The people of this community—like the people of any community—do not speak with one voice, and they have different concerns and opinions. All of these voices, however, are extremely important because they all express the opinion of this community, and none can simply be dismissed. I try to present the various voices because they are all concerned with perpetuating their culture and their identity in the contemporary context. I hold that those who argue for the importance of a primarily economic development agenda and those who have reached economic success are not "quislings," "who have sold out their communities in order to work the system for personal gain, financially, and politically" (Tinker 2004:9, 10). In fact, I think it would be extremely detrimental to make such a judgment and dismiss these voices.

I have said that this is a positive account, and some readers, shocked by apparent conflicts (see Davis 2000:92) or left without a definite closure or solution to the problems apparent in the communities, will be confused as to why such optimism would be warranted. Let me note that my optimism comes from my understanding of these communities as local, participatory societies, and the temporary struggles of buffalo projects, such as Pte Hca Ka, as an expression of this.

Truly local cultures are often the most democratic ones. I do not wish to romanticize peasant societies or other traditional communities because conflict often brews in them. However, this is not grounds to condemn them either: Conflict is normal. I find these communities truly democratic exactly because they allow, and to a certain amount expect, conflict. Radical ideas can be voiced without fear because people accept that there will be a process of working out compromises and that this process is always ongoing. This book follows one of these processes, namely the debate over how best to integrate a society that holds certain particular cultural values into national and global economic and political contexts. This debate is not one that follows romantic notions of indigenous uniformity, and it will disappoint readers who expect that. However, historicity and complexity are taken to be self-evident in nonindigenous societies and cultures, and I would defend the same structures of conflict over resources and power in my own community as vital signs of a complex and valuable democratic tradition. We need to regard social and political debates and even conflicts not as necessarily negative patterns but as matters of course in all vibrant communities.

As Leif Vaage points out in a slightly different context, the work of cultural interpretation is "understood and conducted as one of the many social activities that either help to construct or serve to diminish the local life of particular human communities" (1997:6). What anthropologists do, hopefully, is to look at things from different perspectives. We take information and situate it in a context that is relevant to it, or sometimes we just put it into a context that is interesting. Most of the time, we alienate the subject from its world and situate it in a context that makes it come into our world. In rare instances, we do a good job; we add something to the understanding of our subject and maybe even of the world at large. If this account fails to contribute to an understanding of the world, I do hope that it may in some way help to construct the life of this community or at the least not serve to diminish it. I want to make clear here that I am not trying to blame anybody. I do understand why the different actors in this account felt compelled to act as they did, and I recognize that they all felt they had good reasons to do so.

I am not Lakota, and I do not want to pretend in any way to speak for the Lakota. Neither do I think that my own economic, political, or spiritual preferences have any relation to Lakota culture. I have no assumption that I could, "through some innate cultural or racial superiority, [have] the ability to perceive and master the essential beliefs, values, and emotions of persons from Native American communities" (Silko in Russell 1993:161). Nor do I need to look for my own life or my own love of the earth in other peoples' traditions (Hogan in Russell 1993:161–62). There are individuals who have a need to do that, perhaps those who feel that their own cultures cannot offer them satisfying answers to fundamental questions because they perceive, or are led to perceive, their own cultures as being not only alienated from their environment but even opposed to it. From my own perspective, there are large parts of Europe where people have lived in close connection with their land from "time immemorial." My people have their own traditions, rituals, and ceremonies and have been performing them for centuries. Most of them can be traced to the syncretism that still underlies much of the Catholic beliefs in the rural regions of my home. European peasants have come, in this first industrial and then postindustrial world, to be overlooked, but they are still there. They have a lot in common with other nonindustrial indigenous peoples who have lived in and with the land for as long as they can remember and whose cultures have to be defended against the impact of the postmodern centers. This does not mean that I am in some sort of spiritual relationship with the oppressed people of the world. My people are still very much privileged. What I would like to make clear is that I am grounded in my people's own way of life and traditions and have no motivations to look for salvation in others' cosmologies.

The real experts on the things anthropologists write about are the people we work with, the people we bother. In a peripheral sense, I have been a part of the Lakota community but at the same time am not. I hope to have gained some insight into what living within a Lakota community is like; although I only lived on Cheyenne River for a short period of time, people shared their lives with me, sometimes intensely. I do not know from experience what being Lakota means, but I think I do know some things about it. I do not know more about current Lakota culture than the people who shared their ways with me. In short, this text is not about teaching people "how Lakota are," or how anybody is supposed to be. It is my point of view, my testimony, about what I experienced and learned. As Lévi-Strauss says (1992:410–15), Buddhist meditation and Marxism lead to the same realization of holistic truth. Both are fundamentally based on practice, and I see anthropology as a middle ground between them. If anthropology is a method, as many in the discipline have said, it is based on practice, but its practice is the dialectic between, not the embracing of, either meditation or deconstruction.

Good science does not follow dogmatic guidelines; it follows a desire to explore and explain the world. The world, however, is made up of paradoxes, of which human life is one of the greatest. Science, then, has to take into account and incorporate these paradoxes, and if it explains them away, it is not good science but a cover-up. There is a difference between anthropology and travel writing and between writing science and writing a novel. The difference is that I ask you to trust me, even when I am describing my personal experience. I am not describing things the way they could have been, but the way they appeared to me, the way I understood them: The way they were. Although they might have been different for other people because there are many realities out there, I do not therefore accept the argument that there is no reality. We simply have to understand the limitations of what "reality" means. That understanding might not be a limitation at all, but rather an opportunity.

My own cultural and political values influence this account, and I do not think it would be possible to write anything that would not be influenced by them. This does not mean that the account is bad science, wrong, false, inherently skewed, or deceitful witnessing of what happened. An anthropologist who does not know or is not rooted in his or her own culture, and is therefore paradoxically always influenced by this knowledge, cannot understand other cultures. As long as we know that this influence is there and can for that reason identify the areas in which it might lead to misunderstandings, we are able to try to be respectful of others. Colonized people, of course, might have learned long ago that such an optimistic perspective is utterly displaced and indicative of well-meaning but foolish "Westerners." However it has been ingrained in my cultural psyche (if such a thing exists) that compromise based on cultural understanding is not only possible but necessary and that different cultures can live together peacefully and be respectful to one another.

Ethnologists have to ask themselves why they, as privileged people, think they have the right to describe underprivileged people—and we are always privileged, even if we "study up," simply because we are the ones who describe, and they are the ones described. All anthropologists must answer that question for themselves. My own attempts can be seen in this account. It is through the generosity of the people I have worked with that they have let me ask this question of myself and have not themselves put it to me.

I grew up in a small town in Switzerland, not far from a major city, where I watched the sows being butchered, the cows being milked, and the town rapidly transforming to a suburban space. I later spent my vacations in remote locations in Scotland and North America, traveling with my tent. Mountain biking and backcountry skiing were my passions, not so much for the sport as for the experience of nature. The sacredness of places was never an empty concept for me; this came not from a romantic New Age or Deep Ecology context but from the real and direct understanding that it is but for the mercy of some unknowable forces that we are allowed to return from certain places.

I first came to Cheyenne River Sioux Reservation in June 2000 and camped on and near the reservation for two months, getting to know people and the buffalo operation. Michael Collins gave me invaluable support and sent me to the Tatanka Oyate conference, held that year at Lower Brule Reservation. He also opened a lot of doors for me, allowing me to witness things I otherwise would not have experienced and gave me the moral support to continue on this journey. Fred DuBray and Willetta Ducheneaux helped familiarize me with the buffalo operation and let me go out with the fencing crew. Wynema and Dana Dupris invited me to stay with them for the Iron Lightning Powwow that year. Many other people allowed me insights into their own lives and reservation life; acts of generosity that still leave me speechless with thankfulness and humility. I came back to visit Pte

Hca Ka for a few days in April of 2001, finding that winter can linger for a long time on the northern plains.

My fieldwork began in earnest in late August 2001. At first, I lived in a duplex behind the old Swiftbird Day School, which was at that time the offices of Pte Hca Ka. The duplex had no running water, no refrigerator, and no stove. After about two weeks and after I had proven my fortitude, people took real pity on me. I began to rent the old office, a trailer next to the mobile slaughtering unit on US 212, where I lived for the rest of my stay with Pte Hca Ka, even after the office was moved back into the trailer in November. I stayed on Cheyenne River for almost a year, with trips to other reservations on the northern plains, the bison auction at Custer State Park, the buffalo herds there and in Yellowstone National Park, and several other points of interest for my research, including local bison auctions, the National Bison Museum in Jamestown, North Dakota, and a symposium in Wyoming. During this whole year, through all the difficulties that ensued, I experienced the warmth of support and friendship from the people on Cheyenne River.

Obviously, people have more important things to do than talk with or think about anthropologists, but if one shows respect, they will consider both. It might seem odd, but my experiences in various fieldwork situations have convinced me that to be a good ethnologist, one should not ask too many questions. I tried to explain to people what I was trying to do, but I did not conduct formal interviews with a tape recorder. Respect is the method of ethnology, but it cannot just be a method. One's hosts will sense sincerity or the lack of it. After some time, when people came to trust me in a more personal manner as somebody who respected their ways of life, the exact purpose of my stay came to be less important. What seemed to matter—for opening up avenues of conversation and informal interviews—was not a trust in my professional goals but a trust in my personal integrity. I expressed my interests, and people decided what, if anything, they wanted to tell me. Other than that, I simply tried to be as helpful as I could. In the meantime, people were nice enough to let me pretend that I was not in their way. Tim Pickner, Albert (Swap) Arpan, and Chris Arpan took me along to fix fences; chase, kill, and gut buffalo; hunt deer; collect wood; and grind and package meat. The LeBeau tiyospaye invited me to Blackfoot for Thanksgiving and Christmas. Henry and Willetta Ducheneaux, Tim Pickner, and Denise LeBeau and their families invited me to their houses, and others came to talk with me, had me play pool, and took me places. The game wardens came to drink coffee, warm up, and chat.

I have since continued to talk with people on Cheyenne River and from outside the area. I need to especially mention eye-opening conversations on the practice and philosophy of tribal resource management and on Pte Hca Ka with Dennis Rousseau, the director of the GFPD, Michael Collins of United Tribes Technical College, and James Garrett, of Cankdeska Cikana Community College.

Although I am aware that the American bison is not a "buffalo" in the strict sense of the term—water buffalo or African buffalo are relatives of the bison but not very close ones—I use the terms "buffalo" and "bison" inter-changeably throughout this study. There is a long tradition of the term being applied to the North American animal, and although it might not be the scientifically correct name, probably more people say buffalo than bison. It is also, perhaps, the culturally correct term. As Tim Pickner told me once, "'bison' is the white man's term, 'buffalo' is what they are called."

The public interest for *Bison bison* is rising, and so are the numbers of publications on buffalo. Most of these books are historical, dealing with the slaughter of the buffalo that brought them to the brink of extinction, and the subsequent recovery of the species. It is often overlooked, however, that a tradition of writing on the buffalo has existed at least since the latter part of the nineteenth century (Allen 1876; Hornaday 2002). One can find the extensive bibliography in Roe's meticulous and still seminal study (1951). In his footsteps followed McHugh (1972), Dary (1989) and Haines (1995), all trying to paint a comprehensive picture of the history of the North American buffalo, including biological and ecological information. Rorabacher (1970) concentrated specifically on the state of the contemporary buffalo and is in that regard an exception. Sandoz (1954), on the other hand, set the trend in writing not so much the story of the buffalo as the story of the buffalo hunters.

Since the 1980s, a number of well-illustrated, popular books on buffalo have been published. There has also been a renewed interest in the history of the buffalo, including revisionist perspectives on the near extinction in the buffalo hunts (e.g., Isenberg 2001). In the context of what some perceive to be an agricultural crisis on the Great Plains and following modern ecological problems and movements, there is also a renewed interest in the fate of the region as such. The buffalo have become one of the symbolic points of focus in this discussion. The concept of the "Buffalo Commons" (Popper and Popper 1987) has spawned much response and discussion, both directly related to buffalo (Callenbach 1996; Matthews 1992), and indirectly (Licht 1997), and it has also inspired a novel (Wheeler 1998). The controversy over the killing of Yellowstone buffalo in Montana (Christofferson 2004; Rudner 2000), the conservation of the species as such (Berger and Cunningham 1994), or the birth of white buffalo calves (Pickering 1997) have become subjects of interest in their own right. The growing "Buffalo Industry" has also sparked books on buffalo management (American Bison Association [ABA] 1993; National Buffalo Association [NBA] 1990) and first-hand literary accounts (O'Brien 2001).

Rorabacher (1970) explains the motivation behind his classical study of the renaissance of buffalo on the plains as follows: "An interest in the cultural ecology of the Great Plains led to the study of the bison; the role of the bison in the balance of life on the plains; and to the question of this book— Why do people raise buffalo today, and what is the present role of the buffalo?" It was also an interest in the cultural ecology of the plains that led me to the buffalo. The question for my research is almost the same, though a bit more specific: Why do American Indian nations raise buffalo, and what is the present role of the buffalo for American Indians?

This study looks at and partially answers a question that has been sidelined in almost all of the numerous articles and publications on the subject of buffalo and the Great Plains: Now that the buffalo have come back, what is their relation to the people whose cultures and economies had been centered around them, the American Indian people of the Great Plains? I look at the role buffalo are playing and could play in the balance of life on American Indian reservations.

CHAPTER I

Cheyenne River

The Great Plains constitute an area defined, as historian Walter Prescott Webb said (1981:3), by three characteristics: level land, a treeless environment, and lack of water. All three of these characteristics are generalizations and relative statements. The land might seem level on a first superficial look but is actually surprisingly hilly once one gets out of a car and attempts to traverse some distance on foot. It is mostly the distances between observer and elevations—the predominantly gentle, rolling form of elevations, and the treeless nature of these elevations—that make perspectives deceptive for observers accustomed to woodlands and that trick the perception into seeing a level land. There are also ravines and river valleys—some with flowing water, some without—where, sustained by moisture and out of the constant, drying wind, trees grow in natural parklands. Rainfall diminishes from east to west, from the woodlands east of the Mississippi to the Rocky Mountain front. From an average of forty inches in the east to twelve inches or less in the west (Bamforth 1988:53–54), this gives rise to subdivisions in the plains ecosystem: tall grass prairie in the east giving way to mixed grass prairie and finally short grass prairie in the west. Cheyenne River Sioux Reservation is set within the transitional zone from short grass to mixed grass prairies on the northern plains. The subdivisions are locally diverse, and often, the classification of ecosystems overlap.

South Dakota, in whose north-central part Cheyenne River Sioux Reservation lies, is sometimes divided into two regions, East River and West

River—the river and dividing line being the Missouri (Wagoner 2002:52). Generally, east of the river lie rich, fertile soils (at least in comparison to those farther west), and the land west of the river is poorer and used as range land. This division is based on the dividing line of the 98th parallel, which Webb (1981) used to define the eastern boundary of the Great Plains or the slow beginning of the short grass prairie to its west. Others (e.g., Worster 1977:227), following John Wesley Powell now draw the line at the 100th parallel (Bennett 1996:251), which in South Dakota approximately coincides with the Missouri.

Where the short grass zone or the mixed grass zone begins is a matter of contention and rainfall in any particular year. Historically, mixed grass and short grass prairies began as much as 150 miles farther east than they do today because buffalo grazing impacted the ecosystem (Truett, Phillips, and Kunkel 2001:125). Just like the shifting boundaries between these ecosystems, the Missouri is not an absolute line between agriculture and ranching. East of the Cheyenne River Reservation, whose eastern boundary is the Missouri, climate, land, and socioeconomic consequences thereof are about the same as all around it. In this region, the land east of the river is, for all matters, West River country, too. Agriculture is attempted on both sides of the river, and its decline to the west is a gradual one, measurable in the smaller grain elevators that are spaced farther and farther apart. As with so many other things on the plains, perspective changes the longer one spends on the land and so, too, does the perception of reality. Boundaries and differences that were based on outside assumptions become less clear or even obsolete once one has lived and experienced the land and the people.

The territory that is today Cheyenne River Sioux Reservation is part of the Great Sioux Reservation as defined in the Treaty of 1868. The Lakota people do not need the treaty to claim this land as theirs: whether one follows the academic or the spiritual accounts of Lakota origins, this territory is Lakota. In academic accounts, the Lakota came from the western part of the Great Lakes region and crossed the Missouri between 1750 and 1775 to expand into the hunting grounds of the plains beyond the river, eventually extending their territory into the Powder River lands. In spiritual accounts, the Lakota originated from the Black Hills and extended their lands outward around them.

Although the interaction with Euro-Americans leading up to the establishment of the present reservation began much earlier, the Treaty of 1868 is the basis for much of what is going on in Lakota country today because it constitutes a political and legal benchmark in time. Although the process of colonization began ideologically with the designation of the plains as French and Spanish, only from the nineteenth century on did the United States have the political will and military power to translate the ideology of European ownership into practice.

European exploration of the Missouri started at least as early as the late seventeenth century. French and French-Canadian voyageurs began trading and living with the nations along the lower Missouri, and the plains, between present-day Kansas City and the Southwest, gained in strategic importance as a contested ground between France and Spain, resulting in Etienne Veniard, Sieur de Bourgmont's expedition to the Padoucas in 1722–1724 (Holder 1970:1–14). Ever since the Verendryes came to the upper Missouri in 1742 from Canada, contacts between tribes in that region and Europeans increased. Building on an indigenous tradition of trade that reaches back into Mississippian and possibly Hopewell times, these Europeans were primarily fur traders. They were also primarily French, not only because the French had a long history of relatively peaceful trading in North America, but also because on the maps dividing the world among the expanding European empires, the Great Plains were a part of France. It was the beginning of a phase in which indigenous nations on the plains and European colonial powers lived in parallel universes. Each was claiming the land for itself, but the people directly involved were still able to pragmatically balance these divergent claims on the ground.

After the French had had to give up Louisiana—the Great Plains—to Spain in the Treaty of Paris (1763), they gained it back in 1800, following Spain's appeasement policy to Napoleon Bonaparte. The newly formed United States under Thomas Jefferson was not at all amused or pleased and threatened to side with Britain in the war against France and invade the territory. The French had just put down a rebellion in Haiti and had twenty-five thousand men there, who could have been sent to defend the territory west of the Mississippi. However, the soldiers were decimated by an epidemic, and Napoleon realized he did not have the capacity to fight two major wars simultaneously. He decided to sell Louisiana (i.e., the French lands west of the Mississippi) to the United States (Balesi 1992:320–21; Nobles 1997:116–117). As so many times before and so many times afterward, important decisions that would decide the fate of the Americas and their Native peoples had been made on the basis of European politics and wars.

The Missouri River Valley became the possession of the United States, at least, for the time being, on its maps.

The United States was in a hurry to inspect its newest acquisition. The British had already reached the Pacific over land. Sir Alexander Mackenzie had explored the westernmost part of Canada and reached the West Coast in 1793. Canadian traders were common sights on the northern plains. So, in 1804 the United States sent Meriwether Lewis and William Clark on an expedition to inspect the new territory. The Lewis and Clark expedition marked the beginning of a change in relations between indigenous nations and Euro-Americans. Now, with an independent U.S. state claiming the region, interest in applying actual political power on the plains had grown considerably and would gradually lead to the subordination of Native nations.

In 1832, Pierre Chouteau Jr. brought the first steamboat up the Missouri, which carried George Catlin. With steamboats replacing the old keelboats, the fur trade volume picked up. In the winter of 1854–1855, several trading posts or forts were built on and around what is today the Cheyenne River Sioux Reservation. These posts were located in the area of Fort Pierre, Fort Randall, the mouth of the Cheyenne and Moreau Rivers, Cherry Creek, and Thunder Butte (Biegler 1994:10). The Franco-Canadians often married into the tribes, settling down to run their trading posts. Today, family names such as LeBeau, Dupris, Ducheneaux, LaPlant, DuBray, Rousseau, and Claymore (from the English pronunciation of Clement) are common on the Cheyenne River Sioux Reservation. French names in South Dakota and North Dakota are usually held by American Indian families; it is no accident that the French anthropologist Danielle Vazeille (1977:45) reports to have been mistaken for a Lakota when people heard or read her name.

Although the early traders along the Missouri had integrated into Lakota culture, politics, and economics, pressure began to mount for the Lakota to integrate into the United States after Lewis and Clark's expedition. As everywhere in North America, after the settler society had become strong enough to overcome its own isolation and marginalization, indigenous communities became marginalized and isolated (Reimer et al. 1997:9).

This process was not unchallenged: Plains Indian societies, like Native societies elsewhere, were highly efficient in diplomacy and warfare. The United States learned this when they were defeated along the Bozeman Trail, which led to the Treaty of 1868. The provisions of the Treaty of 1868 — among other things, such as promising the Great Sioux Reservation to the

Lakota—called for several agencies to be built on the Missouri River, where annuities promised in the treaty would be distributed. Cheyenne River Agency was built in 1870 on the west side of the Missouri at the mouth of the Cheyenne River. Here, four bands of the Lakota, the *O'ohenupa* (Two Kettle), *Mnikowoju* (Minneconjou), *Itazipco* (Sans Arc), and *Sihasapa* (Blackfoot), were to receive their annuities. In an 1868 survey, their numbers were established at 6,420 (Hoover 1992:48). In 1871, the agency was relocated into Fort Bennett, a military post on the west bank of the Missouri.

Management of most of the agencies set up in the treaties was inefficient: Many agents were corrupt, and because of transportation problems, annuities rarely arrived on time, so that the commodities were often wasted before they could be distributed. Many Lakota felt betrayed. This also meant that many Lakota had continued their traditional life as best they could (i.e., Poole 1881). The invasion of the Black Hills by gold diggers and their protection by the army led to skirmishes, and finally, when the army decided to round up all Lakota not living at agencies, to the battle at Greasy Grass or Little Big Horn in 1876. This Pyrrhic victory for the Lakota was followed by military action that forced remaining "hostile" bands either into Canada, like Sitting Bull's followers, or into surrender and possibly death, like Crazy Horse.

Many Minneconjous fled into Canada with Sitting Bull, and after they returned, they settled in the Cherry Creek and Red Scaffold area in the years between 1881 and 1886; this was the southwestern corner of the present reservation and lands farther to the west, which at that time still belonged to the reservation. There had been people living in these areas before, but the western half of Cheyenne River was where the "fullbloods" or "traditionals" continued to settle predominantly, in an effort to evade too much control by the agency on the Missouri (Gilbert 1941:15; Ziebach County Historical Society [ZCHS] 1982:73–86). The western region of Cheyenne River would stay, at least in the general perception of many people, more "traditional" in relation to the eastern region along the Missouri River, where, it is assumed, more "mixed bloods" lived and where historically the influence of the agency was more immediate. This perception is still alive today and often shapes reservation politics.

In 1887, the U.S. Congress passed the Dawes Severalty Act, or Allotment Act. Several tribes had undergone allotment before 1887; allotment was not a new policy in itself. The Dawes Act, however, modeled on the Homestead Act of 1862, gave the president of the United States the power to allot lands

(Iverson 1998:30–31). Because even the remaining part of the Great Sioux Reservation included more than double the lands needed for allotments, the procedures for allotment were stood on their head with the proposed Sioux Agreement of 1888. Even before allotments were to be made, the calculated surplus land was to be turned over to the government, which would open it for settlement. "The plan was to set aside six separate reservations — Pine Ridge, Rosebud, Cheyenne River, Standing Rock, Crow Creek, and Lower Brulé — on which the allotment program could be carried out at a leisurely pace" (Utley 1963:44). Finding the Lakota united in opposition against the agreement, the Sioux Agreement of 1889 made more and better promises, and in February 1890, "President Harrison announced acceptance of the land agreement by the required three-fourths majority of adult males and threw open the ceded territory for settlement. The promises had not been carried out. No surveys had been made to determine the precise boundaries of the new reservations. No provision had been made for Indians living in the ceded land to take allotments there. Here was the ultimate in bad faith" (Utley 1963:57).

The Act of 1890 defined Cheyenne River Sioux Reservation as a separate reservation. It also cost the Lakota lands in the northern part of the remaining Great Sioux Reservation, setting the new western boundary at the 102nd meridian and opened two corridors between the Cheyenne and the White Rivers for settlement. Because Fort Bennett — the agency for the Lakota bands now assigned to Cheyenne River — was located south of the now established reservation, the agency was moved upriver to Chargers Camp, immediately to the south of where today US highway 212 crosses the Missouri. This spot, renamed "Cheyenne River Agency," was opposite the town of Forest City, and there was a ferry service between the two settlements.

The effects of the Act of 1890 were felt most strongly in the western areas of the reservation, where many people, more traditional and just returned from Canada, lived on land that now had been thrown open to settlement and was not part of the new reservation anymore. Many of these people, mostly Minneconjou, became followers of a messianic movement, the Ghost Dance or Spirit Dance. The government, suspicious of the movement and of traditional American Indians in general, read a brewing rebellion into the panicked reports from agents, journalists, and ranchers and set out to suppress the movement. After Sitting Bull had been killed in the context of the Ghost Dance movement, one of the leaders of the movement on Cheyenne River, Big Foot (*Si Tanka*), learning of the impending arrest of his people by the army, attempted to flee to Pine Ridge Reservation. The Minneconjous, struggling through a South Dakota December, were intercepted at Wounded Knee Creek by the Seventh Cavalry and surrendered. On December 29, 1890, a fight broke out and the cavalry killed about three hundred Lakota, many of them women and children fleeing the scene (Utley 1963:200–30; ZCHS 1982:15–18).

On the Cheyenne River Reservation, allotments began to be made in 1906, and in 1907, Congress proposed to open the reservation for settlement. In 1908, an act of Congress opened a large area, consisting of the land along the Moreau River and roughly the northern three-quarters of Ziebach County, for homesteaders. Because allotments to Indians took place before the homesteaders came in, they had the opportunity to select the best lands available, which were located along the Moreau, the Cheyenne, and the Missouri Rivers. Fifty-five percent of allotments made to American Indians ended up being on lands that were to be opened for settlement by non-Indians. The designated areas of the reservation were opened on April 1, 1910, but only half of the available land was ever claimed (Fouberg 2000:43–47). Fouberg (47) thinks that this was a consequence of the fact that homesteaders, mostly farmers, recognized the lack of fertility of the soil. This is probably true: by this time immigrants to the plains had ample warning to not blindly believe the promises of land promoters.

Allotment remained the policy of the federal government until the passing of the Indian Reorganization Act, or IRA, in 1934, under the leadership of the new Commissioner of Indian Affairs, John Collier. Although the IRA had been watered down from its original version by Congress, "Collier took solace in what remained: allotment was dead; surplus unsold lands were returned to the tribal domain; Native lands could not be sold or leased without specific tribal approval; and tribes could form their own governments, with their own constitutions, but only if they voted to approve all the provisions of the Indian Reorganization Act" (Iverson 1998:91). The IRA was controversial on the reservations, but Cheyenne River "grasped the opportunities offered under" the act (Gilbert 1941:16).

Many people believed—and still believe—that the IRA was an assimilatory step, one that had the American Indian nations accept the political, economic, and cultural dominance of the United States. Statements that show how the IRA, or at least the underlying ideology, was geared toward assimilation and finally termination are not hard to find, and often, tribal councils themselves seem to have worked toward these goals. Lawrence

Davis (1944:174) applauds plans drawn up by the Cheyenne River tribal council and administrative officials to abolish the reservation by 1959, with the goal of completing "the process of absorbing the Indians into white culture" by 1960. "Sooner or later," Davis concludes (177), "the Indians must become a part of the culture in which they live." His claim that these plans had come mostly from the reservation residents themselves can for example be seen reflected in then tribal chairman's Frank Ducheneaux (1956:24) remarks on language during the Termination period:

> Fifty [percent] or more of the children who attend the reservation schools are not able to speak or understand the English language when they enter school. They must first be taught to think in English. . . . We believe that in another generation this problem will work itself out for the reason that more and more of the younger parents are speaking English in the home and their children can at least speak and understand English before they begin school.

It is important to realize that this is not the isolated opinion of a sole American Indian politician. Many people on reservations, under the threat of termination policies and searching a successful future for their people, took those kinds of approaches to traditional culture, language, and ceremonies (e.g., Fowler 1987 on Gros Ventres strategies). In hindsight these are positions that most people would probably regret, but we cannot interpret history from a present-day perspective. It was also Frank Ducheneaux who worked hard to save the Cheyenne River Reservation from being terminated.

Whether or not the IRA was a step toward assimilation, it was also an important step toward self-governance. Ironically, American Indian sovereignty might have been strengthened by an act that, for many, seemingly required its denial. Once American Indian nations had established federally recognized tribal governments under the IRA, it became harder and harder for the federal and state governments to ignore American Indian governments and issues overall. Before that process started in the 1970s, however, Cheyenne River, along with many other nations along the Missouri, lost tribal land once more, and this time it was land that was ecologically and economically irreplaceable. The consequences and political reverberations of this land loss still dominated the political agenda on the reservation during my fieldwork. The event that led to this loss of land was the damming of the Missouri to form Lake Oahe.

Oahe Dam, just north of Pierre, is but one in a series of dams that trans-formed the entire Missouri River Valley. To address Missouri flood and drought cycles, the Army Corps of Engineers and the Bureau of Reclamation came up with the Pick-Sloan Plan in 1943, which Congress approved in 1944 (Parman 1994:130; Robert McLaughlin Co. 1994:1–17). The plan for the development of the Missouri River Basin was based on the Tennessee River Valley Authority and called for 105 reservoirs to be built in ten states (Cushman and Macgregor 1948:108). The dams on the main stream in North Dakota and South Dakota, however, had the greatest impact, and these dams were placed in such a way that they flooded mostly reservation land. From the Garrison Dam to the Gavins Point Dam, tribal lands disap-peared into the lakes (Iverson 1998:131; Parman 1994:130–31).

On Cheyenne River Reservation, as on other reservations, the tribe was not sufficiently compensated for the land. This was its most valuable land, essential for the livestock economy and as habitat for wildlife (Cushman and Macgregor 1948:131, 163; Game, Fish and Parks Deparment [GFPD] 1999; Robert McLaughlin Co. 1994). In a time of termination policies, the resulting hardships for the reservations were presented as an advantage for American Indians, who were supposedly held back by the system, and would now be forced to adapt to the new times. The dam, the government pre-dicted, would open economic opportunities that would give Indians "full freedom of opportunity and economic independence as other citizens of the United States" (Cushman and Macgregor 1948:158–59; Hoover 1992:77–78). Cushman and Macgregor (163), writing for the Indian Service, mention that "[c]heap electricity will become available" for the tribe. Despite promises, however, the tribe was denied a block of hydroelectric power produced by the dam, although communities throughout South Dakota were and still are given preferential rates (Robert McLaughlin Co. 1994:46–50).

Some 104,420 acres were taken from the Cheyenne River Reservation for the dam and became known as the "Taken Area" (GFPD 1999:2). Congress determined that the tribe was to receive $10,644,014 for land, sev-erance, timber, indirect damages, a rehabilitation program, and expenses (Robert McLaughlin Co. 1994:99). The government had to abandon the agency town, including the school, hospital, and Bureau of Indian Affairs (BIA) buildings; they were moved to Eagle Butte, located in the center of the reservation. Many families had to move out of the river valley, too. During the years of the drought that started in 2001 as a result of Lake Oahe running low on water, one could see the foundations of former towns and houses and of the old agency buildings by the boat ramp south of the highway bridge reemerge from the lake.

In the eyes of the tribal administration, Cheyenne River Reservation received a big boost for the future in 2000, when Public Law 106–511 was signed into law. Title I of the law, "Cheyenne River Sioux Tribe Equitable Compensation," finally accorded to the tribe just compensation for the loss of land to Lake Oahe. This issue is better known in South Dakota as Joint Tribal Advisory Committee (JTAC). The Cheyenne River tribal government had fought long and hard for just compensation, and after Standing Rock had a JTAC bill passed in the 1990s, Cheyenne River sought its own bill. Public Law 106–511 states that "the Oahe Dam and Reservoir project . . . has not only contributed little to the economy of the Tribe, but has severely damaged the economy of the Tribe and members of the Tribe by inundating the fertile, wooded bottom lands of the Tribe along the Missouri River that constituted the most productive agricultural and pastoral lands of the members of the Tribe and the homeland of the members of the Tribe." The government acknowledged that the tribe was never fairly compensated and determined fair compensation at $290,723,000. This money was to be put into a trust fund administered by the Department of the Interior.

CHAPTER 2

The Reservation

Cheyenne River Sioux Reservation lies about an hour to the northwest of Pierre, South Dakota. Its eastern border is the Missouri River, today dammed to Lake Oahe, and the southern border is the Cheyenne River. The reservation, adjacent to Standing Rock Reservation in the north, is the second largest in the state, only slightly smaller than Pine Ridge.

Numbers for the land areas of the reservation differ from source to source. In a 1994 Bureau of Indian Affairs (BIA) publication (3–8), the agency reports that of a total of 2,719,618 acres of reservation land, 1,300,193 acres were privately owned; 1,392,450 acres were trust land; and 26,975 acres were government land. A publication by the National Wildlife Federation (NWF 2001) counts 2,820,751 acres inside the reservation's external borders, "more than half" of which is in trust status. The differences in total reservation acreage may stem from disputes over the boundary in Lake Oahe; depending on whether the middle of the streambed or one bank is taken as the boundary, the reservation is bigger or smaller. To the best of my ability to discern, about 1,400,000 acres are trust land, divided into about 920,000 acres of tribally owned land and 500,000 acres of allotted land owned by tribal members (Game, Fish, and Parks Department [GFPD] 1999:16; O'Brien 1989:155).

The exterior boundaries of Cheyenne River Reservation follow the ones of two South Dakota counties, Ziebach and Dewey. Ziebach County encompasses 1,962 square miles, and Dewey County is a little larger with 2,303

South Dakota

square miles. Ziebach has the form of a thick L and makes up the western part of Cheyenne River Reservation, whereas Dewey comprises the eastern half. The counties were organized in 1911, after the reservation had been opened for settlement under the Allotment Act. A third county, Armstrong, was left unorganized at the time; most of its land was leased to big cattle companies, and there were only eight families, a total of fifty-two people living in the county. In 1953, Armstrong was annexed by Dewey county.

As with most allotted Indian reservations, external boundaries are almost meaningless for practical administration. In reality, and although the Cheyenne River Sioux Tribe (CRST) is trying to change this, the reservation has administrative powers over Indian lands, only—lands held either by tribal members or the tribe itself. On Cheyenne River, Indian lands more or less follow the rivers. Generally speaking, they make up the land along the Missouri and inland to a line west of La Plant. They also follow the Cheyenne River to the western border of the reservation, the Moreau River to west of Whitehorse, and from there in a discontinued pattern to around Thunder Butte and Iron Lightning, where most of the land is again reservation land.

The fact that reservation boundaries coincide with county boundaries makes for complex and differing perspectives in reading the land. From a county perspective, Indian lands are within the county's boundaries but exempt from much of its governance. For the tribe, the same is true in reverse for non-Indian land. This leads to quite a few practical problems. For example, non-Indians living in an area of predominantly tribal lands pay taxes to the county, but the county tax base in that area might be so small that the county cannot allocate enough funds to keep its roads up to normal standards. For hunters, the landscape consists of interlocking land units that have different regulations and demand different permits. Law enforcement is a complex mixture of various agencies. Which agency is responsible for or allowed to uphold federal, state, or tribal laws depends not only on land proprietorship but also on whether one or all parties involved in an investigation are tribal members and on the severity of the crime as defined in the Major Crimes Act. Tribal Police, City of Eagle Butte Police, the County Sheriff, State Highway Patrol, BIA Police, and the Federal Bureau of Investigation (FBI) are some of the agencies involved, and at times competing, in law enforcement on the reservation. The judicial system follows some of the same distinctions. Although the tribe offers many of its services to all people living within the reservation, the Indian Health Service (IHS)

Hospital in Eagle Butte and the various ambulatory community clinics are basically reserved for American Indians, except in life-threatening situations. As Fouberg (2000:163) points out, "a good deal of cooperation exists between the tribe and the counties for provision of goods and services on the reservation." Still, reading the land involves the application of different maps that split up the land in ways that affect almost all areas of daily life. Through the trust responsibilities assumed by the federal government, these divisions pertain not only to the tribe-county level, but also to tribal-state, federal-state, tribal-federal, and finally federal-federal relations. Some would argue that because tribes are independent nations, they also pertain to international treaties and agreements.

According to the 2000 U.S. Census (2002a, 2002b), 5,972 people lived in Dewey county, and 2,519 lived in Ziebach county. The difference between the two figures can easily be explained by the fact that Eagle Butte, the largest town in the area, is rapidly growing and lies in Dewey county. Of this population, 74.2 percent in Dewey and 72.3 percent in Ziebach identified themselves as American Indian. That means that 4,431 residents in Dewey and 1,821 residents in Ziebach counties, or a total of 6,252 residents, are American Indians. Census figures cannot be taken as accurate in total numbers, however; because of remote homes and distrust of the government, many Lakota do not participate in the census, so the figures are usually lower than actual numbers. According to the BIA (1999:6), for example, 10,589 people on Cheyenne River are eligible for their services.

Eagle Butte, the agency headquarters since the flooding of Lake Oahe in 1959, is the largest town on the reservation with a population of about five thousand. It lies almost in the middle of the reservation, on Fox Ridge. The two most important roads on the reservation run through it, US 212 running east and west, and SD 63, running north and south. BIA and tribal offices are located here, as are the IHS hospital, banks, the cultural center, the former Si Tanka College, two motels, gas stations, the Lakota Thrifty Mart, and other stores. Like everybody in central and western South Dakota, residents of Cheyenne River go to Pierre or Rapid City for more complex medical care. Pierre has a mall with a couple of department stores and an airport with flights to Denver and Minneapolis, but Rapid City has more stores and cheaper flights out of its much larger regional airport. The Rapid City area also provides recreational opportunities in the Black Hills tourist attractions. School field trips from the reservation often go there.

About twenty miles west of Eagle Butte is Dupree, county seat for Ziebach county. It has a population of around 450 and has the county offices, a general store, and some gas stations. The county seat for Dewey county, Timber Lake, is located about forty miles northeast of Eagle Butte, in the farming area near the northern boundary of the reservation. About as large as Dupree, Timber Lake has a museum that opened in 2001 and features spectacular fossils; it also has a motel, a grocery store, county offices, and a gas station. To the east of Timber Lake are Trail City and Glencross and to the west are Glad Valley, in the northwestern corner of the reservation, Firesteel, which has a store, and Isabel, with a population of about two hundred with a store, motel, and gas station.

Other communities on the reservation include Iron Lightning, Thunder Butte, Red Elm, and Lantry around Dupree; Red Scaffold, Cherry Creek, and Bridger in the southwest; Green Grass, Whitehorse, Promise, and Blackfoot along the Moreau River; and Parade, Ridgeview, La Plant, and Swiftbird on Fox Ridge east of Eagle Butte.

People from the Cherry Creek area have to shop in Dupree or Eagle Butte, a thirty- to forty-mile drive. People from the east, around La Plant and Swiftbird, might go instead to Gettysburg, about thirty miles across the Missouri, or Bob's Resort, a gas station and motel right across the Missouri. Further north, people from Blackfoot and Promise may go to Mobridge, across the Missouri from Standing Rock Reservation. Although nominally, all of the reservation lies in the Mountain Time Zone, the East End unofficially stays on Central Time, marking its ties across the Missouri. Not only are grocery stores in Gettysburg and Mobridge closer than Eagle Butte but so are hospitals and ambulance services, government offices, hardware stores, and mechanics. Schools, including high schools, are in Eagle Butte, Timber Lake, and Dupree, and two newer school complexes are in Takini for the southwest and in La Plant for the east.

Climate on Cheyenne River is continental: hot summers, cold winters, and dry. The reservation's frost-free season "lasts from about May 17 to September 21" (BIA 1994:3–9). Summer temperatures can easily reach triple digits, whereas winter nights can oscillate around –40° F.

Based on data from High Plains Regional Climate center weather stations in Faith, Dupree, Timber Lake, and Gettysburg, collected from 1948 to 2000, average annual total precipitation is 17.43 inches, with increases in rainfall from west to east. July average maximum temperature on

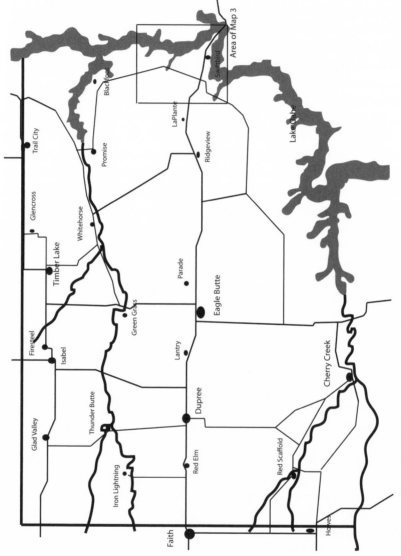

Cheyenne River Sioux Reservation

Cheyenne River is 87.1° F, whereas the average minimum temperature for the same month is 59.1° F. For January, average maximum temperature is 25.4° F, and the average minimum temperature is 4.3° F. Winds are ever present and can easily reach up to fifty or sixty miles per hour for periods of up to a week. They drive dust and dry snow through every crack.

As everywhere on the plains, weather can be highly localized. Summer storms, especially, often affect only a highly specific area and spare others completely. Local experience with weather can take into account geographical and historical patterns. In the summer of 2000, I was at the annual powwow in Iron Lightning. At nightfall on the second day, a policeman showed up and warned of a tornado that had touched down about fifty miles away, with Iron Lightning in the apparent path of the storm. Although everybody else scattered, the locals stayed absolutely calm and tried to assure people that there are neither tornadoes nor thunderstorms in Iron Lightning. They might occur around it but never in the community. Such categorical statements did not assure me at that time, and so I was frantically packing my tent into a basement while people from the community were sitting around the now-deserted powwow grounds, drinking coffee. Of course, the storm came, raged all around, and never touched the community.

Relations between the Indian and the non-Indian communities are relatively good on Cheyenne River, especially for a South Dakota reservation. Many aspects of intercultural relations have improved in the state; however, there is a long list of real and perceived discrimination against Indians in South Dakota, especially from law enforcement agencies (South Dakota Advisory Committee to the U.S. Commission on Civil Rights [SDAC] 2000), and I heard many personal stories of racial profiling. For example, for some police officers, any "Indian car," identified either by the looks of the driver, the general state of the vehicle, or a dream catcher hanging from the rearview mirror, is fair game. During the time of my fieldwork, cars in South Dakota could be stopped for objects hanging from the rearview mirror, a law that was enforced and hotly disputed because American Indians felt it amounted to an excuse for racial profiling.

That being said, the shared experiences and challenges as ranchers and farmers on the plains also create a bond among people on Cheyenne River. This bond is obviously not felt by everybody or in all situations. Issues, like land taxation, always simmer under the surface, but in general, the ranching community gets along without too many bumps in personal relationships.

Some ranchers share more than just their occupational challenges with their Lakota neighbors. One day, I was talking about language revitalization programs with some Lakota men, and one of them mentioned a conversation he had recently had with a rancher from around Timber Lake. That man's grandfather had been one of many Volga Germans settling in the Dakotas, and his father had spoken German fluently. He himself, however, had never learned it because his father had not wanted him to have problems in school. The conclusion the Lakota man drew from this was that the different societies on the reservation are facing some of the same problems.

When I talked with non-Indian people in Timber Lake or Gettysburg, they felt that the two cultures get along pretty well, but when I talked with Lakota people, who deal daily with and in these communities and depend on their services, the stories were often somewhat different. The dominant society often does not understand how others feel treated unfairly, especially if obvious and conscious acts of racism are missing. Lakota people pointed out to me what they perceived as racial discrimination: store clerks would observe their every move in a store just because they looked Indian, for example. Although businesspeople in towns provide the same services to everybody, in my conversations with these business owners, they would sometimes express views of the reservation that were based more on stereotypes than on realities; such misperceptions work both ways, of course. As soon as I hung a dream catcher from my own rearview mirror, motorists off the reservation would raise their hand in greeting less frequently. And when I went to eat in a restaurant with somebody who obviously "looks Indian," we were not served until after a group of locals who had entered five minutes later. These examples do not amount to overt racism, but they are the kind of everyday attitudes that make Lakota feel treated with contempt.

Nothing brought out the mixed feelings of people on the reservation about the United States more than the terror attacks on September 11, 2001 and the response by the government. Many people on the reservation, many of them veterans, were most disturbed by the attacks and most sympathetic to the victims, but they saw the attacks as "the chicken having come home to roost" (this phrase is a quote from conversations at the time and not taken from Ward Churchill). What the United States is doing in the Middle East, many people told me, is exactly what it has been doing, and is still doing, on American Indian reservations. Many reservation residents have relatives in the armed forces; American Indians are percentage-wise the most represented group in the U.S. military, and they have fought honorably in all wars since even before being made citizens. During the war in Afghanistan, one man told me he had been on the phone with a relative somewhere in Central Asia and had told her that she should do her job honorably but to keep in mind that "the Lakota have no quarrels" with people there.

When President Bush gave his speech on September 20, 2001, he stated that, "Americans have known wars—but for the past 136 years, they have been wars on foreign soil, except for one Sunday in 1941" (Bush 2001). In other words, he conveniently forgot to mention not only the Japanese invasion of the Aleuts, which predominantly affected Native peoples, both directly and in refugee camps with conditions more horrible than internment camps for Japanese Americans, but also all the Indian Wars since 1865. These are the wars that understandably make up much of the historical memories of the Lakota because they were the wars of aggression that colonized the northern plains. In the historical memory of President Bush, however, as in that of many people in the United States, these wars apparently do not exist. The existence of two so dramatically different historical memories raises important questions on the viability of a common social, if not political, unity. And perhaps more importantly, given the absence of a historical memory of events so traumatically important to the minority group, the absence of concern for present conditions is easily explained; which, however, does not make it easier on any American Indian people to live with the knowledge that they do not exist in the eyes of the administration and for the sake of a nationalistic memory (Braun 2002).

As I have briefly mentioned previously, the reservation itself is often perceived to be divided into two larger communities, the East End and the West End. This categorization primarily follows the different Lakota groups—Minneconjou in the west and O'ohenupa and Sihasapa in the east. It not only leaves the Sans Arc unaccounted for but also does not reflect the intermarriages between people. Although it is true that residents know which traditional group or band they belong to, there has also been a new identity formed, one of "Cheyenne River Sioux." The categories of east and west are partially based on the communities' different histories. People in the west are often considered to be "full bloods," and people in the east are seen as "mixed bloods."

The classification does not mean in any way that everybody on the East End has adapted to or accepts Euro-American culture or that everybody on the West End is a "traditionalist." It is, however, even among people from the East End, a generally accepted notion that West Enders are more traditional. Certain ceremonies are acknowledged to be more alive, if invisible to outsiders, on the West End, and the Lakota language seems to be spoken more frequently there. That said, however, it is important to point out that many people from the East End are involved in ceremonial practices, many of which are traditional. For example, although Lawrence Davis (1944:135) found that the "practice of scaffold burials has long been discontinued," only a few years ago, as his last request, one man from the East End was placed on a traditional burial scaffold for a year, and a local religious man took care of the body.

Today, with the rise of Eagle Butte as the agency town and its rapid growth, the division between East and West, which was always bridged by marriages and relations, seems to have become a triangular relation. Both East and West Enders see the town, its association with the government agencies, and its problems with gangs and drugs as somewhat of a corrupting force for their children and a depressing place. The town has developed a culture of its own, different from both the West and the East End. With the agency town retaining almost all resources, there seem to be more tensions between the rural areas, both east and west, and the town than between the two regions themselves. There are occasional tensions between East and West Enders, especially pertaining to resource allocations, such as the buffalo program, but these do not reach the intensity of real conflict. Some full bloods expressed to me that things are not going well because mixed bloods are running the reservation, but there is not the same feeling of a real division as sometimes on Pine Ridge, for example (see Kurkiala 1997 for an excellent treatment of these terms and ethnicity politics on Pine Ridge). Eagle Butte, in this view, also serves as a literal and metaphorical meeting place for the West and East End and their different perspectives.

CHAPTER 3

The Idea of Buffalo Cooperatives

The historical significance of buffalo for the peoples of the plains before the arrival of the Europeans and Americans is well known. As Ella Deloria put it (1944:62):

> Indeed, the buffalo was everything to the Dakotas' well-being: food, shelter, fuel, toys, implements, clothing, and much more. His was, therefore, the chief of all spirits serving as mediums for deriving supernatural good. . . . He was the embodiment of sacrifice that others might live. He came when they were starving; he set them the example of hospitality; he was host to the whole nation.

The economic significance of the bison was intertwined with the symbolic meaning of the animals for the Lakota and other Plains Indians. It is essential to understand that the symbolic value of the buffalo was not tied to, and did not emanate only from, its undeniable economic importance. As Joseph Epes Brown says (1997:82), "The role of the bison in Oglala society is not defined by economic determinism. Rather, the bison's central role affirms that the natural world may offer vital, creative input to a society whose members are predisposed to receive it." It was this connection between the symbolic meaning and the economic significance that stood at the start of an idea to better the social, cultural, political, economic, and ecological situation not only on Cheyenne River but also on Indian reservations nationwide: to build and sustain economically viable tribal bison herds as locally controlled and culturally sustainable development projects.

Cheyenne River Reservation and the surrounding area have been of significance to the history of the buffalo for a long time. In 1880, the reservation took part in one of the last big buffalo hunts on the plains, which resulted in some two thousand hides being brought to the agency for sale (Haines 1995:204; Zieback County Historical Society [ZCHS] 1982:10). In 1883, the area between the Moreau and Grand Rivers was the scene for what many agree was the last buffalo hunt in the West, when Sitting Bull led his people from Standing Rock to kill the last remnants of a herd that had been wandering down from Montana. Many white hunters took part in that hunt, too (Haines 1995:204; Hornaday 2002:512; ZCHS 1982:10–13). Frances Densmore reports the hunt to have taken place in 1882 (1992:436), with five thousand buffalo killed and the hunting party consisting of six hundred mounted Lakota. The differences in details can be seen as stemming from the legendary meaning of the event, which brought the final chapter of bison hunting on the plains and the lifestyle of the Plains Indians to their end. Some might see these events as proof that American Indians partook in the extermination of the buffalo, but if they had not gone out to hunt once more, the buffalo would have been killed by whites. As it was, they could at least enjoy one last hunt and get some much needed provisions for themselves.

While the Ghost Dance movement is often claimed as the first vision to bring back the buffalo, the Cheyenne River Reservation can lay a much more practical claim to efforts to save the bison from extinction. This is primarily a result of the efforts of Fred Dupuis, later called Dupris or Dupree. Fred Dupree was a French-Canadian working for the American Fur Company under Pierre Chouteau. He came to Fort Pierre in 1838 and established a trading post near Cherry Creek on the Cheyenne River. By 1860, he had married Good Elk Woman (Mary Ann Dupuis), a Minneconjou. Eventually, he became a successful rancher in the area. In 1882 or 1883, Fred Dupree and some others went to the region between Slim Buttes and the Yellowstone River and returned with five (some say nine) live buffalo calves (Dupree 1982:345–46; Wood 2001:402–403). Harold P. Danz says the hunt took place in 1881 (1997:121), and Fred's son Pete captured the five animals. In any case, the buffalo were caught, and by 1888 Dupree's bison herd numbered nine full-blood buffalo and seven mixed-blood animals or bison-cattle hybrids. Fred Dupree died in 1898, leaving a herd of between seventy-five and eighty-three full-blood animals. After his son Pete died in 1900, the herd was sold to James "Scotty" Philip in 1901 (Danz 1997:121; Dupree 1982:346; Wood 2001:402–403).

Scotty Philip was a Scotsman who had immigrated to the United States at age sixteen in 1874 and joined the illegal gold rush into the Black Hills in 1875. He later married a Cheyenne woman, Sarah Larrabee or Larvie, and settled near the present-day town of Philip, South Dakota. In 1880, he met Fred Dupree, by this time a well-respected businessman in the region. In 1891, Philip with two others founded the Minnesota and Dakota Cattle Company and from 1893 on ranched near Fort Pierre. After he bought Dupree's buffalo herd, Philip slaughtered all the obviously mixed-blood animals, which left him with about eighty full-blood buffalo. This herd had grown to around four hundred animals in 1911 when Scotty Philip died. From 1914 to 1925, buffalo from his herd were used as nuclei for the herds in Custer State Park, the San Luis Obispo Preserve, the 101 Ranch in Oklahoma, the Cimarron Boy Scout Ranch in New Mexico, and many other bison herds that laid the foundation for the recovery of the species. Finally, in 1925, Scotty Philip's son-in-law staged a big hunt on the remaining two hundred fifty animals. Two hundred were killed for a hundred dollars each, and the rest were sold off or given away (Danz 1997:122; Dary 1989:232–33; Wood 2001:407–408). The Houck's Triple U Ranch between Fort Pierre and the Cheyenne River can be seen to be carrying on Philip's legacy today.

The efforts of Dupree and Philip played a major part in the conservation of the buffalo as a species. These two men were successful cattle ranchers and businessmen and kept their buffalo herds out of curiosity and interest. Both married American Indian women, and I think it is only fair to assume that their wives had some influence in their buffalo interests, although both husbands and wives are today largely forgotten by history.

I have not found much information about buffalo on Cheyenne River Sioux Reservation between Dupree's herd and the mid-1970s. I presume, however, that a small number of animals held by individuals have been present for most of these years. Madonna Swan remembers that her father and others from the Cherry Creek and Red Scaffold area went to hunt a buffalo that got lost between the Philip ranch and Custer State Park in 1933 or 1934 (St. Pierre 1991:24–26). She also mentions that Wally Knight was raising buffalo near Red Scaffold in the late 1960s and early 1970s (163–64). Many tribes and individuals on reservations owned small buffalo herds in those years. In the 1930s, at least three tribes had buffalo herds: Taos Pueblo, Crow Reservation, and Pine Ridge (InterTribal Bison Cooperative [ITBC]1998:9). Other herds, however, would later be established.

The history of tribal buffalo herds is difficult to follow because different sources give somewhat diverse dates, but it is clear that tribal buffalo herds grew over the years. The Shoshone-Bannock Tribes, for example, started their herd in 1964 (Hone 1992) or 1966 (Zontek 2003:129). Callenbach reports that Pine Ridge reintroduced buffalo in 1972 (1996:69), after an absence of twenty-five years; other sources maintain that the Oglala herd was reestablished ten years earlier (ITBC 1998:9). The different dates in historic references may perhaps stem from the existence of a number of different herds on the reservations. The important point here is not to establish a historically accurate dateline, but to point out that many reservations preserved a presence of bison on their lands in these years, sometimes reintroducing them after a time of difficulty. In 1964, after the detection of brucellosis, the Crow Reservation herd was destroyed, for example, but the tribe reintroduced buffalo in 1971. All together, sixteen tribes were raising buffalo in 1992, and together they owned about twenty-eight hundred animals (ITBC 1998:9). Ken Zontek puts that number even higher, at twenty-six tribes with thirty-six hundred animals (2003:129).

In the late 1980s and early 1990s, many American Indian activists from the 1970s were looking for a new approach on how to help reservations. After the era of political activism in the 1960s, there was a new emphasis on economic development as a necessary avenue to make political self-determination possible, but in line with the alternative development discourse of the 1980s, these people were looking not so much to repeat the mistakes of the 1960s as toward the idea of holistic, ecologically, and culturally sustainable development. From this perspective, economic development alone carried the danger of overlooking cultural factors, and by way of forced economic assimilation, of worsening the social background on reservations.

In the meantime, bison ranching had become an economic force. From the early 1900s on, raising buffalo had become a profitable business venture, not simply a pastime for eccentric ranchers. The near extinction of the species meant that the remaining numbers became more valuable. This was especially true as public herds were established and as the growing tourist and leisure industry turned the American West and many of its symbols into commodities. After World War II, a market for live buffalo developed

(Rorabacher 1970, 65). The National Buffalo Association (NBA), the first association of buffalo producers, was founded in 1967, initiated by L. R. Houck of the Triple U Ranch, north of Fort Pierre (Danz 1997:157). The Triple U, of "Dances with Wolves" fame, is still one of the larger buffalo ranches and one of a few that early on built their own slaughter facilities. This was important because a small niche market for bison meat developed in the late 1960s. Economically not important, it nevertheless showed a potential path for growth to ranchers who until that time had raised bison mostly to sell to businesses as exotic tourist attractions.

"It is unlikely," Albert Rorabacher predicted in 1970, "that the present bison population will be significantly increased as a result of stimuli derived from a further desire for the conservation of buffalo or the animals' symbolic nature. . . . If buffalo ever become so numerous as to become a common creature, the importance of the symbolic nature of the bison will undoubtedly decrease" (63). With a fast growing buffalo ranching industry since 1970, buffalo did indeed become more common, although they retained, and still retain, much of their symbolic value. Part of the reason for this is probably that few people actually live around buffalo, so that the animals have not become commonplace in the public's perception. Another reason might be the commodification of symbols in general—the symbolic nature of buffalo is actually an economic incentive to increase their numbers. Although Rorabacher was right in that few people ranch buffalo for purely symbolic reasons, buffalo have become marketed heavily as a bearer of symbolism, whether it is in books, for political and social reasons, or simply to attract tourists. On its own, however, symbolism is not stimulus enough anymore, if it ever was. For several years now, the increased availability of buffalo, as live animals and as meat, has indeed led to their increased perception as a normal commodity and as such has also contributed to their devaluation as a novelty item. However, in the late 1980s, driven by a farm crisis, low beef prices, and the resulting search for niche commodities, the buffalo industry was in full swing.

In 1975, the American Buffalo Association, which later became the American Bison Association (ABA) was founded as an offspring of the NBA, and it eventually grew larger than the NBA (Danz 1997:158). The two associations merged in 1996 to form the National Bison Association, the new NBA (Danz 1997:169). These organizations have produced guides to buffalo ranching, organized sales and trophy shows, and have tried to create a bigger market for buffalo products, especially meat. The same is true for the

Canadian Bison Association and a number of state, provincial, and regional associations. Because buffalo have been exported not only to Hawaii but also to Europe, numerous other national organizations have come to life.

In 1993, the North American Bison Cooperative (NABC) was founded. It built a slaughter plant in New Rockford, North Dakota, which was designed to meet European Union (EU) regulations. Completed in 1994, up to ten thousand bulls a year might be processed there eventually (Anderson, Metzger, and Sexhus 1997). In 1998, the buffalo industry created a direct and secondary economic contribution to North Dakota of $50.3 million, with buffalo processing generating another $20 million (Sell, Bangsund, and Leistritz 2000:18). As should be clear from those numbers, buffalo have become established as a factor of some importance in the economies of northern plains states. This is also reflected by North Dakota State University in Fargo's increased research and economic activities centering on bison.

Obviously, the rising buffalo industry would not go unnoticed on plains reservations. For some American Indian people on the plains, this seemed to be the perfect chance for a new, holistic approach to the economic development of their reservations. The rise of the buffalo as a product marketable off the reservation was matched with the bison's traditional cultural importance for the reservation societies and seemed to present a unique opportunity for a combined cultural and economic revival. Many of those who initially became involved with buffalo projects on reservations were not looking so much to become major players in the meat market as to enhance tribal sovereignty and self-sufficiency, both economically and culturally. Because some reservations already had tribal bison herds, the task at hand was not so much to build a new project from the ground up, as to grow an existing base and expand its potential. To coordinate the various already existing projects on reservations and to help others to build their own herds, the InterTribal Bison Cooperative (ITBC) was founded in 1992. Fred DuBray, who at that time had also just started Pte Hca Ka, Inc., on Cheyenne River, is generally credited with playing a critical role in the establishment of ITBC and as one of the first visionaries of tribal bison ranching as a holistic development alternative for reservations. However there were many others, among them Mike Fox from Fort Belknap.

Originating from a 1991 meeting of the Native American Fish and Wildlife Society (NAFWS), ITBC was first operating under NAFWS, but then, from 1993 on, it has operated as an independent nonprofit organization headquartered in Rapid City. The idea behind ITBC was to create an umbrella organization that could organize a support network for independent tribal bison operations. ITBC would also provide support for business education, management plans, and function as a clearinghouse and meeting point for tribal bison practitioners from all over the United States. By providing such a sounding board, a place where different experiences could be exchanged and a site for education for potential new tribal herd programs, ITBC hoped to start a movement toward more tribal bison herds. It met with overall success.

In ITBC's first six years, the number of tribal buffalo programs more than doubled, and the number of buffalo on reservations nationwide increased from twenty-eight hundred to about eight thousand. Around five hundred tribal jobs were created by the buffalo programs, either directly or indirectly (ITBC 1998:9). Even though in some cases, especially with small herds of twenty to twenty-five animals, the goals of the bison operations were more geared toward cultural revitalization, ITBC has always placed emphasis on a sound economic foundation for tribal herds. There are no stipulations on goals for membership in ITBC, which has led to a great diversity of bison operations represented in the organization. Tribes who are members of ITBC do not have to be working in a cultural or traditional manner because the cooperative provides an umbrella organization for all tribal buffalo herds, no matter their objectives. Although this diversity might sometimes create frictions, it is also the strength of ITBC to be able to include so many different experiences from which all its members can draw for their own operations.

Although not all tribes running buffalo and not all buffalo herds on tribal lands are members of ITBC, the organization grew to include over fifty member tribes in ten years. It has also become involved with the brucellosis issue in Yellowstone, the slaughter of buffalo wandering into Montana from the national park, working with the National Wildlife Federation (NWF) in introducing an alternative management plan for the national park's bison. This partnership "marked the first time a formal relationship had ever been established between Native Americans and a national conservation agency" (Torbit and LaRose 2001:175).

The success of buffalo herds on neighboring reservations and throughout the country has also sparked the more recent establishment of new herds. The Winnebago tribe of Nebraska, for example, started their buffalo program in 1994 and grazed not only their own buffalo but also hosted animals belonging to the Poncas and the Santee Sioux of Nebraska (Suzuki 1999:140–41). In 2001, Fort Peck was able to buy one hundred animals from Fort Belknap after a ten-year effort to found a buffalo operation (Peterson 2001).

Although most tribal operations include cultural programs, the simple physical return of buffalo to Native lands by itself is seen by many of those who work toward traditional goals as an irreversible trigger for cultural revitalization. From this perspective, even reservations that do not consciously work toward this goal, then, are inadvertently doing so, anyway. This notion and the connection between the seemingly economic activity of bison ranching and cultural revitalization itself suggest a closer look at contemporary and traditional symbolic connections between Lakota people and buffalo is necessary.

In a spiritual and religious sense, bison—both conceptually and physically—continue to play a large role in contemporary traditional ceremonies. I do not want to say too much about the contemporary use of buffalo in ceremonies because the people who told me about the religious significance of the buffalo asked me not to discuss this topic, and the people who allowed me to participate in ceremonies asked that my participation be spiritual, not anthropological. There are several published accounts of Lakota ceremonies (Brown 1997:71–82; DeMallie 1984; Walker 1991), however, including the use and significance of the buffalo in the contemporary Sun Dance (Feraca 1998; Powers 1982; Steinmetz 1998). Because ceremonies such as the Sun Dance are interpretations of individual visions following broad general guidelines, some of these descriptions match my own experiences, and some do not.

The spiritual significance of the buffalo and the relationship between the Lakota and the buffalo can be seen in myths (Rice 1994; Walker 1983), the most important of which deals with the White Buffalo Woman, *pte san win*, who brought the Lakota the pipe and the sacred ceremonies (DeMallie 1984:283–85; Densmore 1992:63–67) or in other words the religious and social order on which Lakota culture and society is based, and as such can be seen as the Lakota culture hero. As Amiotte says (1987:84), "ancient beliefs that perhaps existed even before the Pipe was brought to us . . . became formalized as a result of the Pipe." Several versions of this myth and several interpretations of aspects of its meanings exist, but the basic tenet remains the same: from the beginning of Lakota culture as it is known historically and today, a special relationship existed between the Lakota (*lakota oyate*) and the bison (*pte oyate*). The importance of the bison for traditional Lakota, from this cultural experience alone, then, cannot be overestimated: it was pte san win who stands at the beginning of Lakota existence as such.

All Lakota hold their own views of buffalo, but I would like to point out what I see as some tendencies in contemporary Lakota perspectives toward bison. These are true for those Lakota who in fact feel a special relationship to buffalo; many other Lakota do not.

Callenbach asserts that "[m]any Indians have no respect for cattle and believe that eating them makes you weak" (1996:74). As a general feeling, this might have been true at the beginning of the reservation period, when people would stage hunts on ration cattle just to keep the thrill of the traditional buffalo hunt alive. Today, there are some Lakota who still hold that idea, but quite a few people I talked to on Cheyenne River and the Crow Reservation—which hold the two largest tribal buffalo herds—prefer beef over buffalo meat because they are used to the higher fat content in beef. One payday, when Pte Hca Ka took their mobile burger kitchen to the Game, Fish, and Parks Department (GFPD) in Eagle Butte to sell lunch, some employees sneaked out the backdoor and went to the tribal Dairy Queen to get burgers instead. It is also true that other tribal members think that beef is at least partially responsible for diabetes and say they would like to replace it with buffalo meat. In general, however, the cattle culture has replaced the buffalo culture on all northern plains reservations. Despite this, people know that as Lakota they should have a special relation to buffalo. Cattle have therefore not replaced buffalo in official and officious symbolism, but they have in practical economics and daily life.

Because economics are coupled with an adoption of "scientific" ecological knowledge and range management practices, in part required by the regulation of grazing pressures and other environmental impacts, the symbolic aspect of buffalo ecology has almost been lost. The symbolic meaning of bison is one of identity politics coupled to remembrance of oppression and a mystical old way of life but almost completely void of practical knowledge. Today, comprehensive traditional ecological knowledge about buffalo is preserved by only a few residents. As one person told me, whereas a 150 years ago every Lakota person had an expansive knowledge about buffalo, today there might be five or fewer people on Cheyenne River who have preserved some of that.

In her discussion of Indian identity centered in an ideal of "really Indians," Theresa DeLeane O'Nell says that this ideal identity is often expressed in the ways and wisdom that previous generations had but which have supposedly been lost (1996:58–59). People are seen to have been healthier, excellent hunters, modest, hardworking, to have known the language, to have had medicinal knowledge, powers to influence the environment, and so on. The ecological knowledge of, and the special relationship to, buffalo, in this context, can be seen as a part of the central values that O'Nell's "really Indians" were ascribed with and around which contemporary Indian identity revolves. Claiming to have a special relationship with buffalo, or other animals for that matter, is a part of claiming Indianness—an outward, expected sign of identification, both within the reservation community and toward the outside, although stemming from different motivations in these two situations. I sometimes had the impression that people had to convince themselves that buffalo are supposed to be or are indeed spiritually meaningful, or *wakan* beings. However, at other times, it became clear that traditional relations with regard to the respect of animals are still alive in most people with whom I talked, and these general feelings can be extended toward buffalo.

To those Lakota and other Plains Indians who are trying to keep the traditional relations and ecological knowledge alive and revive them, buffalo still are a powerful relative. To them, the fate of the buffalo and the fate of the Lakota are intertwined, not only economically, but also in terms of each nation's history. Both the buffalo and the Lakota are seen as survivors of genocidal politics at the hands of the government, and this shared tragic historical experience only deepens the bonds and adds responsibility to each side to look out for the other. This is still true today, as might best be seen in the controversy over the killing of Yellowstone buffalo that wander into Montana. "When you destroy something like these buffalo," DuBray says in relation to Yellowstone buffalo, "it destroys us. Each time one of these buffalo is killed, part of us is killed, too" (in National Park Service [NPS] 2000:757).

Because of this bond, bringing back buffalo to reservations will improve the situation on reservations by the simple fact that buffalo are once again physically present in the lives of the residents: "[T]he buffalo are back and the people have changed. The beginnings changed. They are beginning to grow and they are beginning to understand little things about their lives that they didn't know before. It's beginning to have impacts on Tribes where there are buffalo" (LaRose in NPS 2000:866). I think this is true because the phys-ical presence of buffalo will bring back cultural memories and a rediscov-ering and renewal of cultural traditions relating to buffalo, regardless whether they come from elders or from anthropological texts. As such, the presence of the animals initiates a discourse about culture, a feeling that Indian cul-tures have something to offer to the larger world, and with that a feeling of personal worth that will affect the general well-being of reservation residents. Efforts to revive the buffalo culture on reservations cannot be seen as only an economic or ecological re-replacement of cattle: they have to be regarded in a holistic way, taking into account the cultural and historical implica-tions that are attached to both animals.

As DuBray points out (1993:394–95), buffalo were teachers to the Lakota: "[T]hose animals were our professors. That was our university out there, out on the plains and that's where we learned from, we observed, watched. You look at the family ties the buffalo has, the social structure, the social order, it's very similar to the Lakota structure." Buffalo, he says, are organized in *tiyospayes*, extended family units, which is "real important to their relation-ship to the land" because they dispersed through the plains in small groups. According to many people involved with the bison projects, the Lakota learned their social organization from the buffalo. In other words, the Lakota learned from the behavior of the bison how they in turn could best adapt to the plains environment.

The relation between buffalo and plains nations as teachers and students is not just something of the past but is a notion that has been consciously brought into and adapted to present reservation situations by some tribal buffalo programs. On these reservations (e.g., Fort Belknap), buffalo have been used as teachers and therapists in addiction programs and tribal court systems. From prolonged observation of buffalo interaction, people learn kinship and family values, such as respect and how to treat one's children.

I mentioned previously that buffalo were traditionally considered to be wakan in Lakota culture. The Lakota word wakan is often translated as "sacred." That might come pretty close to the meaning, if sacredness means something like "the wonder and mystery of nature through which God is thus known" (Gilkey 1993:203). However it is essential to understand that beings that are wakan are not in a different realm from secular beings: They are also secular because there traditionally has been no "sharp distinction between sacred and secular. Since every object was believed to have a spirit, every object was believed to be *wakan*" (DeMallie 1987:30). To be wakan was the manifestation of an incomprehensible power, which had to be pleased, but was always "bounded and directed" (DeMallie 1987:29). Sometimes, the translation of wakan as sacred can lead to misunderstandings. This can be seen, for example, by input into the management plans for the Yellowstone bison herd. Arguing against the killing, one respondent at a public hearing said: "The buffalo is really powerful to the people, really sacred" (Wing in NPS 2000:756). This could be interpreted as a general objection to any killing of buffalo because of their sacred status. However, such an interpretation would not be in accord with traditional values. While they are wakan, buffalo are and have been animals and fulfill practical roles in Lakota society: the status of being sacred or wakan does not mean that they cannot be touched. In fact, it is their role to provide food and other practical benefits for the people. In return for their role as providers for the people, however, they deserve respect.

Hunhoff says that "[o]nly the Great Spirit was above *Tatanka*. *Tatanka* was a symbol of the Great Spirit" (1993:12), and similar statements abound in the popular literature. Not only do they emphasize the male aspects of the buffalo—tatanka is the term for the dominant bulls; buffalo in general are *pte*—but they also tend to create the image that buffalo were revered by Plains Indians. Under the influence of some of these ideas, which tie in with notions of "ecological Indians," and of the Christian notion of the "sacred," which tends to be separated from this world, some Lakota have actually become opposed to any slaughtering of buffalo. Something sacred, they argue, should not be used in any way for commercial purposes. The supporters of tribal buffalo herds, however, contend that the buffalo are wakan because of their ecological relationships, which have always included the special relations to humans and the use of buffalo by humans. If traditionally, Plains Indians have lived off buffalo, they say, then how can tradition be used to deny the right to slaughter buffalo? Because buffalo are wakan, this has to be done with respect, but one role of the buffalo is to support their relatives. As Donald Meyers points out (in NPS 2000:818), "Native People do not worship the buffalo, but rather hold this magnificent creature in high esteem and recognize its role in the survival of our species."

Again, it is important to note that these feeling of intense relations and of kinship are held by those Lakota people who either have held on through intergenerational transmission to aspects of the prereservation value system or are trying to reconstruct what they see as a traditional value system. From the late nineteenth century into the early twentieth century, reservations on the northern plains underwent a cultural change to a predominantly ranching economy, and with this change, important cultural values shifted, too. In the efforts to reconstruct traditional cultural values, new ideologies sometimes influence the perceptions of the past; this is true just as much for internal memories of the past as it is for external, stereotypical images of American Indians. I will discuss the consequences and cultural shifts somewhere else. What is necessary to point out in the context of tribal bison ranching, however, is that by no means do all Lakota agree on the significance of contemporary relations to bison.

Many Lakota feel no direct special relationship to the animals, except those that are routinely expressed in the rhetoric of identity politics. One consequence of this is that from the start, tribal bison ranching was perceived from two different perspectives. Whereas most of the innovative thinkers and activists who pushed the idea in the beginning envisioned a potential revitalization of traditional culture, many others simply saw the projects in strictly economic terms. This division in perspective—and consequently in approaches to management of the herds—would become more pronounced as the herds grew and the projects proved that they could actually be successful. The economic, cultural, political, and symbolic significance of a fledgling, innovative experiment is not as great as that of a project that shows promise of being able to influence or represent the future of economic development for a society. Once the projects became more successful, in other words, politics became involved.

Before talking about politics, however, it might be a good idea to look a bit closer at some of the ecological facts about buffalo because those are large determinants of whether bison operations can and should be successful economic development projects, especially as compared to cattle ranching.

CHAPTER 4

Bison Management

"The buffalo had few qualities," says Walter Prescott Webb, who for a long time was regarded as the eminent historian of the Great Plains (1981:44), "save massive size and gregariousness, that fitted it to the Plains. . . . The buffalo was slow of gait, clumsy in movement, and had relatively poor eyesight and little fear of sound." In view of the fact that buffalo evolved with, and lived in, the historical North American ecosystem for at least ten thousand years, the argument seems to be just as ridiculous as functionalist arguments that declare indigenous peoples to be "maladapted" (Edgerton 1992). Compare Webb's statement with the following description: "Carefully crafted by nature and perfectly suited to a grassland and plains environment, the bison was seemingly assured of a near eternal survival in its North American domain. Endowed with great strength and agility, quickness of movement, keen hearing, sense of smell, and resistance to disease, this large horned mammal's only perceived weakness was less than average eyesight" (Danz 1997:65).

The genus *Bison* first appeared in Asia at the end of the Pliocene, and whereas one branch of the family went west, finally becoming the *Bison bonasus*, or Wisent, of eastern Europe, the other moved east and eventually into North America. After constant adaptations to changing environments, the historic *Bison bison* emerged, mostly on the wide grasslands (Berger and Cunningham 1994:24; Haines 1995:1–15; McHugh 1972:27–37). Historically, several subspecies of *Bison bison* have been recognized, especially

Bison bison athabascae, or Wood Buffalo, in Canada. Valerius Geist (1991, 1996:59–60), however, makes the case that Wood Buffalo are not a separate subspecies from Plains Buffalo, but an ecotype, better adapted to their forested habitat. Wood Buffalo have a narrower and longer body, longer legs, and their hump, the muscles for the front legs, is placed more forward. Many of these traits can be seen today in Plains Buffalo because conservation efforts have mixed the two types in many cases.

Buffalo are fabled for their adaptation to the plains. One of the most obvious adaptations is the ability of buffalo to live through winter. This is often attributed to their technique of "facing the storm," or walking into the wind (Dary 1989:36). McHugh puts this into the realm of legends (1972:243). "All the bison I've observed during storms," he says, "have been facing in random directions." William Temple Hornaday stated that "the buffalo used to face the storms, instead of turning tail and 'drifting' before them helplessly like cattle. But at the same time, when beset by a blizzard, he would wisely seek shelter from it in some narrow and deep valley or system of ravines" (2002:423). From my own observations, it seems to be true that buffalo have a tendency to face the wind. Some who do not care to do so might also face away, however. But before a blizzard hit, the buffalo I know always disappeared from the exposed flat lands into the ravines. Frank Gilbert Roe, who has a bone to pick with Hornaday in general, thinks that it might not have been very "wise" to seek shelter from a blizzard in a narrow ravine because the buffalo there "ran the greatest risk of being buried alive" (1951:191). Indeed, one should not imagine buffalo seeking shelter from storms in narrow ravines like troops in a trench; the reason why valleys offer protection is that there are trees and bushes in valleys. I have to add, though, that during blizzards, some buffalo appeared out of and into the snow as if nothing was going on. "As a description of something which buffalo were observed—or even believed—to do on occasion," as Roe says, "the foregoing is of great interest; as a definition of their conduct in all cases under such conditions, it is woefully inaccurate and misleading" (1951:191). All authors agree that buffalo occasionally did fall prey to blizzards and froze to death.

Stories about survival instincts of buffalo abound. For example, one person told me that he observed buffalo walk up a snow-covered hill, lay on their side and slide down, thereby freeing grass from the snow with their hump. It is clear that buffalo use their heads to shovel snow from grass. This method works well to amazing snow depths but not when the snow is covered by a heavy sheet of ice. Buffalo usually migrate in more or less a single file, a trait that gets rewarded in winter because a strong animal will blaze a trail through high snow that the group can then follow. They also have a strong endurance running capacity. Stories of buffalo running faster than racehorses abound, yet they are usually slower, although with top speeds near that of racehorses. Buffalo can run at thirty-five miles an hour for about half a mile. However, whereas a good buffalo horse outran them on short distances, longer pursuits were mostly abandoned because the endurance and agility of the buffalo made up for the speed (McHugh 1972:171; Roe 1951:144–53). The jumping ability of buffalo can be observed easily in corrals or at fences. A buffalo can jump over a six-foot high fence from the stand. Most buffalo ranchers I know agree that a buffalo fence, no matter how high or sturdy, is more of a psychological impediment, for the benefit of the humans outside the fence to feel safe. Buffalo will charge through almost anything, including barn walls, if stressed enough. Despite their bulky appearance and their weight, close observation of buffalo shows sophisticated footwork that reminds me of antelopes. Many people are unpleasantly surprised by the speed with which buffalo can turn on their feet.

Bison are not cattle, and because they are two different species and evolved in different ecosystems, one can expect them to show different ecological behaviors and to have different impacts on the land. Webb (1981:245) states that cattle herding "was a natural occupation which used the land in its natural state and altered it hardly at all." I do not know what exactly he meant by "natural" occupation, but the land, inhabited and altered for centuries by Native societies, was definitely not "in a natural state." Many people do indeed subscribe to the natural state theory, of course. (Ab-)original wilderness, like *terra nullius*, is a welcome concept for settler cultures. Apart from that, some authors agree with Webb that cattle did not alter the land. They make the argument that cattle have simply replaced buffalo on the plains because both species are large grazers. Some actually argue that cattle grazing is saving the ecology of the plains rangelands because some grazing animals had to fill the ecological gap left by the extermination of the buffalo—without grazing, the grasslands would have disappeared long ago (see Donahue 1999:133–34, 137; Wuerthner 1998:374–75). Much of this argumentation circles around what exactly is meant by rangelands.

    Gary Gray, for example, thinks that the term rangeland denotes "a kind of land": land that is so limited by environmental factors that it is unsuitable for any other use than grazing (1993:177). Using this definition, which basically follows Webb's definition of the plains as a region of deficiencies, it does not matter what animals graze the land or how it is grazed. Critical of cattle ranching, Donahue (1999:9), on the other hand, emphasizes that "'Rangeland' is not an ecological term," but that it "refers to lands that are, or historically have been, used by domestic livestock." Using this definition, the land has actually been changed into rangeland from its natural state as grazing grounds for native animals.

Today, rangeland on the plains is under heavy pressure from exotic species, both plants and animals. As Crosby (1986:157–59, 290–91), an environmental historian, points out, the successful invasion of the region was only possible after the buffalo, which had evolved with the native grasses and were in a symbiotic relationship with them, had been removed from the system. If that is true, then cattle have obviously not ecologically replaced buffalo, and on the contrary played a crucial part in a dramatic change in the ecosystem. Ecologists agree that cattle grazing alone is not responsible for this change: exotic plants "colonize open sites where competition by native species is reduced by excessive grazing, excessive trampling, insufficient grazing, fire, or other stresses" (Weaver, Payson, and Gustafson 1996: 72). Because insufficient grazing can truly present a problem for the ecosystem, cattle grazing can indeed be a good management tool, as long as seasonal variables, intensity, and frequency of grazing are taken into account (Bragg and Steuter 1996:63; Manning 1997:222–23; Plumb and Dodd 1993). As Licht says (1994:70), "it seems safe to say that livestock grazing is neither inherently good nor bad for biodiversity conservation. It becomes an issue when it is practiced in a manner not analogous to the way grassland species evolved." This last point needs to be emphasized. Already the conservationist Aldo Leopold was aware that overgrazing does not only consist of the mathematical problem of placing too many cattle on a piece of land but also has to take account of and is dependent on the specific local ecological circumstances (1991a:108–12).

Although the specific management of livestock plays a significant role in their impact on the ecosystem, the fact remains that from a strictly biological perspective, cattle are not an ecological replacement for buffalo. "The near elimination of the bison," say Benedict, Freeman, and Genoways (1996:155), "has had a substantial impact on prairies. . . . Although bison have been replaced by cattle and other livestock in most regions of the prairie, the impact is not the same." Buffalo not only prefer to graze different plants, but also their grazing habits are different from cattle. For example, whereas cattle tend to stay around water sources, thereby damaging riparian areas, buffalo go to water sources once a day and then spread out (Belsky, Matzke, and Uselman 1999; Donahue 1999:134–39; Plumb and Dodd 1993; Wuerthner 1998). Therefore, although "[m]odern grazing pressures . . . may be comparable" to historic ones (Weaver, Payson, and Gustafson 1996:68), by "feeding selectively on certain plants, grazers reduce the dominance of these species and allow subdominant plants to become a more important component of the vegetation" (Benedict, Freeman, and Genoways 1996:153).

Other than grazing itself, behavioral differences also play a role in different impacts on the ecosystem. Buffalo like to wallow, for example, thereby creating "unique microhabitats that cattle do not replicate"; these microhabitats can become miniature wetlands and persist for over a hundred years (Licht 1994:70–71). Buffalo also had a direct impact on wildlife and plant populations. Birds and mammals are affected by grazing and behavioral patterns and benefited from the vegetative mosaic resulting from the presence of buffalo (Truett, Phillips, and Kunkel 2001:129–34). These effects on the environment are not reduplicated by cattle; their introduction thereby altered the ecosystem to some degree, no matter the management methods.

Reintroducing bison to the plains, many advocates, including those on reservations hope, will allow for a return of ecological conditions representative of the landscape before the advance of Euro-American settlement. From that perspective, bison ranching offers a large advantage over cattle ranching. There are some problems with this notion, however.

In sheer numbers, buffalo had to have had a huge impact on the plains ecosystems. Although the estimated numbers of protohistorical buffalo are debated hotly, ranging from less than 30 to 60 million, historical accounts describe grasslands so full of buffalo that they were black (Danz 1997:16–22; Dary 1989:20–29; Haines 1995:32–34; McHugh 1972:13–17). This is a powerful image, and many times it is used to create a feeling of awe for the animal, without providing much context. For readers, it becomes implied that buffalo lived in such huge herds all over the pristine grasslands. Applying this image to the wider ecology of the grasslands, however, creates another image: that of the ecological devastation that has to follow. The question, then, is this: how could these millions of buffalo graze the plains without degrading the grassland in much the same way that cattle, if left grazing in great numbers, overgraze it today?

One part of the answer to that question lies in the social organization of buffalo. Buffalo are social and live in family groups for much of the year. Colonel Dodge (in Roe 1951:357) describes the following, "classic" scene of what, according to Roe, "appears to have been the largest herd ever recorded:

> The whole country appeared one mass of buffalo, moving slowly to the northward; and it was only when actually among them that it could be ascertained that the apparently solid mass was an agglomeration of innumerable small herds of from fifty to two hundred animals, separated from the surrounding herds by greater or less space, but still separated.

Probably describing a similar scene, yet more restrained, Rudolph Friederich Kurz (2005:51) wrote in 1851: "We rode into grazing lands that extended farther than the eye could see and over the wide extent of which were scattered the dusky forms of bison, ranging in herds." Both authors thus describe not a contiguous, massive herd, but a collection of smaller herds that, in its collectivity, forms the larger, stereotypical buffalo herds of the popular imagination. In summer, during the rut, and during the time that Euro-Americans would travel the plains, buffalo came together in huge herds, yet separated into smaller units. During the year, however, buffalo lived in these smaller groups, dispersed across the grasslands. Bulls actually often graze alone or in pairs and threes (see Berger and Cunningham 1994:74–75).

Whether or not the smaller groups, usually consisting of cows, calves, and young bulls, with a few older bulls hanging around nearby, are actually family groups or "clans" has long been contested. From my own observations, I am inclined to believe that they are. Certainly, other people do so, too (Wood 2001). Bison rancher and Yellowstone ranger Bob Jackson is one of the most ardent proponents of the family group thesis and manages his buffalo according to this principle (2001a, 2001b, 2002).

The second part of the answer is the migratory behavior of buffalo: they were constantly on the move. Father Hennepin gave one of the first descriptions of their migratory habits in 1683 (in Danz 1997:24–25). He was also one of the first authors to think that buffalo migrated south in winter and north in summer: "These wild cattle or bulls change country according to season and the diversity of climate. When they approach the northern lands and begin to feel the beginning of winter, they pass to the southern lands." In his 1887 report, Hornaday elaborated from there, assuming that there were different herds, and that at "the approach of winter the whole great system of herds . . . moved south a few hundred miles, and wintered under more favorable circumstances than each band would have experienced at its far-thest north" (2002:424–25). These popular theories were following the migratory patterns of birds, of course, but unfortunately for the theorists, they were wrong (McHugh 1972:174–75). Although buffalo usually seek pro-tection from the harsh winter climate, they do not necessarily go south but might actually go north, from the windswept plains into the boreal areas. Roe takes it to be possible that certain regions saw "more or less regular migra-tion" but disputes this for the buffalo range as a whole (1951:521–600). Although there were no truly regular north-south migrations, the buffalo were still constantly on the move.

Together with the social organization in small groups, the constant migra-tion of buffalo made their grazing pressure bearable for the land. As Wuerthner notes (1998:379), the "shifting mosaic of grazing pressure result-ing from near constant movement, along with periodic population decline due to variability in climatic condition almost ensured that heavily grazed areas would be rested, often for months or even years. Such lengthy rest is seldom emulated by most livestock management schemes which tend to focus on maintaining constant numbers with at most a reprise of a year or two from grazing influences."

Today, no buffalo are free to wander, especially not in the lower forty-eight states. The Yellowstone buffalo are sometimes called the last wild bison, but as should be clear by the controversy over allowing them to cross into the state of Montana, they are not. Most buffalo live on immensely smaller pieces of land. They do not enjoy free range, and most of them are culled for productivity. In other words, the family groups are broken up. Holding buffalo on relatively small parcels of land alters their behavior and their eco-logical impact as compared to cattle: "When comparing bison grazing with cattle grazing one must keep in mind that the nomadic nature of bison was perhaps the most significant difference between the two herbivores. . . . Replicating such a regional grazing pattern on a landscape comprising numerous small private holdings is improbable" (Licht 1994:71). Many peo-ple think of buffalo as free-roaming animals and compare the ecological impact of migratory times to the ecological impact of cattle. But as Plumb and Dodd point out (1993:639), "differences between the influence of free-roaming bison on pristine grasslands and semi-free-roaming bison on a fenced natural area must be much greater than those of the latter and domestic cattle."

Only if the buffalo pastures are big enough, in other words, to allow at least a modest replication of migrations and only if they are managed in accordance with their social organization into smaller family herds can the different ecological impacts of buffalo be felt. For example, on small pastures, buffalo might still not destroy riparian areas as much as cattle do, but the full advantages of having a native grazer impacting the land, rather than a foreign one, cannot be experienced. Because smaller pastures are the norm rather than the exception for bison ranches, the ecological advantages of buffalo ranching over cattle ranching are relativized accordingly.

There is another way in which buffalo are influenced when they are fenced in relatively small (or even more so, objectively small) pastures and are generally treated like cattle. Buffalo become domesticated. By this I do not mean the various attempts, which have gone on at least since the late eighteenth century to crossbreed buffalo with cattle (Hornaday 2002:451). Formal experiments in hybridization began in 1815 in Kentucky and have been going on ever since (Roe 1951:706–14; Rorabacher 1970:95–105). Even without crossbreeding, however, some people maintain that buffalo will become domesticated in captivity, especially in situations of intensive management.

This is a tendency that should worry environmentalists but must be especially worrisome for tribal practitioners because bison that become domesticated, or in other words lose their natural or, depending on the perspective, cultural instincts and behaviors, cannot serve in their intended role as teachers anymore. The traditional roles cannot be fulfilled beyond the immediate economic ones if buffalo are domesticated. Phrased in terms of culture, it will be impossible to bring back aspects of Lakota culture through the introduction of buffalo on reservations if the buffalo themselves have undergone a culture change. There is, therefore, for these practitioners, a definite need to keep bison as wild as possible, which in turn means the maximal absence of herd management.

For Fred DuBray (1993:395), one of the most intense critics of domestication, the problem begins "when we start this intense management kind of stuff, where we take out all the older bulls, take out the unrulier ones, take out all the problem animals and we have this nice little gentle herd that we can control." Domestication occurs under conditions of "intensive, selective predation," which are, according to ecological anthropologist Tom Ingold (1980:239), the very "ecological dynamics of ranching." A rancher who is faced with shipping some of his animals to slaughter will probably select the ones that give him the most trouble, eliminating their genes from the remaining pool. Dale Lott sees several factors involved in the future domestication of buffalo: "Humans will handle bison, will establish breeding populations with a strongly female biased sex ratio, will encourage rapid body growth and will sometimes sharply increase local population density. Each of these features of domestication will tend to modify bison behavior away from the wild type through natural selection, artificial selection and developmental phenotypic change" (1998:104). In addition to an increased female sex ratio, there is also a trend in the buffalo industry and in public herds to retain only younger bulls and females. Custer State Park (2001:7), whose buffalo herd provides much of the revenue needed for the park's operation, "removes animals from the herd when they are 10 years old. The females are sold at auction, and the bulls are hunted." All of these management techniques represent a change from situations in the wild, where older, stronger bulls are usually the ones who have gained the right to reproduce and educate the young, and females can have calves up to the age of forty-two. Even if older cows do not bear calves anymore, they can still provide leadership and experience to younger buffalo. This experience gets lost in a managed situation and will lead to inevitable change in behavior, or as some Lakota would see it, in culture.

More factors than selective management techniques affect bison domestication. Buffalo are known to succumb to stress much quicker than cattle. In my own experience, they might be compared to deer: to capture a deer, even without harming it, can induce so much stress in its system that it dies from it, even after having been released. Buffalo react in much the same ways to chutes and confinement. By confining buffalo in feedlots or on a small acreage, their natural curiosity and their mental development will be impaired. This can lead to poor maternal care and generally more sickness. Odds for passive selection go up if one adds grain diets and weaning of calves at an early age. Animals that can deal with stress better, or in other words have a calmer temperament, will be favored by both active and passive selection; in a few generations the wilder genes will be lost, and according to many people, buffalo will not be wild anymore.

There are also other selective goals than the one of making buffalo more effective ranching animals. Some ranches are trying to bring back what they see as the "typical" buffalo—big and muscular bulls. These might be ranches that adhere to a hands-off management but still use selective predation (e.g., in hunts) to breed back what they see as the fittest and strongest animals. This approach still selects for outside interests. As Michael Collins pointed out to me, it is not always the big or aesthetically appealing animals that are the leaders or the fittest or the most adaptive animals. In his view, the herd should be allowed to make these judgments on its own, and humans should not intervene with their own criteria. Only then will the herd be assured to be healthy.

Although DuBray says that ranchers "don't have to do anything with these buffalo"(1993:394), and experienced buffalo ranchers applying hands-off management methods have assured me that their buffalo are a lot healthier than those run through vaccination chutes every year, many ranchers see themselves under much pressure to run buffalo like cattle. Not only have many buffalo ranchers switched to buffalo from cattle ranching for primarily economic reasons and apply their old experiences because they worked, but market forces and interstate transportation laws seem to require the culling of older animals, weaning of calves, and yearly vaccinations. In fact, running buffalo through a chute does not necessarily hurt the animal, as long as people keep in mind that these are not cattle. Understanding buffalo behavior can lead to low-stress handling methods and low-stress facilities (Grandin 2001; Lanier and Grandin 2001; Patterson 2001a,b, 2002a,b). Of course, even if "stress-free," these procedures still present human interventions in the lives of buffalo.

For somebody who believes that buffalo are relatives and thus equal to humans, with their own social organization in families, providing education and leadership for their young, the point is not so much whether buffalo are calmed down before undergoing stressful events or are trained to endure them. What becomes important is that buffalo are treated with respect: that they are asked for permission before their lives are impacted. Ingold says that in contrast to wild animals, domestic animals "have no free soul, either individually or collectively, as distinct from the souls of their respective human masters. Otherwise put, the spirit of the domestic animal is the soul of man, controlling the animal from without" (1987:255). To assume that buffalo have no free soul is to see them as domestic animals; wild animals are not controlled, even if their territory might be limited. It is this notion that tribal practitioners like DuBray expressed when they called for hands-off management practices. It is the expression of the values of cattle ranching when others on the reservation called for branding, vaccination, and seasonal culling of the bison herd.

From the start, Fred DuBray drew a definite distinction between the practices Pte Hca Ka would use in raising buffalo and those used by other buffalo and cattle producers. "We don't believe you can treat buffalo like domesticated animals. When we say we're bringing the buffalo back, we don't mean to do it like [other] producers have been doing. That way of raising these animals is just as big a threat as extinction itself. . . . This is more than an economic venture; it is a deep-rooted venture. What we're trying to do is to fit a traditional belief into a modern situation" (DuBray in Porterfield 1995:B1). "We're not interested in buffalo ranching if it's done in the way that cattle ranching is usually done. Many ranchers, for instance, might spend a lot of time killing off prairie dogs and coyotes—animals they see as pests. But the buffalo don't see them as pests, and neither do we. We're working to restore the whole habitat" (DuBray in Crum 1997:41). In essence, the objectives of the corporation were holistic, and as DuBray told me, a narrowing down to categories, such as economics, ecology, culture, or health, would have only artificially broken up the larger goal the corporation was trying to reach. For DuBray, the buffalo were part of a larger harmony of people living with the land in a right way, and if they did, then positive consequences would undoubtedly follow from that, affecting all other aspects of their existence.

Having situated buffalo ranching in this larger perspective, for DuBray there is no excuse for people who do not treat the buffalo right. Many ranchers tell him it is unfortunate they have to dehorn their animals, wean the calves, or raise them in feedlots, but DuBray answers: "[T]hey say well it's really unfortunate that I have to do this but I have no choice, well I'm suggesting that you do have a choice. . . . [T]he easiest way is to just fit in to what is going on now, 'it's not my duty to try to make change', but it is, it's every one of our duty to try to make change, because this earth is the only one we have and it can only do so much" (1993:397). DuBray draws a direct analogy between the treatment of buffalo and the treatment of the Lakota and asserts that buffalo have a culture that can be broken (1993:395–96). Buffalo act on instincts, "but some of that [behavior] is learned behavior from their peers, just like us, same thing. That's what happened with Indian people, they put them away in boarding schools to break the culture. . . ." The fact that buffalo have culture and act on the same basis of rational thought as humans also has consequence for a respectful approach: "When I was first planning this project, one of the elders said something that stuck with me. He said that before you bring the buffalo back you must ask the buffalo if they want to come back" (DuBray in Kelley 1993:8).

To say that non-Indian bison ranchers in general have adopted a different management philosophy than Indian bison ranchers would be an inexcusable misrepresentation. Management philosophies adopted by individual ranchers have no correlation to ethnicity. There are non-Indians who subscribe to the notions laid out by DuBray, and there are Indians who could not disagree with the notions any stronger. Cultural values to the land and to animals are varied and defy cultural stereotypes. Most ranchers on the plains—Indian or non-Indian—have the same time length of family history in the profession and have developed their management philosophies based on these professional cultural experiences and professional interactions with the land.

This important point notwithstanding, it was clear from the start that the InterTribal Bison Cooperation (ITBC) would adopt different tendencies from the National Bison Association (NBA) or the North American Bison Cooperative (NABC), simply because the people in control of ITBC at the time were placing so much emphasis on cultural revitalization. It should not come as a surprise then, that at least in the rhetoric employed, the philosophies of ITBC and NABC emphasized different things. As DuBray explained (in LeMay 1993), slaughter plants and commercial operations took away the required respect with which, in his perspective, buffalo needed to be treated, and which prohibited ITBC members to participate in NABC:

> Before we build the herds to a point where there is enough available for a viable market, we have a need within our own community. It's very important that we raise them as natural as we can on open prairies where the animals have access to plants they have evolved with; just because they are buffalos that doesn't mean they provide a healthy food source. That's where we differentiate ourselves from most of the commercial producers; our tribes have a greater responsibility than just an economic enterprise (DuBray in Murg 2003:B4)

DuBray always expressed to me his opposition to the management practices of feedlots and meat finishing, but he also connected that to a larger agenda: that bison operations should not just be focusing on economics should not be read as an opposition to an economic use of buffalo. It would be more true to say that even the economic aspect of tribal bison operations, in many practitioners' view, should serve larger goals, primarily that of extending tribal sovereignty.

As I mentioned previously, ITBC always placed a lot of emphasis on the economic well-being of its member organizations. Tribal bison operations then definitely should be participating in the market, but they should partake in the market on their own terms. After all, the buffalo are not simply an ephemeral religious or spiritual entity but a practical sign, just as much if not more than a simple utilitarian tool, of a return to general tribal political and economic sovereignty. For many years, for example, ITBC was looking into building its own permanent slaughter facility. Finally, in 2003, Fort Belknap was able to purchase a meat packing plant approved by the U.S. Department of Agriculture (USDA) in Malta, Montana, and ITBC intended to use this facility to establish tribal buffalo meat brands (Perez 2003; Selden 2003).

CHAPTER 5

Pte Hca Ka, Inc.

The Cheyenne River Sioux Tribe (CRST), as an official entity, requested the allocation of surplus buffalo from either the National Park Service (NPS) or Custer State Park as early as 1969. Besides receiving buffalo from the parks, CRST also bought a few buffalo from private owners in the 1970s to increase its herd. The tribal buffalo were kept in a pasture by the highway bridge over the Missouri River. Through the 1980s, the herd number oscillated around one hundred animals. The buffalo were sold for meat, mostly to Westside Meats in Mobridge, donated for funerals and cultural events, and sold to individual owners and ranches around the country. Some trophy hunts were also held, at least one of which was videotaped by the tribal college for promotional purposes. Fences and corrals were constructed, and additional animals came from Theodore Roosevelt National Park and Custer State Park. From 1987 on, the tribal buffalo program was known as the Buffalo Run Game Reserve. Besides a herd manager, several other full-time jobs were supported by the buffalo herd. In 1991, the herd was grazing on twenty-five hundred acres around the Swiftbird community, between US 212 and Lake Oahe.

As mentioned previously, in the late 1980s and early 1990s, people on American Indian reservations noticed the growing market interest in buffalo, and it was exactly the potential to combine economic with symbolic value and economic opportunity with cultural revitalization that led to increased activities in Indian buffalo ranching. On Cheyenne River Sioux Reservation, it was Fred DuBray who came up with a plan to turn the existing Buffalo Run Game Reserve into an economic, cultural, and ecological tribal enterprise, Pte Hca Ka, Inc. Pte hca ka can be translated as "the real buffalo" or "all the buffalo" in English, although I have heard numerous other translations.

DuBray, a tribal member and Vietnam veteran, was working as tribal economic planner and as a coordinator for the Administration for Native Americans (ANA) with the CRST in 1991 when he was charged with devising a new tribal development strategy. He conducted a general assessment and analysis of the previous approaches to economic development, their pitfalls, and the general situation of the reservation: "I looked at everything— our geographical isolation, the cost of shipping, the cost of setting up an artificial economy. I studied all the failures" (DuBray in "Bringing Back the Buffalo" 1995:32). In his conclusions, DuBray came to see the buffalo as a potential way to economic and spiritual restoration.

The plan was for the existing tribal herd to be expanded, and the buffalo to eventually be restored to their role as a backbone of the economy, while at the same time restoring aspects of the old buffalo culture. In DuBray's analysis, the reservation had two resources: land and people. An agricultural solution therefore made sense, but in his eyes, this could not simply be an expansion of the cattle industry. Because the solution had to be holistic, including the social problems on the reservation, a true Lakota solution had to be found, and that was the buffalo. If approached correctly, the buffalo could be sustained by the two available resources and would not only draw on the resources but in turn become a resource themselves, not only for their own restoration, but also for the reservation as a whole.

If buffalo have a culture and an ability to make their own decisions, then ranching buffalo is no longer simply an economic activity or a biological interaction but a social interaction. From this perspective, the consequences of buffalo ranching become readily understandable: social actors in turn interact with people, reacting in part to human approaches to them. Everybody takes for granted that the social actors they encounter can be helpful in ways that are not directly linked to the "professional" area in which the main interaction takes place. To treat buffalo in the right way, then, can have positive implications for a whole range of social and cultural issues; if the buffalo are treated with the culturally appropriate respect and their culturally appropriate role, then the buffalo will in turn help the people—as they have done in the past.

Like all reservations on the northern plains, Cheyenne River has had and still has its fair share of social problems involving poverty, health, and abuse. It is essential to put these problems in a historical and cultural context. Too often, people rush to judgments about how American Indians have no choice but to adapt to a "modern" environment or leave the reservations if their economy is bad. Historical and contemporary contexts of catastrophic culture change, disenfranchisement, genocide, and unresolved grieving are fundamental to any understanding of problems on reservations and are essential in attempts to solve them.

The Cheyenne River Reservation has a much higher poverty rate than the rest of South Dakota. In all of South Dakota, which encompasses several other Indian reservations with high poverty rates, around 14 percent of people live in poverty. Some sources put the poverty level of the Cheyenne River residents as high as 68 percent (Humphrey 2001a). This is probably not too high, if one looks at some Bureau of Indian Affairs (BIA) figures. According to these (BIA 1999:6), 78 percent of the tribal labor force on Cheyenne River is unemployed. This number went up in 2002. According to an Economic Trends Report prepared by the University of Kansas and using BIA data, of 13,961 tribal members, 9,841 were available for work, of which 1,462 were actually employed. This puts the true unemployment rate at 85.1 percent (Kansas Center for Community Economic Development [KCCED] 2004:21). The labor force participation rate, or the indicator of the number of people who would like to work but have given up looking for a job, on Cheyenne River is low. From 1990 to 2002, labor force participation rose in Dewey county from 37.5 percent to 43.1 percent but has actually fallen in Ziebach county from 32.7 percent to 27 percent. The rate for South Dakota rose from 49.9 percent to 55.3 percent, whereas the rate for the United States overall stayed at a stable 66.6 percent (KCCED 2004:15, 20).

In a report for the Economic Development Administration of the U.S. Department of Commerce, Velarde Tiller gives the per capita income for Cheyenne River Sioux Reservation as $4,077 (1995:555). The U.S. Census reported per capita income in 1999 for the reservation at $8,710, and the poverty rate for individuals at 38.5 percent (table 1). In 2001, per capita income had come up to $13,597, but Ziebach county still had the fifth lowest county figures of all counties in the United States. It should come as no surprise that even of those people who are employed, a staggering number live below poverty guidelines. According to one statistic, of the 1,462 tribal

Table 1
Poverty, unemployment, and household income
in Dewey and Ziebach counties

	South Dakota (%)	Dewey county (%)	Ziebach county (%)
County-level unemployment rates, 2001[a]	3.3	16.1	14.4
People below poverty level, 1997 model-based estimate[b]	14	32.9	46.4
County-level poverty rates, 1999[c]	13.2	33.6	49.9

	South Dakota ($)	Dewey County ($)	Ziebach County ($)
County-level median household income, 1999[a]	35,282	23,272	18,062
County-level per capita income, 2001[d]	26,566	17,583	9,610

Note: The U.S. Census and Economic Research Service(ERS) numbers count only those who do receive unemployment benefits, or in other words, they discount the long-term unemployed.
[a]Data from ERS 2002b.
[b]Data from U.S. Census 2002a and 2002b.
[c]Data from ERS 2002a.
[d]Data from Kansas Center for Community Economic Development (KCCED) 2004: 30, 32.

members employed on Cheyenne River in 2002, 100 percent fell below the Department of Health and Human Service's Poverty Guidelines (KCEED 2004:21). Although the exact numbers reported differ slightly from agency to agency, "it is clear that what money there is, is spread very thin, and that the lack can not help but have an adverse affect [sic] on quality of life" (KCCED 2004:30).

Although the economic indicators do not look rosy, the population is growing. From 1990 to 2002, population in Dewey county grew 9 percent, and the population in Ziebach county grew 17 percent. This growth is not mirrored in surrounding counties (KCCED 2004:3). Compared to the whole state of South Dakota, which, according to the 2000 Census is 88.7 percent "white", Cheyenne River, like all Lakota reservations, has a higher birth rate. It also has a much higher percentage of people under eighteen

Table 2
Birth rates and percentages of young and old people in population

	All U.S. races, 1997	All Indian Health Service areas, 1996–1998	Aberdeen Indian Health Service area, 1996–1998
Per 1,000 population:			
Birth rate[a]	14.5	24	29.5
	South Dakota (%)	Dewey County (%)	Ziebach County (%)
People under 5 years old, 2000[b]	6.8	9.2	10.8
People under 18 years old, 2000[b]	26.8	38.9	40.6
People 65 years old and over, 2000[b]	14.3	8.3	7.5

[a]Data from Indian Health Service (IHS) 2002.
[b]Data from U.S. Census 2002a and 2002b.

years old. On the other hand, however, fewer people reach age sixty-five or older than in the rest of South Dakota (table 2). This means, on the one hand, that the problems with unemployment will persist or grow more acute in the future. On the other hand, it also means that fewer people can fulfill the traditional leadership and advisory roles of elders.

Despite the high percentage of young residents on reservations, Aberdeen Indian Health Service (IHS) Area, of which Cheyenne River is a part, also has a high infant mortality rate. Problems with health care issues are in general much larger in American Indian communities than elsewhere and are mirrored in a lower life expectancy rate. Of all IHS areas, Aberdeen IHS Area has the highest or second to highest rates for deaths overall and for deaths from alcohol, diabetes, and suicide (IHS 2002). What the figures show, at least in the abstract, is the constant presence of hope and death in the communities, a feeling of joy and mourning that is, for the outsider, almost unbearable in its paradoxical reverberations (table 3). But in this close-knit society it is the closeness and familiarity of people affected by births and deaths that leave a mark.

I do not list these figures to paint a desolate picture. Poverty rates, substance abuse, and other statistics have to be approached critically, especially in a cross-cultural setting. "[O]utsiders," as Pickering points out (2000:68),

Table 3
Infant mortality, death rates, and life expectancy

	All U.S. races, 1997	All Indian Health Service areas, 1996–1998	Aberdeen Indian Health Service area, 1996–1998
Per 1,000 live births (adjusted):			
Infant mortality rates for infants under 1 year	7.2	8.9	12.5
Per 100,000 population (adjusted):			
Age-adjusted death rate	471.9	715.2	1009.4
Age-adjusted suicide death rates	10.6	20.2	33.1
Age-adjusted alcoholism death rates	6.3	46.5	87.4
Age-adjusted diabetes mellitus death rate	13.5	52.8	82.9
Life expectancy:			
At birth, both sexes	76.5	70.6	65.4
At birth, males	73.6	67.4	61.2
At birth, females	79.4	74.2	69.9

Data from Indian Health Service 2002.

"chiefly see the reservations as impoverished, even though many Lakotas are happier and doing better with little cash than Americans in wealthier conditions." There is alcohol and drug abuse on the reservation, and there is a high suicide rate and a lot of poverty. Eagle Butte, at least, also has a problem with gang violence. Although they mirror problems of many non-reservation rural counties on the plains, these facts are a part of reservation life, a part of the reality of what it means to be Lakota in the United States. But they are also the background of continued generosity and fortitude and of people who refuse to have their humanity and dignity stripped away from them. Huffstetter (1998) shows how people from Cheyenne River try to deal with their feelings of grief and mourning. He also wants to show "that Lakota people have hope and courage and generosity in the midst of their grieving" (8). If anything, I want to say that the hope, courage, and generosity of the Lakota I know is some of the best I have ever experienced.

As I mentioned previously, the problems of the reservation have to be seen in both cultural and historical context. Lakota people are still grieving the traumatic loss of ancestors, land, language, and ways of life (Huffstetter 1998:7–8). Yellow Horse Brave Heart and DeBruyn (1998) show how contemporary discriminations do not stand alone but exacerbate unresolved historical traumata. A report by the South Dakota Advisory Committee to the U.S. Commission on Civil Rights (SDAC) points out that "[t]he expressed feelings of hopelessness and helplessness in Indian Country cannot be overstated. . . . Despair is not too strong a word to characterize the emotional feelings of many Native Americans who believe they live in a hostile environment" (2000:39).

Alcoholism, drug use, a high suicide rate, rampant unemployment, and instances of racism go hand in hand. To state this is not to make excuses; it is to make an effort to understand why things happen and why it is exceedingly hard to change them. Quite a few people off the reservation think, and told me implicitly and explicitly, that Indians are alcoholics and therefore deserve their lot. That is not so (see Medicine 2007).

Although alcoholism is a huge problem, many Lakota on Cheyenne River are alcohol free and are well respected for that. Even those who do drink know that they should not and are embarrassed about it. The very few public alcoholics are socially sanctioned outcasts, and sometimes even their own families will not speak with them. Constant excessive drinking is not accepted partly because it prohibits people from fulfilling their social responsibilities. "The ultimate aim of Dakota life," Ella Deloria says (1944:25), is to be a good relative; "Without that aim and the constant struggle to attain it, the people would no longer be Dakotas in truth. They would no longer even be human." Although alcoholism historically is sometimes seen as resistance in a certain way—resisting acculturation by fleeing from a reality too cruel to endure—and some people see alcoholics as warriors, a warrior's first responsibility is to protect and be an example for his people.

Most people who do drink, whether alcoholics or not, are social drinkers and can control their habits to various degrees. Many know that they will not be able to stop once they start but have control over when they start. Some people drink nonstop for three days over a weekend but have no problem staying sober for a month. Others drink more often. Drinking is a social habit partly exactly because people know they should refrain from it. In my experience, abstinence is highly respected. If one is present when others drink and does not participate, however, not only might one feel asocial, and perhaps be seen as asocial, but also one elevates oneself over the others morally, something that runs counter to Lakota culture. The best way not to drink, then, is not to be in places where people drink, which often makes it hard to be social, a mainstay of Lakota culture.

Drug use is often also a social affair, although it is easier to decline. Marijuana is about as ambiguously accepted or not accepted as alcohol, although around 1970, it was virtually unknown on Cheyenne River (DeMallie personal communication; see also Vazeilles 1977:117). I have heard from researchers familiar with the situation on Pine Ridge that this is not probable but would like to make the argument that both a more assimilated ranching society and traditional Lakota values might have made Cheyenne River society as a whole more conservative. Marijuana does not present the real danger of drug use today, but crystal methamphetamine does. Methamphetamine is imported to, and produced on, the reservation, and some people have become severely addicted. It is in a different category from alcohol and marijuana, and its use is not accepted by most people who drink or smoke.

It is important to remember that the appearance of methamphetamine, just like many other problems on the reservation, is a mirror of the surrounding counties and most rural areas of the plains. The patterns of drinking and drug use follow the patterns off reservation in that they are in part a response to the social realities encountered in all of South Dakota. This is also true for suicides. As Osha Gray Davidson points out (1990:94), the farm crisis of the 1980s sent suicide rates in rural plains areas soaring. Social realities on Cheyenne River are simply harsher than for most people off reservation and have been so for at least three generations. Davidson says (94), "The constant downward ratcheting of expectations, the grinding, daily battle against largely unknown but seemingly invincible enemies, the dissolution of families, communities, and dreams are taking a toll on rural people that will last for decades." On reservations, the conditions that rural farmers are fighting against have been in place for a century. Again, I do not mean to say by this that people cannot cope with life without drinking. But in an environment where traditional cultural mechanisms—especially ceremonies—to deal with psychological pressures have been suppressed both by external and internal dynamics, and depending on the social network might be difficult to obtain, and the reasons behind these pressures are hard or impossible to explain, the burden becomes too heavy to bear.

In a small community with a culturally tight kin network, almost every person who dies is related to everybody else. That by itself imposes a heavy bur-

den of grieving on people, given that there is a funeral to attend about every
two weeks. If deaths were mostly older people with fulfilled lives, they would
be bearable because we can accept what we can understand. But how are
relatives to understand the many deaths and near-deaths of younger people,
who often leave their families behind? How are they to understand that a
successful young woman tries to commit suicide in the shower? How are
they to understand that a family father gets crushed by his car a mile outside of town? How are they to understand that an eighth grader, an honored
school athlete, hangs himself in the closet three days before graduation ceremonies? As if it was not difficult enough to come to terms with such events
in the most ideal situation, most people on Cheyenne River cannot spare
time and energy to grieve because they need to fulfill their other social
responsibilities: to keep the living alive. As Greg Ducheneaux comments
(in Bordewich 1996:250), "We accept these deaths as normal. Suffering is
normal. Violent death is normal. They just shrug it off. It's our way of life."

The people who are strong enough to bear these burdens and refuse drug
use are often those who have the support of deep involvement in the traditional ways of healing such grievances. On the other hand, those who have
acculturated to the dominant culture and are at ease with it also have fewer
pressures. For a future with and in a continued Lakota culture, however,
redress for the contemporary and historical traumata cannot mean total
assimilation but has to include traditional methods of healing, and more generally, aspects of traditional culture and spirituality. I do not mean by that a
romanticized New Age interpretation of traditional spirituality and healing.
As Yellow Horse Brave Heart and DeBruyn say (1998:74): "What we advocate is the development of a spirituality that does not serve as a defense
against experiencing painful affects. Rather, a healthy spirituality embraces
the range of one's feelings—grief, shame and pain to joy, pride, and resolve
to maintain balance—in order to regain personal wellness and the power of
community self-determination."

This power of community self-determination, which means the liberation from exterior oppressive forces, is essential. "To be genuine, liberation
must not only remain comprehensive in scope, but it must also and primarily be achieved by the poor themselves," says the liberation theologian
Leonardo Boff (1997:108). To be able to rely on themselves to achieve their
liberation, however, people need first to realize and acknowledge that they
can trust themselves, their own ideas, histories, and traditions. In a society
of institutionalized discrimination and disdain toward poor people, this is

an essential but difficult step. To trust one's own traditions even though one has been taught for over a century that they are worthless is not easy yet invaluable. After all, as Boff writes (108), "The poor are not simply those who do not have; they *do* have. They have culture, ability to work, to work together, to get organized, and to struggle. Only when the poor trust in their own potential, and when the poor opt for others who are poor, are conditions truly created for genuine liberation."

The same argument is true not only for the cultural but also for the economic and political spheres. As Cornell and Kalt point out (1990:119), "economy follows sovereignty. . . . For some time federal officials and other analysts have argued that if tribes wish to be truly sovereign, they first need to build viable economics. This is backwards." In fact, the idea that economic development on American Indian reservations must be based on political and economic sovereignty is not a new finding. In 1976, the American Indian Policy Review Commission's (AIPRC) Task Force on "Reservation and Resource Development and Protection" came to the conclusion that, "without control over their own affairs, the Federal Government cannot expect total Indian economic development. . . . It is impossible to attain economic self-sufficiency and political self-determination in a system which perpetuates economic dependence" (AIPRC 1976:2).

If to be liberated and sovereign, communities need to think of themselves as having ability, culture, and tradition, then education and cooperative work can play huge roles in this process. Community health and sovereignty can be built through education, and if this education should be combined with cooperative ventures, it can center on symbolically powerful animals, such as buffalo.

Therapists have found animals to be useful allies in efforts of healing. As Fadler says (1995:145), "Today, therapists and educators are integrating animals into their work with both adults and children, recognizing that animals can be powerful catalysts in human transformation." Although he concentrates on the direct connections between pets and human health issues, this is easily transferable to other symbolically important animals. Wiebers (1995:137), an experienced neurologist, argues that health should not just focus on biologically identifiable diseases: "The concept of wellness representing not only absence of disease but also an inner harmony of body and spirit, and a harmony with the environment, is a profound one from which western medicine can learn a great deal." It is the reintegration of health issues "within a whole where everything is meaningful" by recourse to mythical language that contributes to healing, as Lévi-Strauss points out (1963:197). Healing can be seen as the process of finding a language that is "making it possible to undergo in an ordered and intelligible form a real experience that would otherwise be chaotic and inexpressible" (198). This can be readily applied to tribal buffalo projects and their expected ramifications on community social health issues.

In the context of American Indian reservations and cultural restoration, education in traditional ecology, encompassing social relations and the general value system, can be seen as an act of resistance and liberation. Depending on where people stand on issues of modernization and economic development, this can be seen as a positive or a negative trend. In general, however, education is necessary for achieving sovereignty: not just political sovereignty but also personal sovereignty, the ability to make choices for oneself. In the long run, education—and I do not just mean formal schooling—is irreplaceable. As such, education has consequences well beyond the return of the buffalo.

Children who are surrounded by a dysfunctional, alienated, oppressed, and unhealthy environment, both social and natural, will learn how to be oppressed and how to oppress and how to adapt to alienated, dysfunctional circumstances. The restoration of a healthy social and natural environment then is an essential part of any restoration of cultural health. If children can observe an environment in which people treat each other and the natural environment with respect—especially in cultures in which there might not be such a strict distinction between social and natural environment—they will grow up to treat their own environment with respect. Pooley and O'Connor (2000:712) have found that environmental education based on abstract ecological knowledge "results in little attention being given to values and the development of analytical skills and environmentally conscious behavior." Instead, they say (719), "both emotions and beliefs" should be specifically targeted "in educating people about the environment."

Education in social and cultural values, or in other words, education in total ecology, through, with, and about buffalo not only provides a respectful learning environment but also an applied setting. This in turn connects to traditional American Indian ways of education. Obviously, it is important that students learn the tools to thrive in the ways of the dominant society. But integrating cultural values and knowledge in education, such as in curricula that integrate traditional notions about bison, is an important addition to teach American Indian students "in a way which would make [each of them] a happy, useful, and important individual" (Pike 1974:36).

Nobody thinks restoration of culture means to go back in history: Lakota culture, like any culture, has changed too much for the historical past to be an alternative to the present. But the seeming division between traditional values and those of the dominant society needs to be addressed and resolved. If the Lakota want to stay Lakota and not become Euro-Americans— something that is likely impossible to be accepted by outside forces, anyway, in a society that puts so much emphasis on seeming biological difference— traditional values and aspects of traditional culture must play a large part in this resolution. The solution must be one informed by *wolakota*, all that which it means to be Lakota. "Poverty," says King (2001), "starves you of personality and integrity, morals and values. It is only through spirituality that all these issues can be balanced."

Without trying to imply any cultural similarities between Lakota and Buddhist cultures (see Paper 2001 on misguided attempts of doing so), the complexity of the situation might be exemplified by a Buddhist puzzle:

> The Zen master Fayun once said to his disciples: 'Suppose you were in a situation where if you were to move forward, you would lose the Dao [or here, wolakota], if you were to move backward, you would lose the world, and if you were to do neither, you would look ignorant as a stone. What would you do?' 'Is there any way we can get away from looking ignorant?' 'Abandon both rejection and attachment and act out your potential.' 'But if we act, how can we keep from losing the Dao and the world?' 'Move forward and backward at the same time.' (Tsai 1994:124)

To move in two directions at the same time, to live wolakota and thrive in the dominant society, is the complex problem that the Lakota—and other indigenous peoples all over the world—have to solve every day.

To some visionary activists on American Indian reservations in the late 1980s, tribal buffalo operations, with their economic possibilities coupled with a potential for cultural revitalization, seemed to be a perfect way to integrate aspects of traditional economic, cultural, and ecological values with the real- ities of a global, industrialized economy and the cultural and ecological values that are associated with that. Many tribal bison cooperatives have stayed, through their histories, a perfect manifestation of these issues, and maintained the balancing act that is required to keep momentum going and not to lose either the path or the world. Theoretically, the solution had been found, and the path to redress designed. The bison cooperative had been founded. Now, it was a question of whether the plan would work.

Social problems on reservations, just like anywhere else, do not exist in a political vacuum, and not everybody agrees on the right approaches to solve them. On reservations, for various reasons, the political process in general is closely intertwined with notions of kinship, ethnicity, and personal identity, and the stakes for solving pressing issues are often higher than in an off-reservation environment. This can lead to tribal leaders taking direct influence in schools, courts, and other institutions because they do not like the direction these institutions are taking. Such influence, or interference, can lead to disruption of long-term programs. Often, tribal leaders are under pressure from their electorate to achieve progress during their terms as presidents or councilmen or to steer institutions in a certain direction.

For Pte Hca Ka to become a valuable enterprise and to achieve long-term success, Fred DuBray realized, it had to become separated from the political process. On September 19, 1991, Pte Hca Ka, Inc., was founded as a tribally chartered corporation. All assets and authorities to oversee the buffalo were transferred from the Land and Natural Resources Office and from the Extension Committee of the Tribal Council to Pte Hca Ka, Inc., on October 8, 1991, under tribal resolution #211–91-CR. The decision to create a bison cooperative that would maintain as much distance as possible from the political leadership of the reservation—whoever the leader was going to be—was lauded in retrospect by the Harvard Project on American Indian Economic Development (HPAIED): "Certainly, Pte Hca Ka's success can be attributed to its innovative business strategy, but it has also depended on an arms-length relationship with the CRST's political leaders and a strong connection with the reservation community" (HPAIED 1999:13).

At the inception of the corporation, the buffalo were grazing on the twenty-five hundred-acre pasture near Swiftbird, at the eastern edge of the reservation, whereas the office was located in Eagle Butte. It is hard to determine the original number of buffalo: I was given and found figures ranging from 80 to 172. The most accurate numbers seem to lie between 80 and 100. However many animals there were already, the main goal for the corporation in 1991 was the expansion of the herd to a size that could make a viable contribution to the reservation economy. Projected benefits to the reservation community included job creation, attraction of tourism, range improvement, and an increased capacity for meat distribution. With the help of an Administration for Native Americans (ANA) grant and a strict priority to increase herd size, the number of animals had reached 420 in 1992. In addition to the natural increase, 255 buffalo had been donated to the corporation by the National Park System (NPS). By then, Pte Hca Ka had a permanent pasture of three thousand acres and was leasing an additional five thousand acres, with an option on another five thousand acres for expansion. The corporation also provided jobs for five employees. It was a promising start.

In a 1992 business plan, a range of economic possibilities for the corporation were discussed, including "commercial meat production, sale of breeding stock, trophy hunt, production of arts and crafts from by-products, and promotion of tourism." Social benefits to the reservation community were identified to "include a revitalization of traditional and cultural values, in turn providing a strong framework for all types of tribal interactions, including governmental." The founding of the corporation and its possible consequences for the reservation had been discussed in detail, not only within the tribal council but with all of the district councils and grassroots people. Each of the six reservation districts was to be represented on Pte Hca Ka's board of directors. From the beginning, it was clear to DuBray that the sweeping changes he envisioned as a final goal could only be accomplished with the support of the people.

The plans for the future were indeed sweeping, if not grand; the Prairie Management Plan mentions that the goal for the Bison Enhancement Project "is to use 100,000 acres of tribal land for bison production within five years" (CRST 1992:13). Although 100,000 acres of 1,296,613 acres of livestock grazing area on the reservation may not sound like a revolutionary change (BIA 1994:3–10), the goal of building a program from twenty-five hundred to one hundred thousand acres within five or six years makes clear the scope of the plans at that time. It also shows why some of the established cattle ranching interests on the reservation would come to see Pte Hca Ka as somewhat of a threat, not only against their land base, but also against the by now traditional, established cattle culture, and the management philosophy and ecological values that go with it. The vision to integrate buffalo ranching into the reservation economy as a viable economic alternative to cattle ranching on a large scale rested with Pte Hca Ka for the following years, even though such acreage numbers were not achieved. During the next few years, the herd size was constantly increased, until it reached about nine hundred animals in 1996.

The program moved its office out of Eagle Butte in 1994 and into a mobile home along US 212, across from the buffalo pasture. On the one hand, this move meant an elimination of the commute between the office and the herd and therefore resulted in better supervision. When buffalo break out of a pasture, they are usually on the move, and if the response time is at least an hour, they can move a long way from the place they were first or last spotted at. It was also, however, a move toward more independence from the political climate in Eagle Butte. Although some people might have interpreted this as an evasion of proper tribal oversight, a feeling that influenced the events leading up to the reorganization of Pte Hca Ka in 2001, the corporation had been founded to run the herd without getting entangled in tribal politics. There was a discussion about whether the program should move into a planned casino and resort complex, but that was decided against; as it turned out, this was a good decision because that casino was never built.

Several key characteristics had been established with the creation of Pte Hca Ka and guided its first years. The foundation of the project's philosophy consisted of a commitment to a holistic approach, on one hand emphasizing economic viability and on the other hand equally stressing the importance of aspects of the historic culture. Second came a commitment to growth: this commitment had as its end goal an admittedly utopian reservation-wide replacement of the cattle culture with a buffalo economy. Third was the conscious disengagement from the official political process. Although all these characteristics made Pta Hca Ka successful, they, and the success they fostered, also raised the profile of the organization as a target for the political leadership of the reservation. To understand why politics inevitably caught up with Pte Hca Ka, a look at identity and ethnicity politics on the reservation is necessary before continuing.

CHAPTER 6

Reservation Identities

As I mentioned previously, many reservation residents have a persistent notion of a division of the reservation population into mixed bloods and full bloods. These notions carry over into tribal politics because they in turn carry associations of people being more assimilated into the dominant society or more traditional and resistant to assimilation. It should be obvious how such notions become important quickly once the object of a conversation or a political decision becomes a project like Pte Hca Ka.

Whether a resident of the reservation is considered to be a full blood or a mixed blood depends not necessarily on one's origins or blood quantum but on whether one is seen to live in accordance with traditional values. As already Gordon MacGregor points out (1946:25), these initial, contextual labels are cultural at least as much as, if not more than biological (see also Kurkiala 1997:167–78). This can be seen easily by understanding that the usual Lakota word for mixed blood is *iyeska*, meaning "translator." Historically, many translators were in fact of mixed parentage, often children of French traders. But more than that, a translator is somebody who can mediate between cultures, who lives on the fringe of both societies, belonging yet not belonging. A translator is a "culture broker" (Wagoner 2002:14). This, the cultural meaning, is the more important aspect of the term and of the interpretation of mixed blood.

The question at hand then seems to be, to put it crudely, what criteria should be employed in the decision as to whether one is a real Lakota, or who, in general, is a Lakota and who is not. This is a difficult question because perceptions on this point may differ, and traditionally, or perhaps better, for exactly those people who are still rooted in traditional values, self-promotion may in fact be seen as a sure sign that one is not "really" Lakota. Theresa DeLeane O'Nell's excellent discussion of Indian identity on the Flathead Reservation is largely applicable to the Lakota context, too (1996:56–71). She sees Indian identity as revolving around an unachievable ideal, manifested in the lives of the ancestors related in stories. According to her, the community agrees that "there are people who are 'more' Indian and others who are 'less' Indian," and that there is "a generally agreed upon sense of who belongs at the extremes." Everybody else's identity is constantly renegotiated and redefined.

It is important to realize that this does not mean that identities are up for grabs or that anybody can pretend to be whatever they want. Medicine says that "educationists have always claimed that Indian peoples' self-image is extremely weakly developed" (1987:160). I see such claims as a misunderstanding from the point of view of the dominant culture, in which self-image means the necessity to constantly state who one is, mostly in a positive light. Quite necessarily, this criterion, when applied to a society in which self-image is rather displayed in actions toward others than in words for oneself, will result in misinterpretations.

Lakota identity, says Kurkiala (1997:220), "is not only true to a historical heritage, but to the natural order of things. From this perspective, identity is a non-negotiable essence manifested in history but ultimately rooted in the sacred." If it is true that "Indian is primarily a moral category" (O'Nell 1996:58) and that identity is rooted in the sacred, Gregory Bateson's concept of the "sacred" can explain why "Indianness" cannot be defined but can be situationally described, as in using metaphors or telling exemplary stories. Silence, he says (in Bateson and Bateson 1987:81), "can be used as a *marker* to tell us that we are approaching holy ground." Instead of constant verbal affirmation, some cultures can choose silence as an affirmation of deeply held values: therefore, "*noncommunication* of certain sorts is needed if we are to maintain the 'sacred'. Communication is undesirable, not because of fear, but because communication would somehow alter the nature of ideas" (Bateson and Bateson 1987:80).

Attempts to define Lakota identity would delimit the concept too much: instead of inclusive moral guidelines, explicitly defined identity markers would become exclusive checklists. George Allan notes that "for concepts such as truth, goodness, and beauty; liberty, equality, and justice; faith, hope, and love; and being, becoming, and perishing their significance is beyond measure" (2000:107–108). I would argue that being, becoming, and perishing incorporate concepts like culture, person, and identity. And just like Allan's list, these concepts, too, "and the notions to which they refer are significant for the very reason that, and this is foremost among the qualities that give them power, they are vague. They are vague, these notions, not for arbitrary reasons but because they are features of the most general contexts important to us, contexts logically, causally, and temporally fundamental, contexts at our outermost horizons of knowledge and action and aspiration" (Allan 2000:108).

I find that the sense of identity instilled by the constant, situational renegotiation as described in O'Nell (1996) is strong, as in general, identity is strongest if it needs to be constantly redefined and weakest if it is governed by a set of strict rules, for example by biological definitions. This might be why many "white" Americans do not have a sense of "American" culture, whereas minorities in this country and other people outside of it have a stronger sense of community. Lakota identity might not be definable by two or three key words, but this does not mean that the Lakota do not know who they are. The fact that today American Indians need to prove their Indianness in a legally prescribed and mostly biological way is not consistent with cultural notions of identity (O'Nell 1996:72–73). In this context, Kurkiala points out that although "Oglala" (and "Indian") are emic and legal categories, "Lakota" is not legally defined (1997:168).

Although the constant renegotiation and orientation of cultural identity at the hand of historical, "real" Indians makes it impossible for traditional Lakota to define Lakotaness, on the other hand, it makes it easy for nontraditional people, who are not bound by traditional values, to pretend that they are traditional. They simply have to convince people, especially those who are not sure about traditional cultural values, that they adhere to a list of values in general associated with Indian identity. For example, if ecological knowledge of bison behavior is seen as a characteristic of a true Lakota, then those people who are perceived to have such knowledge are seen to be "more" Indian. As a perceived identity of being more Indian can lead to social, and therefore political capital, it becomes important for those with political ambitions to profess traditional values or knowledge as a political strategy, even if they might not hold these values to be true or might not possess the knowledge.

Reservations are a lot like any other society in which people have by now become alienated from their traditional knowledge. Changes in culture are inevitable, but if the standards to determine cultural identity depend on knowledge and values associated with a culture that has since passed, and if those who still know and abide by this knowledge and these values are in the minority and are prohibited or feel prohibited by these same values to speak out against those who falsely identify with the traditional culture, then the door to abuse is wide open. Marshall points out that while leaders traditionally had to be humble, these days "the process of selecting leaders apparently leaves no room for humility" (2001:12–13). Instead of the people approaching somebody they believe would be a good leader as in the past, today, those who think of themselves as great leaders approach the people. Humility is not something that gets rewarded in the dominant society of the United States. With the old institutional checks and balances gone and replaced by new ones that reward the key values of the dominant society, the old values are not enforced anymore. Generosity, wisdom, and humility are not in demand in a short-term oriented, capitalist society. "Today, in these days," Marshall says (2001:196), "men want to be leaders for the power and glory of it, and not always because they have the good of the people truly in their hearts." Many people, especially those trying to live traditional values, have turned their backs on the political system. There still are traditional leaders on the reservation, and many of them are influential, but they are mostly working outside institutional politics.

As with most moral categories, whether one is perceived to be fitting into a concept of Lakotaness or not depends on personal views on the importance of various aspects pertaining to this category. Distinctions are made, or rather allegiances are chosen, depending on each situation (see Kurkiala 1997:167–246). Consider the case of a man who wears "traditional" dress and is seen in the community, and to outsiders, to be a religious man, perhaps a leader. Somebody else—who is seemingly not traditional—told me that he doubts his Lakotaness because he tried to prohibit a small child from wandering onto the dance floor at a powwow. One of the Lakota values that I have heard most often is that "Children are wakan." They cannot do harm and should be left exploring if they so wish. The violation of this value, however minor or major it was, and for whatever reasons it was committed, was enough to cast doubt on whether this man was indeed incorporating wolakota. The reasoning behind the action was seen to be "white," that is, counter to traditional Lakota values. However, to people not familiar with

Lakota values, the dress code and self-promotion of this person might still convey a strong sense of Lakotaness.

"Native religion," Powers writes for Pine Ridge, "enables people to identify themselves and each other as Oglala" (1982:129). Traditional religion is certainly a marker for being Lakota on Cheyenne River, but not exclusionary. Powers says that "we find a correlation between full-bloods and Native religion on one end of a scale, and the mixed-bloods, non-Indians, and Christianity on the other" (129). This statement is obviously true if the categories are cultural rather than biological, yet they cannot be taken to mean that there is no overlap. People who self-identify as Lakota and belong to or go to a Christian church also profess traditional religious values, and vice versa. It is important to keep in mind in this discussion that traditional religion, although bringing to the forefront the discussion about values that is useful in looking at identity, is not just an identity marker. Although identity is rooted in the sacred, the sacred is more than a giver of identity. Medicine points out that Indian people "are searching not so much for identity but for a viable, believable system" (1987:164).

In view of the latter point, approaches to identity exclusively through the sacred must fail. Many Lakota both go to church and practice traditional ceremonies; for most, there is no sense of one excluding the other because both are expressions of spirituality. Hilbert points out that although many Lakota may still see Christianity and Native religion as opposites, there is a rapprochement from both sides, with Christians trying to incorporate Native aspects into their services and Lakota spiritual leaders also practicing Christianity (1987:143). Although this rapprochement seems to have come to a standstill or has been reversed, important here is that for the constitution of Lakota spirituality and identity, religious traditions are still not exclusive to the point of rejection. At one Sun Dance, I witnessed an invitation being extended to Aztec visitors from Mexico to perform their own ceremony during a break. No one present ever made any comments about this being inappropriate, although it caused the time schedule of the ceremony to be disrupted. It was just another way of expressing spiritual connections and therefore deserved respect (see also Bucko 1998:176–96; Feraca 1998; Huffstetter 1998; Steinmetz 1998).

One is not less or more traditional because of institutional choices but because of what values one incorporates into one's daily life. Lakotaness cannot be professed or institutionally adopted. It has to be lived and proven daily.

This is not so much a matter of outward appearances but of actions and reasons behind them. Many people who could superficially be seen as having adapted to Euro-American culture hold traditional values close in their daily lives, even though they do not practice traditional religious ceremonies. Not participating in ceremonies might, in fact, actually be a consequence of respect. One woman told me that she does not participate in Sun Dances because she drinks and smokes and does not want to desecrate the event. In this case, the reason for not participating in religious ceremonies was not informed by a rejection of traditional values but by a deep respect for them. In other words, participation cannot be taken as a direct indication of values held. In a culture in which religion is not separate from daily life, participation in religious ceremonies is not only problematic to measure but also problematic to use as a variable of values. If one's life is actually the expression of spiritual values, individuals can make personal choices to not attend public ceremonies. And in a culture that places value on not talking about religious ceremonies in public, participation in these ceremonies is not likely to be easily revealed to an outsider.

One problem that has arisen from the stereotypical status of Lakota culture as "Indian culture" is the appropriation of Lakota ceremonies by outsiders employed in contexts different from those for which they were originally intended. Organizing sweat lodges and vision quests for tourists from overseas, New Age sympathizers, or offering classes on these ceremonies in Europe has become an increasingly profitable business for not only Native Americans but also people who pretend to be so (see Wernitznig 2003). "Real and imagined 'medicine men' have become hawkers of 'spirituality', breaking the old circle of people and introducing anyone who can pay the entrance fee," says Deloria (1997:213). This appropriation has increasingly been seen as a consequence of allowing the participation of non-Indians in the ceremonies. Whereas "militant" "traditionalists" have always protested the participation of outsiders in ceremonies (Steinmetz 1998:31), the increasing perception of a general sellout of sacred ceremonies and traditions and misuse of them by outsiders has now become a major concern for many religious leaders.

In March 2003, a meeting of spiritual leaders on Cheyenne River Reservation, under the leadership of Arvol Looking Horse, the Keeper of the Sacred Bundle, decided to limit participation and leadership in the seven sacred rites. The leaders from the Arapaho, Northern Cheyenne, Cree,

Dakota, Nakota, and Lakota nations cited strong concerns over abuse of ceremonies by non-Natives who have only a superficial understanding of the powers involved. Looking Horse emphasized that although participation in the center of the Sun Dance would be limited to Native peoples, support from around the circle is essential to the ceremony. This notion—that one does not have to be in the center to contribute fundamentally to any given event—seems to underlie all Lakota philosophy; it also clashes with some of the notions about participation in U. S. culture. In essence, the gathering decided to reestablish respect for and control of the ceremonies without excluding anybody. If people wish to participate in rites in ways that help the ceremonial community, they are still able to do so. This is also what Arvol Looking Horse (2003) emphasized.

Other people saw it differently. *Indian Country Today* featured a stinging editorial cartoon depicting Arvol Looking Horse as a king sitting on a throne, proclaiming "No white guys-in-the-sweat lodge Day," with the subtitle "Too much power" (editorial cartoon, 2003). The elders of the Afraid of Bear/ American Horse Sun Dance maintained that their Sun Dance and ceremonies would stay open for everybody (Cook 2003). "Tiospayes," they point out, "are inherent sovereign entities in matters of life and religion." Therefore no tiospaye, or extended family unit, is bound to decisions made by others. Their response, like the cartoon, seems to be a political statement of tiospaye sovereignty against an attempt at some sort of regulation just as much as it is concerned with the exclusion of people along a problematic distinction between Native and non-Native. The debate is important enough, however, to warrant some further discussion because it defines not only how social boundaries are marked or unmarked in Lakota society, but, more important for this study, shows tendencies of assimilation and adaptation and their opposites. The New Age movement in Indian Country, although emphasizing Native culture or aspects and derivatives of it, can be seen as an assimilationist movement because only those aspects are marketed that are acceptable and desired by the dominant society. Sovereignty, on the other hand, needs markers of difference and should focus on all aspects of the culture, no matter whether they fit into the ideology or desires of the dominant society. As such, the debate shows many structural parallels to the discussion about methods of buffalo ranching and the paths of economic development.

The "issues involved in the Looking Horse Proclamation have to do with Hunka," Cook says (2003:A5), referring to the Lakota Making of Relatives ceremony. He cites Afraid of Bear (Walker 1991:201): "I can perform the ceremony for anyone who is chosen in the right way. I can do it for a white man," and Sword (Walker 1991:200): "White men were not invited unless they were to be made *Hunka*. A few white men have been made *Hunka*." If non-Natives can become hunka, or broadly said, relatives, his argument seems to go, they should also be allowed to partake directly in the center of other ceremonies because the distinction between Natives and non-Natives becomes meaningless in a ceremonial dimension.

What Cook does not cite (2003), however, is what Afraid of Bear went on to say after that (Walker 1991:201, 202):

> I must first seek a vision to learn if I can do this for a white man. A white man would be like an Indian if he becomes *Hunka*. I do not know whether the spirits would aid me if I were to undertake to perform the ceremony for a white man or not. I could find this out by seeking a vision. I would have to have presents before I would seek a vision. A white man would be my brother if he became a *Hunka*. The *Hunka* are not what they were in olden times. They do not look on each other as they did before the Indians came onto a reservation. The spirits do not come and help us now. The white men have driven them away. . . . I can not tell the secrets of the *Hunka* to a white man, but if he becomes a *Hunka* I will tell them to him.

And Sword said (Walker 1991:200):

> It is no help to be a *Hunka* now. The *Hunka* ceremony taught the *Hunka* to be what the Indians thought was good. The Indians' way of being good is not the same as the white man's way. The white man's way of being good is now accepted by the Indians.

Several things seem clear to me from these extended statements. First, that the hunka ceremony had changed and lost some of its relevance with the beginning of the reservation period and that it was partly for this reason that objections to making white people hunka were generally becoming irrelevant. In other words, if the object of regulating the contemporary ceremonies is to regain relevancy, then perhaps the general limitations on access are also becoming relevant and important again. Second, although the distinctions in hunka were becoming generally irrelevant, making white men hunka was still to be an individual exception, just like it probably always had

been. Third, Afraid of Bear and Sword saw a distinction between Lakota
and Euro-Americans, and contemporary issues of openness or closedness of
ceremonies are really old. Fourth, somebody who became a hunka became
a Lakota, and more than that, became a member of a special group within
Lakota society (Walker 1992:63). Keeping in mind that Lakota society, like
most American Indian societies, was traditionally open to outsiders, there
was probably no need for a hunka ceremony to become accepted in the
society. Sword and Afraid of Bear make clear that the ceremony lost its traditional relevance with the general culture change under U. S. cultural dominance. Its meaning might then have become more of a general adoption
ceremony instead of carrying the earlier, deeper implications. Together with
the greater need to distinguish Lakota from others, especially non-Natives,
this would have made it on one hand less important in the society and on
the other hand more important for relations with others because it became
a marker for general acceptance into the society.

The debate about participation in ceremonies shows how important the
discourse about wolakota, or Lakotaness, as an identity marker has become.
To maintain a relatively open society, according with cultural traditions, contrasts with the need to assert cultural and political sovereignty and authority,
and therefore a need for distinction. As is always the case when cultural boundaries are drawn, however, what this distinction is based on becomes the issue
contended because whom the boundaries will exclude and include depends
on the paradigms applied. As Kroeber pointed out for culture areas (1939:5),
adjoining peoples who are separated by a classificatory boundary have usually
more in common with each other than with the peoples that supposedly make
up the center of the classification. "It would be desirable, therefore," Kroeber
concludes (6), "to construct cultural maps without boundary lines, on some
system of shading or variation of color; but the mechanical difficulties are
great." To measure culture by material traits, as in the classification of culture
areas, is difficult—how much more problematic, then, does a classification of
cultures based on the measurement of values have to be.

In a discussion, a fellow anthropologist mentioned that in her view, one
of the main problems of the Looking Horse proclamation was its lack of definition of what is meant by a Native and a non-Native. These terms are open
for interpretation, and it is up to every leader of a ceremony to draw his own
boundaries of participation. As I see it, this is exactly not the problem. To
the contrary, it is an expression of how and why traditional Lakota society
works. The problem is that the dominant society insists on definite markers,

such as dress, hairstyle, language, or skin color, without being able to evaluate these markers. The list of supposed ethnic markers then becomes empty in its meaning: it is open to anybody slipping into these markers to appear as a "real" Indian. It is the insistence of the dominant society on measurable ethnic markers and its inability to decipher symbolic meanings that create the confusion.

In his dissertation about Cheyenne River, Mizrach says (1999:198), "One would expect that a more acculturated Lakota person would know less about their own cultural history, attend fewer ceremonies, have engaged in fewer traditional practices, hold fewer traditional Lakota values, and be less fluent in the Lakota language." He proceeds to describe Lakota people leaving Pte Hca Ka's mobile buffalo processing facility during the slaughter of an animal, "apparently driven away by the pungent smell or the splattering of blood and bone, while I and other cultural center members casually filmed the event. In several ethnographic accounts on the Lakota, they are often described cheerfully carving up a bison into all its useful parts . . . . Yet here I observed several Lakota people fleeing the scene of a slaughtering which probably, by comparison, was less 'gross' and more clean and surgical" (1999:270). The question is, whether this may be taken, as Mizrach assumes, as a sign for disappearing culture and traditions.

People may leave a slaughter, just like they may not participate in a ceremony, for more reasons than one, and especially more than the one that seems obvious to a cultural outsider. For many Lakota, the contemporary symbolic value of buffalo is religiously, culturally, and emotionally so overwhelming that they prefer not to be present at a slaughter. This is a direct consequence of symbolic values changing with the times; to assume that they stay the same is to make a grave mistake. The fact that Mizrach was able to "casually" film the slaughter just means that he had enough distance to buffalo to not get upset by the death of an animal. "Fleeing the scene" had probably not much to do with the slaughter not being "clean and surgical" enough, values that, again, are etic rather than emic. I hope it is clear from what I have said so far that measuring cultural values by indicators, such as participating in ceremonies or in "culturally appropriate" events, is not a good method. Leaving aside the problems with measuring cultural values as such, this is even less feasible if one tries to apply the method to a culture that does not divide the cosmos in categories easily compatible with one's own.

Acculturation to U. S. or European culture is not necessarily coupled to a lack of knowledge of Native cultural history. This should be especially clear to anthropologists, who presumably have knowledge of a people's cultural history and yet are not of that culture. It is also hardly important for the average Lakota person to know "certain key events in Lakota history, such as the Indian Reorganization Act of 1934" (Mizrach 1999:198). What all Lakota know, I am sure, are the consequences of this act on their daily lives, and to know that, one does not need to know the date it was passed. Were we to judge Americans not to have U. S. values if they did not know the dates or the historical events of World War II or other key events in the history of this country, we would come up with an amazing number.

Fluency in Lakota is also not a reliable indicator of a person holding traditional values and neither is lack of knowledge of the language a sign of more acculturation. Fluency might be an indicator for a more traditional upbringing, and one can hardly be a religious leader without speaking the language. But many elders, for a variety of reasons, did not pass on the language, yet passed on cultural values to their children. On the other hand, speaking Lakota does not necessarily mean that one is not more acculturated to Lakota society than others who do not speak the language. As the language situation on Cheyenne River is today, I knew how to speak Lakota better than many people I encountered, and I think it would be a hugely arrogant assumption of mine to conclude that they must hold fewer Lakota values for that. Many indigenous peoples—including my own—point out that without understanding the language, one does not understand the culture, and yet, the convergence between language fluency and "cultural fluency," as one might call it, is not absolute and is becoming less so (Mignolo 1998:41–42). Ramerstorfer reports from Fort Totten (1997:308), "For many individuals, having an 'Indian identity' does not necessarily mean that, as a Devils Lake Sioux, one needs to speak Dakota, since there are a number of other cultural elements to chose from."

Language fluency for sure is becoming an important social sign of cultural membership, increasingly so to outsiders, but also as a pièce de résistance against cultural encroachment. This can be seen in the aforementioned decision to allow only fluent speakers to lead a sweat lodge ceremony. "I and most Native people I know hesitate to embrace the radical version of this view—that without our languages we are no longer Native people— but on the other hand," says Christopher Jocks (1998:219), "I fear that without our languages it is all too easy for us to become cartoons, caricatures of ourselves." Although language is an important element in cultural identity, "the value of language as a symbol can remain in the absence of the communicative function," or in other words as a "language which is connected with group identity but which is not used regularly or, indeed, known at all" (Edwards 1996:227).

Historically, one only needs to look at people such as Black Elk to understand that seeming acculturation to *wasicu* culture in one or more aspects does not necessarily go hand in hand with rejection or ignorance of Lakota culture. Iyeska, or middlemen between cultures, although perhaps lacking identity markers deemed important by outsiders, still know Lakota culture and need to know it to fulfill their roles. Lakota society, like every other society, is not a living museum: aspects of the traditional culture are alive and well, but that does not mean aspects of the dominant culture have not been adopted. Culture, after all, changes constantly. Only for fundamentalists is identity a zero-sum game, and I have rarely met a Lakota who was fundamentalist about anything.

I said previously that religious and cultural allegiances are chosen depending on the situation. This is also true for political viewpoints, which are often seen in a dualism between "traditionals" and "progressives," or those who want to revive or retain traditional culture and resist the ways of the dominant society and those who see the future in assimilation to them. In the complex world of identity formation on reservations (e.g., Kurkiala 1997; Wagoner 2002), the two strategies are not always, as might be expected, mutually exclusive. It is important to understand that both traditionals and progressives—if one wants to put such labels on them—are working to help their people in their own ways, which are sometimes, but not always, diametrically opposed. Categorizing people based on their peculiar stances on one issue does not work. Rather, people have many connections and when forced to choose among these potential allegiances, make a situational decision, mostly, as I think, with family, or tiospaye ties ranking high among their priorities. I see this as a continuation of traditional decision making in North America (Braun 1998), and probably in many small-scale societies in general.

"All the answers," as one elder explained on the community radio, KLND, "are in the tiospaye: the tiospaye gives all the answers." The problem today, he said, was that people lack knowledge of their identity because many elders do not pass on the kinship knowledge. To know who one is, then, one has to go and work with one's relatives, the tiospaye, or extended family group. This, and a primary responsibility to and allegiance with one's tiospaye, might constitute a traditional perspective in itself. Truly progressive politicians, who perhaps do not know their place in the larger kinship system, might make decisions based on outside party politics and ambitions that are larger than the reservation. This is often seen as not being compatible with Lakotaness. Some critics might point out that decision making based on family responsibilities leads to a client-based political and social power hierarchy, nepotism, and corruption. Indeed, charges of nepotism and corruption are plenty on the reservation, but it is hard for an outsider to make a judgment on them. Mostly, I see these problems springing from a system forced to work theoretically through institutional checks and balances, like the separation of the judicial and the executive branch of government, although living in a practical and moral world that places much more emphasis on social, than political control. It becomes easy in this situation to abuse the system by quoting traditional values and implying that institutional checks and balances are not only part of the colonial system but really hold the reservation back. It is sometimes hard to figure out whether politicians are truly devoted to traditional values or whether they just profess to be so to get elected; however, this is hardly a unique characteristic of Lakota politics.

Different actors in a society can be viewed as conservative or creative cultural forces: conservative forces, for example, institutions of a society, carry, transmit, and try to preserve the status quo, whereas creative forces work toward changing aspects of a given culture. The result is usually a compromise in which short-term or mid-term stability leads to long-term change. In the case of the Lakota and other indigenous peoples, the connotation, traditionalists, signals a conservative force, and progressives, a creative force. In my opinion, this is somewhat misleading.

As a result of extraordinary outside and inside pressures, Lakota culture has changed rapidly over the course of the last century. The plains buffalo hunting culture, itself the result of deep changes, has been replaced by a settled ranching culture, and for many Lakota, especially those who are not ranching but live in reservation towns, that has again given way to a culture dominated by outside control. I think it is important to understand that Lakota ranching culture is not to be equated with white cowboy culture. Although there are many similarities, especially in economic aspects, ranching culture on the reservations is Lakota culture and not simply an adoption of the values of the dominant society. The same case can be made for reservation towns. Although many young people on the reservations are seeking similarities with historically oppressed minorities in big cities and express themselves, for example, through rap culture, the specific contents with which these signifiers are filled are Lakota. The status quo for a majority of contemporary Lakota is a culture that has many superficial similarities to the dominant society and yet has retained its distinctiveness.

In this context, both traditionalists and progressives are creative forces, but creative forces that follow different and sometimes opposite directions. I want to emphasize that neither of these directions is more oriented toward the past than the future. Traditionalists are simply trying to change the society by incorporating certain aspects inspired by the historical culture. Progressives, on the other hand, try to change it by incorporating aspects from the dominant culture. The labels put on the two movements, if one can use this term, are clearly inspired by a dominant society that sees cultural change as an evolutionary progress with itself as the teleological goal. In this model, contemporary culture forms are not important for consideration because culture change is not relative but absolute on an ever "progressing" scale from the "traditional" (i.e., earliest described historical culture). Any change in culture that does not follow the progressive scale can thus be declared traditional, no matter how much the actual culture has already changed from the historic culture.

It is somewhat ironic that the implicit connotation of traditionalists as conservative forces and progressives as creative forces is all the more misleading if one regards Lakota culture from the perspective of assimilation. There is no question that Lakota society, particularly its institutions, has been assimilated to an important degree into the cultural system of the dominant society, and that what the progressives are arguing for is a further continuation of this assimilation. From this perspective, then, the progressives are actually the conservative cultural forces, or at least more conservative than the traditionalists, who want to change the status quo.

For a general understanding of contemporary cultural, social, and political discourse on reservations, these dynamics of culture change are essential. Creative forces are always working from the cultural periphery. Both traditionalists and progressives are trying to shape the changing cultural landscape according to their own perspectives, but it is important to remember that resistance to both has to be expected from the majority who carries the cultural status quo. Resistance to "traditionalism" is thus easily explained: it is not the puzzling event of a society turning somehow against its own traditions, but the normal resistance against culture change.

With these notions in mind, it is not surprising that despite its leadership's attempts to disengage from tribal politics, Pte Hca Ka started to attract more and more attention from all sides of the political spectrum. First, here was a program that showed evidence of growth and future potential, and every politician wants to be associated with such a program. Second, the progressives, which made up most of the tribal leadership on Cheyenne River, grew suspicious of the traditional aspects of the program, but on the other hand realized that association with buffalo would open opportunities to gain social and political status by becoming more Indian. Third, the traditionalists grew weary of the economic goals of the program, as participation in the national or even global market seemed a potential threat to the support of traditional cultural values and the culturally appropriate management of the buffalo themselves.

Pte Hca Ka thus became embroiled in identity politics, and these identity politics were linked to an old battle over economic politics on reservations. The bison operation came to be seen as a prize by both sides: whoever would control the operation would be in a position to partly define the economic future of the reservation. In reservation politics, however, whoever defines the economic future is in a good position to define the cultural, social, and political future as well.

CHAPTER 7

Pte Hca Ka

Expansion

By 1996, it had become obvious that Pte Hca Ka needed to expand its rangeland to be able not only to continue growing the herd but also simply to accommodate all the animals in the existing herd, which numbered between eight hundred and one thousand buffalo. In January 1996, a philanthropist from Minnesota, Jennifer Easton, made it possible for the tribe to buy six thousand acres for additional buffalo pasture (Carlin et al. 1997:174).

At the same time, plans were underway to buy a mobile slaughter plant from Sweden. Reindeer herders in Lappland use such mobile units in remote locations, and a Swedish company, Sandstrom's Transport Producers AB, had offered to build a unit for buffalo. This unit had to be custom built on two trailers, one for the slaughter unit and one for the processing and packing unit. It came equipped with electrical generators, water supply, electrical saws, complex technology that allowed up to twelve buffalo to be processed in one slaughter event, refrigerated storage rooms, lockers, and an inspection station. All of this equipment was installed in such a way that various parts of the installation could be hydraulically extended from and retracted into the trailers. In addition to the challenge of adapting a facility developed for reindeers for the use of buffalo, the U.S. Department of Agriculture (USDA) also imposed various requirements on the unit. After a long development and planning process, the slaughter plant was acquired with a $1.1 million grant from the USDA and finally arrived on Cheyenne River on July 10, 1997.

The decision to buy a slaughter facility was based on the fact that animals had to be processed off the reservation. The nearest slaughter plant that processed buffalo was Westside Meat in Mobridge. Not being able to process animals on the reservation meant a loss of control over the final products, including by-products, no control over slaughter methods—important in the context of traditional handling—and a real economic loss, including availability of jobs to the reservation. Had economic development been the only concern, however, there would have been the much simpler and cheaper possibility of building a slaughter facility on the ground; the Triple U ranch just south of the Cheyenne River operates one, for example.

The innovative decision to look for a mobile facility was taken for two additional reasons. One was the concern over minimal impact on the buffalo. Animals that have been shot cannot be transported very far or for a long time, which means that live animals usually have to be transported closer to a traditional slaughter plant and kept in holding facilities until they are killed. This is, of course, how the cattle industry generally operates. However, for all the differences in management philosophy mentioned previously and primarily because buffalo are easily stressed, this was not compatible with Pte Hca Ka's notion of treating bison with respect. The third alternative, besides transporting either dead or live animals to the slaughter facility, is to bring the slaughter facility to the animals. This allows the buffalo to be shot on the range and processed on the spot. The other reason for opting for a mobile slaughter unit was that many other reservations also did not have slaughter plants. With the envisioned expansion of buffalo operations on reservations nationwide, a mobile slaughter plant would be able to be driven to other reservations to facilitate their operations. If this were to happen the initial cost of purchasing the more expensive mobile plant would be offset by the services it could provide throughout the region.

Once the unit had arrived on Cheyenne River, it was set up next to the office. In practice, it was not moved from that spot for the next five years. Because it was constantly exposed to the tough South Dakota climate in its ready-to-slaughter state, the hydraulic mechanisms deteriorated, and after some turnover of employees, nobody was too sure about how to fold the units back to their transport size. To be fair, there was also no immediate need to move the facility because it was sitting right across the road from the main buffalo pasture. It was not necessary to move it onto that pasture: the transportation of the dead animals from that pasture to the facility did not take longer than five or ten minutes. Because the facility was not moved, however, over time its tires and hydraulic stabilization poles sank into the rain-softened earth, which made it off level and opened up cracks between the components. Its main loading doors were oriented to the north, and winter storms blew snow into the slaughter unit. The cold wind also made it a general hassle to load buffalo into the unit, especially during winter. Built in Sweden, with European components and technological specifications, the unit also became hard to maintain. If anything went wrong with the equipment, spare parts had to be ordered directly from Europe because U.S. spares were mostly not compatible. Local electricians had to study the blueprints to understand the system before making any repairs.

However, these are problems that developed over the years. Overall, the plant proved to be invaluable for Pte Hca Ka. It enabled the corporation to enter commercial production and provide more jobs, both full-time and part-time, for the reservation. It was also invaluable as an investment in the future, when, it was hoped, it could be used to its full potential. Although a stationary plant could have fulfilled its economic functions, which prompted criticism of waste—not taking into account that the plant had been purchased with a grant—the mobile slaughtering plant was also a concrete and visible symbol of Pte Hca Ka's buffalo management philosophy. As such, it was also a visible sign of the program's general approach to economic development on the reservation and therefore signified a difference of high political importance.

The expansion of the project necessitated and triggered an expanded involvement in the broader political and economic affairs of the reservation. How to best approach economic development on reservations is an old question: it is the question of formalist versus substantivist economic theory (Sahlins 1972:xi–xiv).

From the New Deal on, peaking during the 1960s' War on Poverty programs, economic development initiatives in Indian Country concentrated on bringing industry to the reservations (Pickering 2000:17–18; Vinje 1982:87–88). Under the "vacuum ideology," which saw reservations as areas of cultural loss, now without a distinctive culture, the theory was that U.S. values could and should be imposed on American Indians to fill that "vacuum" (Pickering and Mushinski 2001:47; Ramenstorfer 1997:302–303). This formalist approach undeniably created jobs: in 1970, about 12 percent of reservation wage employment on the twenty-four most heavily populated reservations was provided by manufacturing plants (Vinje 1982:87). But by the 1980s, most of the factories on reservations had been closed. In most cases, the isolation of reservations and the lack of transportation infrastructure became a serious problem. The only plants willing to open on the reservations were basically those that could not survive without federal incentives. Tribes were pushed "toward small-scale, under-financed labor intensive operations that can easily be jeopardized by a small change in technology or a small change in import laws" (Vinje 1982:88).

Northern plains reservations' relationships to global economic centers resemble those of other peripheral nations, which has led to them being sometimes called "Third World islands in a sea of relative prosperity" (Bland 1994). The impression that reservations are islands of poverty is becoming more and more a relative statement—socioeconomic indicators are still worse on reservations than in surrounding communities, but there are signs of rapprochement. It is therefore also becoming a political statement, used and misused in battles over limited funds and limited attention from the federal government to its rural constituency. The term is evocative and politically useful when looking at reservations, which can be seen as internal colonies (see Davidson 1990:159–70). Off-reservation rural areas seem more hesitant to use the label for themselves, although a careful analysis of economic conditions and power structures would probably find just as many conditions of the label met as for reservation communities (see Edmondson 2003).

It might be a sign of the times that the first fact to mention about the economy of Cheyenne River Reservation is that the reservation does not have a casino. When I first came to Cheyenne River, I heard a speech given at the Victory Day powwow on June 26, 2000, saying that the reservation keeps on fighting and does actually not want a casino because the people do not want a contract with the state government, that people chose to be poor by not having a casino, and that they are proud to be poor. It was a powerful speech and received a lot of applause. I was impressed, but I wondered during the speech if people anywhere are really proud to be poor, and if one day of rhetoric and remembrance of the victory at Little Big Horn can be comfort enough. Later, I found out that the realities of the casino situation are slightly different and much more complex.

The tribe had come up with plans for a casino several times during the 1990s, and another public hearing on a gaming compact with the state of South Dakota was held in August 2000. The favorite location for a casino had been the surroundings of the US 212 bridge across Lake Oahe as a ploy

to attract fishermen and hunters. These plans also included a resort for con-
ferences and a golf course along the lake, and the project had gone so far
that a groundbreaking ceremony had been held. Other plans called for a
casino in Eagle Butte. Of course, different people see different reasons as to
why these casino projects ultimately failed. Then tribal chairman Gregg
Bourland (*Around Lakota Country* 2001) quoted concerns about giving up
sovereignty and moral issues as the reason why his administration pulled out
of already signed compacts with the state. Former tribal chairman Wayne
Ducheneaux (2001), on the other hand, claimed that although the compacts were ceding sovereignty, the reason for failure was that the tribe could
not find any investors who trusted its creditworthiness. In 2005, new visions
arose for a casino on lands neighboring Fort Pierre and Pierre, which would
make for a much more attractive location but would also create tough competition for the Lower Brule and Crow Creek casinos.

Like other tribes, Cheyenne River has established an array of tribally
owned businesses on the reservation, most of them in Eagle Butte. The tribe
operates, among others, a Super 8 Motel, a gas station and convenience store,
the Lakota Thrifty Mart, and the telephone company, including a cable TV
and Internet access provider, a propane company, and an office supply store.
The model of economic development on the reservation, and symbolizing
the way into the twenty-first century under the Bourland administration,
was Lakota Technologies Inc. (LTI) in Eagle Butte. JD Williams, LTI's
CEO, was planning to "bring the offshore outsourcing model onshore," and
to convince U.S. corporations to "send LTI the same data-entry, call center
and document-imaging jobs they're currently sending overseas to India and
the Philippines" (Field 2001).

Chairman Bourland's administration, in place throughout the 1990s, was
placing high hopes on new information technologies as a way to improve
economic conditions on the reservation and invested heavily in electronic
infrastructure and broadband technology. This supposedly resulted in the
reservation being "more infrastructurally sound than all of India . . . where
power and telephone services fail regularly" (Field 2001). Although that
soundness might have been true for Eagle Butte, during my fieldwork,
Internet connections from the communities were failing regularly, especially
at peak hours. With this infrastructure, Bourland (*Around Lakota Country*
2001) saw LTI as providing "an opportunity for Cheyenne River to produce
hundreds and hundreds of jobs, not just in Eagle Butte but across the reservation." Indeed, LTI achieved a number of successes and was able to open

a new facility in Eagle Butte in 2002. Plans for expansion facilities in the east and west end communities, however, had to be postponed. Outsourcing ventures feel economic downward trends first, and beginning in fall 2002, LTI had to downsize considerably. As long as businesses are dependent on economic trends and decisions off the reservation, a secure, sustainable economy is hard to build.

Osha Gray Davidson makes the convincing point that high-technology rural development is more often than not a sham because the term "is too fuzzy" (1990:138–41). Cheyenne River will most probably not become another Silicon Valley but, like other rural areas, attract industries that use high-tech but employ mostly manual labor. Reservations attract industries by low wages and nonunion policies, competing with other areas for any jobs they can get. "Economic growth" might not be the best standard to measure success for a community in that situation. As Davidson points out (1990:139), increasing costs of living most often hurt the people relying on fixed incomes and benefit those who are educated and already better off. In the setting of Cheyenne River and other rural communities across the plains, many people, Indian and non-Indian, live on fixed incomes, and low-wage operations do not add enough to the economy to start a cycle of true economic growth (see DeMallie 1978).

An alternative approach to the attraction of low-wage corporations is to give people help for the establishment of small private businesses. Most communities, for example, do not have stores, and the resulting long trips to buy commodities are a burden for people in terms of both time and money. Starting a business, however, requires capital and technical assistance, and to help with that, loan funds have been established on reservations, many modeled on the Lakota Fund on Pine Ridge (Tyndall 2000). On Cheyenne River, the Four Bands Community Fund is trying to tackle the problem. Founded in 1997, the fund runs a mandatory training program for all applicants, family financial planning courses, and credit analysis classes. In 2002, the fund made its first two micro-enterprise loans for business startups (Fogarty 2002; Fogarty and Taylor 2002). The community fund provides just as valuable services with its classes as with loans. One of the problems of a nonexistent reservation economy is that people cannot gain experience without leaving (Pickering 2000:38). Both the community fund classes and tribal businesses, such as LTI, provide much needed managerial education (Fouberg 2000:165). In addition to this, the tribe also operates a Tribal Business Information Center.

Unfortunately, technical advice and loans are sometimes not enough to get a business running. One of the two businesses receiving a micro loan was a proposed convenience store in Swiftbird, the easternmost community. Swiftbird—or Marksville, as it was known then—had had a store, which went out of business soon after a nearby low security correctional facility was closed. After that, people went to Bob's Resort right across the river; to Gettysburg about thirty miles east; or Eagle Butte, about fifty miles west. The proposed convenience store was to sell basic necessities, and future plans included takeout food and bait supplies for fishermen. Bob's Resort sells all of this and includes a gas station. It also sells beer. A liquor license was granted to the proposed store but because of protests from the community was denied at a subsequent hearing. The store never opened.

Rural reservation economies, to an even greater degree than rural plains economies around them (see Edgcomb and Thetford 2004), are to a large degree informal economies, or in other words work on the principle of *bricolage*. Claude Lévi-Strauss introduced bricolage as an anthropological metaphor (1966), but from my own cultural perspective, in which *bricoler* is a valid concept, his definition can be taken quite literally in the context of reservation economies.

> The 'bricoleur' is adept at performing a large number of diverse tasks; but, unlike the engineer, he does not subordinate each of them to the availability of raw materials and tools conceived and procured for the purpose of the project. His universe of instruments is closed and the rules of his game are always to make do with 'whatever is at hand', that is to say with a set of tools and materials which is always finite and is also heterogeneous because what it contains bears no relation to the current project, or indeed to any particular project, but is the contingent result of all the occasions there have been to renew or enrich the stock or to maintain it with the remains of previous constructions or destructions (Lévi-Strauss 1966:17).

This is not a negative or condescending comment. Reservation residents know extremely well what they are doing and how to do it. The point is that people rely more on technique than on technology—a strategic cultural choice (Dumond 1980:41–42) not to be misunderstood as an evolutionary value judgment or need for change (e.g., contra Müller 1970:126–27, who characterizes this as a *"Fortwursteln des Zufalls"*; see also Pickering 2004 on time regimentation). In the current situation, it is essential for people to know how to make do with what they have, and their strategies for survival are geared toward this. In reservation communities, "the development of strong and dependable family and friendship networks might be a more rational response to uncertainty than the learning of skills which require and demand mobility. We expect that in such circumstances, all elements of the economy are more bound up with informal networks than those of formal nature" (Reimer et al. 1997:4). This is especially true for cultures that traditionally place an overarching emphasis on kinship networks, such as the Lakota.

The primary industry on Cheyenne River is educational, health, and social services, followed by public administration. This emphasis on social services and administration is a recent development (Murray 2003:7, 28); the economic mainstay of the reservation in many ways is still agriculture, and direct access to subsistence resources is the primary goal for many people. This is why the issue of land and land rights is so important. According to Velarde Tiller (1995:556), 28,000 acres of trust land are farmed, primarily for corn, wheat, barley, and alfalfa, whereas 915,000 acres are used as range. These data agree with my own impression that farms on Cheyenne River are mostly operated by non-Indians. They are located on Fox Ridge, the heights between the Cheyenne River and the Moreau River, and on the uplands north of the Moreau River, around Timber Lake and Isabel.

The Bureau of Indian Affairs (BIA) gives 1,296,613 acres as livestock grazing areas (1994:3–10). In 1994, according to the BIA report, this acreage was divided into 256 range units, averaging 5,075 acres and ranging from 250 acres to 16,517 acres. Murray counts 267 tribal range units, from 200 acres 1,700 acres (2003:33). The difference in numbers can be explained by political processes in the ten years or the use of different data determinants. The tribe has been extremely interested to undo the negative effects of allotment policies; consolidation of the tribal land base and land purchases are of high interest to any tribal government on the plains.

The attempt to rebuild a viable reservation economy would be difficult enough if reservations had only been consciously underdeveloped in terms of infrastructure and economic initiatives. But in addition, the archipelago of the reservations was in general also built from the land that was considered too worthless for anybody else to desire. "The 48 million acres of Indian lands [in 1937] consist by and large of the poorest lands yet remaining in the United States. If they had been anything else, they would probably not have been set aside as Indian reservations, or if set aside, the white men would have gotten them through the workings of the allotment system" (Marshall 1937:160). If the quality of land on reservations is better than that off reservations, as some people say, this probably has more to do with the history of land use than with the original quality of the land. The lack of means of industrial agriculture, in other words, results in less exploitative land-use practices, and poverty does not necessarily lead to environmental degradation but on the contrary may contribute to conservation.

Grazing land, on the other hand, is just as degraded on the reservation as off reservation. As Anantha Duraiappah points out (1996:17), "the absence of secure land tenure may be the primary factor" behind degradation. The BIA reports an average stocking rate for the grazing units of 2.7 acres per animal unit month (AUM), which they interpret to mean that "the range units are probably in at least fair to good condition on the average" (1994:3–10). This is one way to interpret it, as the stocking rate indicates "the number of acres of forage to support a cow/calf pair for one month." The other, more cynical way to interpret the number is that the range is not in good condition, but a rancher still puts that many animals on it. One Lakota rancher admitted to me that he consciously overgrazed his land because, he said, he did not know whether the tribe would renew his lease for the next year. He therefore tried to squeeze as much use out of the land as possible. Murray points out that eligible leasers of tribal land "are selected by Tribal Council" (2003:33). Although there obviously has to be a process of ensuring eligibility, the close association of the tribal council with land leases gives rise to rumors of nepotism and corruption in the determination of eligibility.

Not everybody overgrazes their land, but enough people do for others to notice. With much of the land leased to outside cattle during the summer and many pastures miles away from roads, it is easy to have too many animals on the land or to use winter pasture that has already supported its full year-long contingent in summer. McNeal, in the context of another reservation, thinks that tribal officials have to neglect enforcement of policies, as it would be "political suicide to enforce the grazing regulations" (Jones and Platts 1995:11). As one tribal official with Prairie Management told me, the BIA and the tribal political powers that be are definitely not interested in downgrading the land. Political pressure is rather working to upgrade grazing units (i.e., to allow more AUMs on the range). Such numbers also allow for mathematical games: people argue that if a unit can hold one hundred cattle for a year, it should graze two hundred for six months or four hundred for three months. This translates into sound mathematics, questionable politics, and bad ecology, especially because such numbers do not take into account that the climate on Cheyenne River does not allow for sufficient recuperation periods and that some ranchers graze four hundred cattle for three months and then some others for the next three months. BIA data for 1992 show "livestock grazing revenues of $1,104,425 from range unit permits and $531,044 from leases" (1994:3–12). With ranching being so important to the local economy, moves that could be seen as anti-ranching are bound to be highly unpopular.

During the drought conditions in summer 2006, some ecologists on the reservation were extremely concerned about readily apparent conditions of desertification. They blamed this on a large part on the failure of the political process that regulates grazing pressures and the short-term economic interests of ranchers.

Another important part of the economy, although not generating monetary revenues, is the more informal, direct subsistence activities: hunting, fishing, and gathering. Hunting is still important in more than one way. Hunting licenses pay for some of the staff of the tribal Game, Fish, and Parks Department (GFPD) and provide its only stable revenue not linked to grants. But hunting not only generates income; tribal members also have the right to hunt deer for subsistence, and those who cannot go hunt for themselves can have somebody else hunt for them. "Hunting for the elderly" is a common activity. Apart from both mule deer and white tails, people hunt coyotes and other smaller animals, both for meat and by-products. Some residents also still run trap lines.

Fishing is important, especially along the Missouri, but also in various dams all over the reservation. Fishermen from all over the country come to fish in Lake Oahe, but most of them stay on the east shore, using their powerboats to look for the best bays. Most of these people do not want to go to the trouble of buying a tribal license and are afraid to camp on reservation land. On the reservation, fishing is most visible in winter, when people ice fish on Lake Oahe. Much of the summer fishing is not done from boats or with reels but with fishing lines. These lines, with up to ten hooks, are spanned across a small bay and are checked every day. The hooks are baited with spawn caught in great quantities from the lake. Bait stores on the east shore make quite a bit of money, too, and I heard of many plans where one might open a bait store on the reservation side. To get fishermen to cross the river more often would mean a welcome influx for the economy, but many Lakota also like the privacy around their fishing lines. The habitual location of line setups is usually kept in the family.

Gathering includes gathering of commodities, such as firewood, taken from downed trees along the creeks. Wood is also gathered for other purposes: one man for example, made beautiful diamond willow walking sticks with antler or buffalo horn grips. People also gather food for subsistence. Sometimes farmers allow them to go into cornfields before the harvest and fill a few garbage bags with corncobs, which are then preserved for consumption through the year. Berries and other plants are of course also gathered, some for ceremonial purposes and some for food. The buffalo cooperative fit in with these activities in supplying meat and by-products for ceremonies and, eventually, for tribal members at a reduced price.

Political involvement in Pte Hca Ka had been held at bay for some years, partly because the office was moved out of sight and partly because the buffalo program seemingly could not offer much as a political asset until 1996. As I mentioned, the tribal administration focused on the development of Cheyenne River as an information technology and outsourcing service center. With the growing success of Pte Hca Ka, both as an economic potential and a cultural symbol, the cooperative was bound to become an interest for politicians. It had much to offer as a political, cultural, and economic asset for the more traditional people and for those who worked to integrate the local economy in the global markets.

Chairman Bourland became a member of Pte Hca Ka's board for a brief period, which ended in 1997. In the severe winter of 1996–1997, he held a press conference during which he said that the "Cheyenne River Sioux Tribe buffalo herd has either wandered off or has perished in the storm," and that "during a fly-over he saw buffalo that had succumbed to the blizzards" (Melmer 1997). In fact, some of the buffalo had walked across the ice-covered Lake Oahe and had to be herded back by Pta Hca Ka's employees. But the only buffalo that perished that winter was one that, for reasons unknown, but probably frightened and stressed, jumped from the bridge across the Missouri on the way back. Several employees told me that they were upset by the chairman's comments to the press because they shed a negative light on the buffalo program; in their eyes, they made it look as if the buffalo operation did not know how to take care of its animals. When he was asked why he had implied that many buffalo had died, Bourland reportedly reasoned that this was a way to get more financial aid and support for the reservation: if even the buffalo had died, then the blizzards had had to be really severe. Whatever the reasons for the chairman's statement had been, it is clear that the political spotlight had found the buffalo operation, and it had been deemed an asset.

CHAPTER 8

Honors and Visions

With its innovative, holistic approaches to combine and revive traditional culture with modern technology, Pte Hca Ka was undoubtedly a model for numerous other tribal buffalo programs in the late 1990s. This leadership role was honored by two prestigious awards in 1999: a National Congress of American Indians award for Effective Indian Development Projects and Practices and a High Honors Award from the Harvard University's Project on American Indian Economic Development (HPAIED).

In its award statement, Harvard specifically mentions the job creation, the education programs—about which I will say more in a moment—and the continuing donation of buffalo to the communities and to the nutrition programs for elderly and children on the reservation (HPAIED 1999:12–13). The combination of these efforts with commercial success, the Harvard project finds, "proves that it is possible to combine modern technology, indigenous traditions, and economic success." One reason for Pte Hca Ka's success that the award emphasizes is its independence from the political process, and its "arms-length relationship from the CRST's [Cheyenne River Sioux Tribe's] political leaders." Specifically, "the enterprise's charter and by-laws prohibit elected officials from involvement in day-to-day program management. Because the Tribal Council and President uphold this agreement, Pte Hca Ka's managers are able to focus on long-run enterprise success rather than short-term political goals." As I have explained, at the time, Pte Hca Ka had already become an interest for political leaders on the reservation: soon after, the political leaders would increasingly begin to pressure the corporation to adhere to their management philosophy. This process, which eventually led to the complete reorganization of Pte Hca Ka, can be seen as to have started with another expansion of the program, the purchase of the VE Ranch.

The VE Grazing Corporation range consisted of about twenty-two thousand overgrazed acres, with US 212 as the southern boundary, and was roughly situated between Promise, Blackfoot, La Plant, and Swiftbird in the eastern part of the reservation. In 1998, this land came on the market. Pte Hca Ka was situated close to the land and was already using a pasture along the Blackfoot Road that bordered on the VE: this made the land all the more attractive to the buffalo program. With the generous financial aid of Jennifer Easton, again, Pte Hca Ka set up a corporation that acquired the land at auction and made the down payment.

This land was not tribal land but fee land. On the one hand, this offered the chance to enlarge the tribal land base. It is also true, as Fred DuBray points out (2000), that the purchase of nontribal land was "the only chance for the buffalo herd to grow without interfering with current land use politics." In other words, were the buffalo program to have expanded on tribal lands, it would have been in direct competition with other tribal members over land use, primarily cattle ranching. The VE offered the only possibility to expand and not jeopardize the economic future of tribal cattle ranchers. On the other hand, taxes apply to fee lands, and it was clear that the taxes would exert quite a heavy toll on Pte Hca Ka, a nonprofit organization that was run financially independently of the tribe and mostly on grants. DuBray, however, had a plan.

The purchase of the VE land would not only allow Pte Hca Ka to grow but also to tackle several other visions that DuBray had for the buffalo operation. Part of the reason for acquiring the VE land was to establish a tribal park, which would eventually serve to attract tourism and could be used for ecological research purposes. This goal fit perfectly into the federal Land Legacy program, under which the land acquisition could have been paid for with no costs to the buffalo program. In 1999, the corporation had everything cleared for the program. Unfortunately, however, the tribal council, which had to apply for this, did not act on the opportunity until it was too late, so that Pte Hca Ka had to carry the whole burden of the purchase and the future taxes.

Plans to build a tribal park, sometimes called the "Sioux National Park," with the buffalo herd at its center, existed at least since 1997 and probably ear-

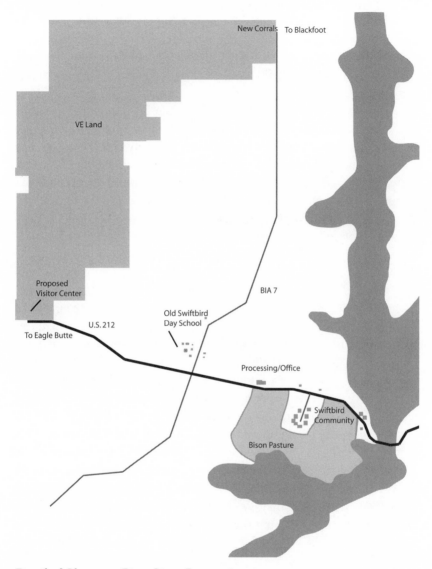

Detail of Cheyenne River Sioux Reservation

lier. This effort, intensified after the purchase of the VE, partly in Pte Hca Ka's drive to apply for the Land Legacy funding, was concurrent with other initiatives to attract more tourists to the reservation and to restore the grass-land ecosystem on reservation land. Pte Hca Ka, with public awareness at the center of its mission, had always worked toward creating opportunities for people to visit the buffalo. To run the buffalo in a park also fit perfectly with other objectives of the cooperative. A tribal park would create jobs for the reservation and would underline the sovereignty of the reservation — national parks are a powerful public symbol of sovereignty over land and showcase a government's stewardship of land and people. Because of their status, however, and as a consequence of their economic value both in cre-ating tourism revenues and in excluding the land from other uses, parks are also fertile grounds for special interest involvement.

Pte Hca Ka envisioned the park as a drive-through experience, much like the National Bison Refuge in western Montana. Together with an inter-pretive center and the expansion of the gift shop, selling crafts from local artists on commission, it would have created jobs and an understanding of the buffalo culture not only for tourists, but—and this was an essential part of the original plan—also for the local people. Game, Fish, and Parks Department (GFPD) basically agreed with this vision but slightly shifted the emphasis on the park as a tourist attraction with guided wagon tours, a heritage village, a campground, and powwow grounds. There were even plans, put forth by a German visitor, for building a remote cabin resort. Pte Hca Ka's plan had been to complete a road through the VE range by 2003 to capitalize on the Lewis and Clark expedition bicentennial. Tribes all along the expedition's route were hoping to profit from the expected increase in tourists following in the footsteps of the historic explorers (Krist 2002).

In 2003, the Interagency Working Group on Environmental Justice (IWGEJ), part of the Environmental Protection Agency (EPA) Office of Environmental Justice, cited the park project as one of fifteen new revital-ization demonstration projects. "The intent of these projects is to examine lessons for the development of collaborative models that ensure problem-solving and sustainable solutions to a range of environmental, public health, social and economic issues associated with environmental justice" (IWGEJ 2003a). The park project on Cheyenne River was presented as a collabora-tive effort between the National Wildlife Foundation (NWF), the tribe, the National Park Service (NPS), the U. S. Fish and Wildlife Service, and EPA Region 8. The park, "is viewed as a re-creation of the lands of their ancestors—a wild, sacred place for all *Lakota* people and others to come, listen, and learn about a living and vibrant *Lakota* culture" (IWGEJ 2003b:23, italics in original). As part of the efforts, the Native American Scenic Byway, already in existence on the Crow Creek and Lower Brule Reservations, was extended to Cheyenne River and Standing Rock, including the Blackfoot Road, BIA 7, leading to the east entrance to the VE buffalo range. With improvements to existing areas and construction of new ones, the tribe hoped to be able to attract overnight visitors.

The CRST had offered a recreation area and campground by the US 212 bridge across Lake Oahe for years, and the South Dakota Department of Tourism lists the facility as "Forest City Campground" (n.d.:7). But although, or perhaps because, the area is a popular spot for recreation by reservation residents, those grounds are not frequented by off-reservation tourists. Campers prefer the amenities of West Whitlock Bay State Park, although that is about ten miles off the main highway. In contrast to the state park, the tribal recreation area offers no running water, water toilets, or park rangers in attendance, and although the camp sites are still discernible in the little forest that covers the grounds, they are far from obvious. Little Moreau State Recreation Area lies within the boundaries of the reservation and offers several small lakes, camping spots, and a park, but its primary access is through Timber Lake. Although the tribe offers several other designated recreation areas along Lake Oahe, these are more remote and difficult to access.

In 2005, a Sioux Falls landscape architectural company finished a design for a visitor center. This design includes a fifteen thousand-square foot tent amphitheater, hiking trails, a recreational vehicle campground, and rental cabins and tepees. I saw the model for the visitor center complex in 2006: it was basically ready to be built. However, because of Pte Hca Ka's debts of over $6 million, which had been left to the GFPD after the reorganization, nobody could tell when the money for the implementation would be at hand.

With popular interests in American Indian cultures and native wildlife on the rise, tourism, and especially ecotourism, would seem to be a strong economic possibility for Cheyenne River Sioux Reservation. After all, two hundred whooping cranes in Texas generate $1.2 million of tourist revenues every winter, and the Santa Ana National Wildlife Refuge in Texas attracts $14 million in tourist dollars for local economies (Youth 2000:14). But these tourists are mostly bird watchers who follow the objects of their admiration to warm southern Texas, so it is hard to imagine that similar revenues could be generated for windswept South Dakota. Even Ted Turner's six hundred thousand acre Vermejo Park Ranch, which generates $6.5 million from hunting and fishing fees, is located in New Mexico (Fabrikant and Strom 2003). But in 1996, "77 million adults—about 40 percent of the U.S. adult population—participated in some form of wildlife recreation," and the sales of equipment, permits, lodging, transportation, and food generated $100 billion (Youth 2000:14–15). These numbers include hunters and fishermen, but people in South Dakota, or on the reservation, do not usually have issues with those activities. One could assume, then, that a part of that $100 billion could be attracted to Cheyenne River. There are two problems, as I see it, with this assumption.

The first is that part of that money is already spent on the reservation, namely part of the revenues created from hunting and fishing permits and lodging. I have already outlined how money for food, transportation, and equipment does not make it onto the reservation. The point is that hunters know where Cheyenne River is and do not represent a big potential growth factor for the local economy.

The second problem, this one having to do with those people attracted to wildlife watching, has to do with issues in location and infrastructure, which make it hard to attract visitors. The major highway through South Dakota—and most tourists view the plains as a transitory landscape—is not only more than an hour south of the reservation but also closer to Rosebud and Pine Ridge reservations. Pine Ridge, one of the most famous, or infamous, reservations in the United States is also adjacent to Badlands National Park, a significant tourist attraction, and Wall Drug. Passersby can thus experience buffalo, American Indian culture, plains environment, and "free ice water" without having to divert too long or far from the interstate.

Cheyenne River boasts no famous historical places, such as Wounded Knee, or places associated with famous leaders, such as Red Cloud or Sitting Bull, and there is no casino that could lure passersby to spend some money. True, some of the world's best preserved dinosaur remains have been uncovered on Cheyenne River, but with the exception of some beautiful specimens exhibited in the local museum in Timber Lake, they are to be seen in Chicago or even Switzerland. In short, all Cheyenne River has to offer is its natural beauty. One might think that this is enough. The crux, as I have said previously, is that this beauty can be seen in other places in addition to attractions that make tourists stop in the first place. The few tourists who take US

212 are mostly from western Minnesota and eastern South Dakota, and they have no great incentives to stop on the reservation. Cheyenne River has largely remained an insider destination, which, of course, has both, negative and positive consequences.

Although the discussion of tourism as a pathway to sustainable development has grown beyond a treatment in this study (e.g., Hall and Richards 2000), I would like to point out some practical problems that develop from the unique character of American Indian reservations, at least those without casino resorts. A United Nations Educational, Scientific and Cultural Organization (UNESCO) study pointed out almost thirty years ago that the building of tourism infrastructure involves "the import of expensive finished products" (1977:24–25). "In most cases," the study reports, "the State takes part in the financing of these projects (directly or indirectly by granting payment facilities or subsidies) even if doing so means running into debt." Because reservations are under federal control, such support is hardly a possibility; tribal governments on the northern plains are not in the position of sovereign nations who can run up foreign debts in the hopes of eventual returns. Tourism is also a competitor for water and land, no matter how eco-friendly it is conceptualized.

Although ecotourism requires less infrastructural adjustments than traditional tourism, in regard to potential profits from tourism, the UNESCO study also points out that "the multiplier effect of tourism, very considerable in some industrialized arid countries, requires a specific socio-economic context" (1977:25). That context, I fear, is not in place on Cheyenne River, so that an eventual tourism development might not profit the reservation community but rather other interested parties from the outside. This does not mean that I would discourage efforts to develop tourism but that the reservation stakeholders should be aware of limited opportunities of such projects and study them carefully before rushing to implement them. In how far the park development as presented is indeed a "sustainable solution[s] to a range of environmental, public health, social and economic issues associated with environmental justice" (IWGEJ 2003a) is a question that needs to be answered in concordance with the management philosophies associated with the buffalo, the pattern of investment that will develop, and the presentation of local culture at the park facilities.

In terms of potential tourism development, Lake Oahe plays a double role. It provides a man-made natural attraction, with opportunities for fishing and other water recreation. As such it is the best spot for either direct use for tourism or as a point of attraction for tourist opportunities in its neighborhood. On the other hand, its existence has deprived the reservation of its most attractive land along the Missouri River, and the equitable compensation act, or Joint Tribal Advisory Committee (JTAC) of 2000, will bring much needed funds to the reservation. As mentioned previously, fair compensation was set at $290,723,000. The tribe was also given another trust fund for ecological mitigation, and these moneys can be used to fund tribal environmental management activities. Quite some controversy has developed over these acts, however, and it is necessary to look at them, and the meanings they were assigned on the reservation, a bit closer.

The JTAC compensation sum was placed in a trust fund for the tribe, "to be managed by the Secretary of the Treasury in order to make payments to the Tribe to carry out projects under a plan prepared by the Tribe" (Public Law 106–511 2000). The money will not be available until eleven years after the passage of the act (i.e., 2011), when the original sum plus the accrued interest will be available in the trust fund. From this time on, the secretary of the treasury will judge what money will be made available to the tribe. Cheyenne River had to come up with a plan for the money eighteen months after the passage of the act; this plan can be updated annually by the tribal council. The tribal administration saw the passage of the act as a huge success that will help ensure the tribe's future. The reaction from tribal members and other Lakota reservations, however, was mixed to negative.

This is mostly a result of another act that was passed in 1999, Public Law 106–53, Title VI, "Cheyenne River Sioux Tribe, Lower Brule Sioux Tribe, and State of South Dakota Terrestrial Wildlife Habitat Restoration," commonly known on the reservation as the "Mitigation Bill." Former Senator Tom Daschle and Former Governor Bill Janklow were instrumental in this bill, as they drew it up and offered it to the reservations. This bill gives the reservations another trust fund, this one for "terrestrial wildlife habitat restoration" to mitigate damages to the environment inferred by the dams. This money, in other words, can be used to fund tribal environmental management agencies, as long as the case is made that they address problems created by the establishment of Lake Oahe. Also, land that had been acquired for the dams but that lies above the flood pool and inside reservation boundaries is given to the secretary of interior in trust for the reservations. Cheyenne River received thirty-three thousand acres in trust. The state of South Dakota, however, received the land and recreation areas along the rivers that had been acquired for the Pick-Sloan Plan and that are outside contemporary reservation boundaries (Public Law 106–53 1999).

Crow Creek, Standing Rock, Rosebud, and Pine Ridge reservations—all the Lakota reservations that had opted out of the mitigation—and other Lakota organizations, such as treaty councils, protested the mitigation law because of this land transfer. For a while, people occupied Framboise Island, a popular recreation area off the east shore next to Pierre. Because the treaty of 1868 put the boundaries of the Great Sioux Reservation on the east side of the river, this area and others that were affected by the law are seen to be treaty land. This means that under the treaty provisions, they can only be transferred out of federal status by the consent of three-quarters of the male Lakota population. In other words, by accepting the mitigation bill, Cheyenne River's leadership was seen to accept the division of the Great Sioux Reservation. By doing so, the leaders came to be seen as selling out to the government. Chairman Gregg Bourland (*Around Lakota Country* 2001) denied the feared transfer of treaty land to the state and assured listeners that the federal government would retain title to the land; the state would only be allowed to use the sites. However, Public Law 106–53 indeed states that the land shall be transferred to the state "in perpetuity" and "shall be transferred in fee title."

It is important to understand that many people saw the two laws as one event, although resistance was mostly directed against the land transfer provisions in the mitigation bill. People on Cheyenne River told me that the chairman "had sold the river" for $290 million. They argued that this was a sellout and that the money would disappear soon enough, while the land would stay. The Lakota, many people reasoned, should not sell any land or rights to lands. The tribal administration, of course, pointed out that these lands had already been taken and flooded. But the Black Hills have also been taken, and many people pointed out that no reservation has yet accepted the money the government finally paid into a trust fund in the 1980s as compensation.

Although the mitigation bill benefited only Cheyenne River and Lower Brule—the two reservations that decided to go along with it—because of the historical implications of the Great Sioux Reservation, the other Lakota reservations saw themselves as just as much involved. They saw what, under the Great Sioux Reservation and under the assumption that the Lakota are one people, they considered to be their lands being taken against their objections and without any benefits to them. Eventually, Crow Creek and Pine

Ridge brought two separate lawsuits against the government to stop the land transfers to South Dakota. Pine Ridge also aimed to stop land transfers to Cheyenne River and Lower Brule, arguing that those lands should also belong to all the Lakota and should be given to the Black Hills Treaty Council. These lawsuits have so far not been successful (Melmer 2001a, 2002a, 2002b; White Face 2002; Woster 2002a).

The consequences, however, went much further. When Senator Daschle was honored at the Labor Day Powwow in 2001, inducted into the Fools Soldier Society, and given a blanket and an eagle feather, people with more traditional views were aghast. They saw Daschle and Governor Janklow, with whom South Dakota Indians had always had a problematic relationship, as "the enemy" because they had again taken land from the Lakota and broken a treaty. Chairman Bourland, who seemed to be courting his own political ambitions beyond reservation politics in his honoring speech, repeatedly mentioned that Daschle, Senate majority leader, was the third most powerful man in the world and possibly the next president. Many people perceived this acclamation of power and the close association between a Lakota tribal chairman and somebody they considered had just robbed them as frightening and considered the tribal administration as being involved in a conspiracy against their own people.

Despite the fact that reservations in South Dakota usually vote Democratic and that crucial U. S. Senate and House of Representatives races had been won by Democrats in 2002 because of the support from reservation voters, Senator Daschle lost his 2004 race to the Republican contender, largely because of a shift in voting behavior on the reservations. Many analysts saw this as evidence that reservation voters increasingly support Republicans. However, I think the specific history of Daschle's crucial involvement with the JTAC issue was much more to blame (Braun 2005:86). The people had not forgotten that he had worked to transfer treaty lands to the state.

With the purchase of the VE Ranch and plans for a park, Pte Hca Ka finally came firmly into the spotlights of the political and economic establishment. The operation was now in the business of not only raising buffalo but also of managing and developing a huge area of land. Other agencies, closer to the tribal political hierarchy and thus arguably better controlled from the perspective of the tribal government, had viable interests in the land and the park. Based in Eagle Butte, the tribal Game, Fish and Parks Department

(GFPD) and the tribal Prairie Management Program (PMP) are both involved in restoration efforts on the reservation. These restoration efforts, as discussed, became stronger with the allocation of the Lake Oahe mitigation money, and the establishment of a tribal park could definitely be seen as falling under ecological restoration. Potential overlaps in interests and management duties among the three agencies concerning the future park became apparent, and although they were never played out in direct conflicts between the agencies themselves, the political establishment began to wonder whether three agencies were really needed. Paradoxically, although the purchase of land for a park ensured the survival of the buffalo program and opened the possibility of expansion, it also created strong incentives for a takeover of Pte Hca Ka, which was perceived as out of reach of, and out of step with, tribal political agendas.

The tribal GFPD was established in 1935. It is responsible for managing natural resources on tribal lands, including wildlife and fish. That task includes "population and production monitoring, habitat restoration and development, harvest monitoring and management, game code enforcement, hunter education and depredation management" (National Wildlife Federation [NWF] 2001). Hoover attributes the strong tradition of the Cheyenne River GFPD in part to the dire socioeconomic situation on the reservation (1992:49): "With the average annual income per family down to only $1,620 by mid-century, it was hardly coincidental that this reservation group—settled on some of the least arable land on the northern Great Plains containing substantial natural bounty—made an effort to conserve and manage its fish and game for the benefit of tribal members." With JTAC, a major task for the GFPD has become the mitigation of environmental consequences from Lake Oahe under the Habitat Restoration Plan (GFPD 1999). With a historically strong department, the mission of the Habitat Restoration Plan and the VE land in direct vicinity to Lake Oahe, it was only natural that the GFPD would be seen as having an interest in the future park.

The PMP was founded in 1993, "after the U.S. Fish & Wildlife Service identified opportunities for 33,000 acres of black-footed ferret habitat" on the reservation (NWF 2001). The main goal of PMP is the restoration and conservation of the grassland ecosystem, with the ferret reintroduction program as its main achievement and goal. With the ferret program came an emphasis on prairie dog and integrated land management. Identifying the holistic Lakota worldview—"based on a recognition of the interrelationship and intrinsic value of all species, which is necessary for the health and harmony of the environment"—as a quest for biodiversity, PMP describes itself as "an example of integrating Native American values with scientific techniques to promote restoration of prairie ecosystems" (PMP 1999). The Prairie Management Plan Phase II, which started in 2000, also carries installments for "Buffalo Enhancement." Because the VE land harbored some prairie dog towns, PMP not only helped fence the southern half of the range but also became involved with the buffalo program in general.

"It is worth noting," Licht says (1997:41), "that although bison are commonly thought of as the preeminent Great Plains grazer, the truth is that the prairie dog probably has the most influence on the ecosystem." About 140 vertebrate species are associated with prairie dog colonies, along with many invertebrate species. However, control measures, especially poisoning, have "reduced prairie dogs to only 2 percent of their historic range from Mexico to Canada" (Donahue 1999:129). Of six known black-tailed prairie dog colony complexes over five thousand acres in size in the United States in 2001, two were on National Grasslands, and four were on Indian reservations. Many ranchers still see prairie dogs as competing with cattle for grass and fear that cattle might break their legs in dog holes (see also Bureau of Indian Affairs [BIA] 1994). Actually, large grazers prefer the constantly rejuvenating grasses in dog towns, and there is no nutritional drawback from grazing in prairie dog areas. However, prairie dog towns cannot be hayed. One acre of range on Cheyenne River can produce about a ton of hay, which is worth about $130.

In 1998, the National Wildlife Federation (NWF) petitioned for the federal listing of the black-tailed prairie dog as a threatened species. There are an estimated one hundred fifty thousand acres of prairie dog towns in South Dakota, most west of the Missouri, and an additional one hundred fifty thousand acres on the Lakota reservations, with about seventy thousand acres on Rosebud alone (Woster 2002b). As Kevin Woster reports (2002b), on Rosebud, "feelings about the prairie dog are mixed. Indian ranchers want the rodents controlled, but many tribal elders respect the prairie dog as a sacred creature," and some esteem them as highly as the bison. The same range of opinions is evident on Cheyenne River. Although some people work for the protection of the dogs, a former cowboy told me he suspected the federal government was behind the plans to protect the prairie dogs: first they took the land, and now they destroy what they could not take, he said.

Reservation policies toward prairie dogs reveal these ambiguous feelings. Cheyenne River history shows annual campaigns to "treat" and "clear" thousands of acres (BIA 1994:Appendix G). These treatments were undertaken with strychnine before 1950 and with zinc phosphide and aluminum phosphide after 1950. For fiscal year 1991, Congress still funded prairie dog control efforts on Cheyenne River with $96,000, following a tribal council request for help. However, the appropriations bill that year mandated the Bureau of Indian Affairs (BIA) to search for control measures and environmental management programs that would "avoid poisoning" and "allow coexistence with prairie dog populations" (BIA 1994:1–4). The BIA tended toward an abandonment of poisoning since the late 1970s but became caught in court action when the American Farm Bureau sued the BIA for "failure to control prairie dogs" on Pine Ridge (CRST 1992:5). The congressional mandate of 1991, however, led to new environmental assessments, especially in regard to the effects of prairie dog poisoning on possible black-footed ferret reintroductions (BIA 1994:1–4, 1–5), and eventually to Cheyenne River Reservation looking for new prairie management policies.

Whereas in 1992, the Rosebud Reservation tribal council "passed a resolution . . . supporting a prairie dog control program using both chemical pesticides and range management on the reservation and opposing any black-footed ferret reintroduction efforts," Cheyenne River went the opposite way, although not without opposition. The new policy looked to maintain a minimum acreage of prairie dog towns and to specifically conserve ten thousand acres of prairie dog towns along the Moreau River as black-footed ferret habitat (BIA 1994:1–6, Appendix F).

The black-footed ferret, an endangered species, depends on prairie dogs as prey for at least 90 percent of its diet and on dog burrows for habitation, thermal cover, and hiding. Believed to be almost extinct, a small population of black-footed ferrets was captured and brought to a research center in Maryland in the early 1970s, but the last of them died in 1979. In 1981, a new population was discovered on a ranch near Meeteetse, Wyoming. Further decimated by disease, eighteen survivors were taken to a breeding center in Sybille Canyon, Wyoming, between 1985 and 1987. The breeding program was exceptionally successful, and efforts have been underway since the early 1990s to reintroduce black-footed ferrets into their historical range (BIA 1994:2–58–2–64). This, however, obviously requires an adequate number of prairie dogs to ensure ferret survival.

After adopting the new prairie management policies, Cheyenne River Reservation was ranked high on an U. S. Fish and Wildlife Service list of potential black-footed ferret reintroduction sites, and in 2000, seventy-five ferrets were released in an area northeast of Whitehorse, under the auspices of the PMP. The fact that PMP was responsible without oversight by federal agencies was a substantial gain in tribal ecological sovereignty, one of the goals of the 1992 prairie management policy. As a PMP biologist explained to me, the tribe wanted to make an official commitment to permanently preserve twenty-five thousand acres for prairie dogs. The reasoning behind this was that if they got it through the bureaucracy before the prairie dog was declared an endangered species, the federal agencies would not be able to regulate species management on the reservation. Although the tribe preserved some prairie dog towns, they did control the populations around human settlements and especially schools because the animals can carry the plague (see BIA 1994).

With the purchase of the VE land, that range became a new possible area for prairie dog preservation and black-footed ferret rehabilitation. Although there were some dog towns on the VE land, at the time PMP wanted to enlarge them to a size big enough for ferret survival. The best way to enlarge prairie dog towns is to overgraze the land for about two years. There is a direct relation between grazing pressure and prairie dog expansion because the animals thrive with good visibility, being safer from predators, especially coyotes. The VE land was an ideal place for PMP's ferret and prairie dog program: not only was there no conflict with cattle ranchers, but the plans for the park added to the incentive of resettling the animals there because they attract tourists all over the West. However, overgrazing was not directly in line with what Pte Hca Ka wanted to do with the land, having allowed it to rest for two years to restore it.

In October 2001, eighty wild horses were set free on the VE land as part of an arrangement between CRST and the International Society for the Protection of Mustangs and Burros (ISPMB). Before this release, ISPMB had operated a wild horse herd on Pine Ridge, with a tourist operation that offered guided tours. After the move to Cheyenne River, they also shifted their planned "Sunka Wakan" tourism project there. Some tribal members, however, complained that the tribe was not involved in these activities and would not profit from them, although the horses grazed on the VE. Others thought that the tribe was receiving money from ISPMB for hosting the horses.

The horses released on Cheyenne River in a ceremony on November 3, 2001, came from the Virginia City area in Nevada. ISPMB emphasized that wild horses were a part of the historical landscape of the northern plains and that the Lakota traditionally had a "horse culture" and not just a "buffalo culture." In a press release for the first "Tribal Cup Charity Polo Match," held in Boca Raton, Florida, to benefit the Sunka Wakan project (Tribal Cup 2002), the proceeds of the event are said to be benefiting the CRST, "by protecting and preserving the Lakota Sioux horse bloodstock for future generations;"

> Just 150 years ago, wild horses roamed the northern plains along with the indigenous Lakota Teton Sioux people. The prairie with its tall grasses and beautiful clear rivers and streams was home to nearly three million wild horses. . . . According to Lakota folklore, returning the horse to the Lakota people is pivotal to bringing about healing and reestablishing a link between nature and the Lakota Sioux Nation, whose relationship with horses formed a human-animal bond that was the font of legends. . . . Visitors to the Lakota's sovereign land will be able to observe tribal culture first-hand, including beading, tanning of buffalo hides, and sculpting pipes. Their aesthetic existence in teepees and the Lakota's connection with nature is sure to have a profound impact on all who visit. In homage to the wild horse, a living symbol of our nation's past, Lakota guides will escort visitors on a tour of the final resting place of the last of the original wild horse bloodstock

One can easily detect in this language the aesthetic essentialization of the New Age and Deep Ecology movements. According to these ideas, the Lakota apparently had lost their connection to the horse at the beginning of the reservation period, when those millions of wild horses with which they had coexisted were killed. Perhaps because the Lakota are supposed to have been "wild" and "free," the horses of their horse culture also must have been wild horses (see Terkildsen 2002), an assumption that does not only defy common sense but also historical and contemporary testimony.

In an interview on the *Native America Calling* radio program (Native America Calling 2001), Karen Sussman, the director of ISPMB, talked about the need to restore the "wonderful nobility" and the "oneness . . . of a Native American on a horse." She assured the listeners that the Lakota had lost their horse culture, and to underline this, she related an anecdote of how, when a friend rode up on horseback to some Lakota children, they were afraid, presumably of the horse. Dennis Rousseau, the director of the CRST GFPD, however, noted that from his "observations on different reservations, as well as Cheyenne River, . . . the presence of the horse has always been there. There's our local ranchers who still use horses, numerous families . . . 75–80 percent of the families that own land do have horses, so the tie to the horse has . . . been there, and it will never go away."

It is interesting that although ISPMB is trying to make the connection between traditional Lakota culture and wild horses (from Nevada), the aesthetic used is that of "a Native American on a horse," which implies that the horse is not wild at all but tamed. Cheyenne River is famous all over the West for being cowboy and rodeo country, and several residents pointed out to me that a wild horse is really a waste because a horse is supposed to be trained. In other words, they had no use for the aesthetic argument of reviving "ecological Indians" and celebrating the connection to nature by having horses run wild: their connection to the horse—practical and spiritual—was exactly that horses can be trained and used. In a pamphlet for the wild horse release ceremony, the CRST wrote that "horses were a vital part of the Lakota way of life, they were important for transportation, hunting, and protection of the people. The Lakota people have always had a spiritual connection with the horse." These sentiments fit with those on other reservations all over the West (see Iverson and MacCannell 1999).

A previous program on the reservation that used horses to restore traditional values of respect and responsibility, the Cheyenne River Healthy Nations, had offered opportunities to youth to ride and take care of horses, especially during summer vacations. Healthy Nations had also offered a space for adolescents to congregate. In communities like Eagle Butte, where recreational opportunities are sparse, the combination of teaching responsibility by firsthand interaction and offering a safe space was a much needed and potentially successful approach. Unfortunately, the grant money for the project ran out after four years. Dana Dupree, the director of Healthy Nations, was also trying to revive the tradition of bareback cross-country horse racing at the 2000 Iron Lightning Memorial Powwow. The horsemanship and enthusiasm of the participants was an impressive testimony to the importance that the horse culture has retained.

Although historical accounts of interactions between Plains Indians and horses support a strong tradition of training horses (Roe 1955; Ewers 1955), the classification of Plains Indians as hunting societies and the popular notion of them freely roaming the land might contribute to the impression that they did not have a strong tradition of relations to domesticated animals. James Downs (1973:171), however, takes the position that "the classification of the Plains tribes as pastoral is essential to a proper evaluation of these societies (or cultures) in a worldwide context." "[T]he horse," he asserts, "is not a tool nor is it a trait. It is in fact a large animal with distinctive patterns of behavior to which man must adjust before the various potentials of the horse can be made useful to human groups."

> Plains culture historians have frequently failed to note that many plains tribes had begun to shift their attention from the dwindling buffalo supply to the herds of White owned cattle coming onto the range. Obscured in the limbo of 'acculturation' these post-reservation or immediately pre-reservation events would appear to be the type of response which we would expect of a pastoral people (Downs 1973:172).

In other words, the horse culture might be the transient between the buffalo culture and the cattle culture; this horse culture, however, is not one of wild but of tamed horses. The emphasis on wild horses is probably inspired by popular culture concepts that mix geographical and cultural areas and extend Monument Valley to South Dakota. Such concepts, if they become popular enough and carry economic incentives, reinvent traditions.

I do not mean to dismiss the horses as meaningless for the local communities; the fact that the reservation did welcome the horses with a ceremony showed that they carry some meaning. Whether they are valued in the same way by locals as they are by the ISPMB people, however, remains questionable. In contrast to the latter, no Lakota present at the ceremony was moved to tears. The meaning of the presence of wild horses can be seen from a pragmatic standpoint, too; if everybody expects Indians to have such a deep relationship to them, they are at the least definitely assets in the presentation of the reservation community to the outside. Still, most people on Cheyenne River I talked with about this issue were well aware that wild horses did not play an essential part in traditional culture. It is probably easier for a horse culture, such as the Anglo-American society, to invent this tradition than for a buffalo culture. As long as the cultural memory of the importance of buffalo is alive, it is hard to overlook the fact that horses were introduced and became central to traditional society as trained animals, traded and fought over as objects of great pride and prestige.

Cultural memories, however, change. As an addendum to this observation, I was extremely surprised to be told by some of my American Indian students in an Indian Studies class that traditionally, nobody in plains societies had owned horses; they "just passed through people's hands," my students claimed. They were adamant that although individuals had owned material goods, such as tepees, horses could not be owned because they were animals, and the relationship to animals was sacred. I see this as an example of how unclear definitions and translations of terms, such as "sacred" and "ownership," fueled by the urge to be different from the mainstream society and by popular expectations of new-age providence, can change the meaning of events and the historic past to such an extent that the new meanings, embedded in the mainstream Native knowledge, will unavoidably clash with an academic — and a traditional — examination of history and culture.

While the GFPD, PMP, and Pte Hca Ka were trying to figure out how they could work together for the benefit of the buffalo, ecological restoration of the VE lands and the future park, Pte Hca Ka came under scrutiny from the tribal administration for its activities and plans in another field, namely education.

At a board and staff planning retreat in December 1999, Pte Hca Ka adopted as its vision statement, "Total restoration of the buffalo culture," and as its mission statement, "Restore buffalo back to their ancestral homeland in a manner which preserves and protects our cultural relationship." In November 1999, together with the purchase of the VE land, the corporation was able to move its office into the old Swiftbird Day School, a couple of miles away from the old office and the slaughter unit, along the Blackfoot Road. The new location allowed the corporation to expand its gift shop and to hold seminars or host school field trips and summer language immersion camps. This engagement in educational programs was nothing new. Beside the economic and ecological focus, Pte Hca Ka and many other tribal buffalo projects have been involved in educational efforts. If the projects are to succeed, especially those that stress the cultural aspects of bison, they will have to reach out to the younger generations and reacquaint them with the buffalo culture.

InterTribal Buffalo Cooperation (ITBC) had long been involved with this process with the so-called "buffalo box." With this program, a team of employees travels to schools and events with a box of traditional tools and implements made from buffalo parts. They tell culturally relevant stories about the buffalo and educate the audience about the importance of buf-

falo in the historical and contemporary culture. By passing around the implements, children get to know firsthand how the buffalo supported the people
and also that their ancestors knew well how to survive without the amenities brought by the dominant society. Education in buffalo culture is thus
always also aimed at installing cultural and personal pride in an environment that all too often denies this. Indigenous alternatives to the dominant
society's material culture are shown; these alternatives are not only antidote
to a feeling of unworthiness caused by poverty and the inability to buy into
the capitalist society but also point the way to a more self-sufficient life. Apart
from the buffalo box, ITBC has also authored a CD-ROM and "Gifts of the
Buffalo Nation," an "educational coloring book" (ITBC 1996). This book
educates its audience about the behaviors and the history of the buffalo in
the United States, their cultural importance to American Indian nations,
and how ITBC is working to restore buffalo herds to help the people regain
their healthy lives. With the book, ITBC reaches a wide audience that is not
limited to American Indian reservations because it is sold in many localities
where buffalo herds attract tourists.

Pte Hca Ka's involvement in the educational process increased with the
expansion to the VE land and the move to the new office compound. Among
other activities, the buffalo project supported a language immersion summer camp held in the compound. After I had arrived at Pte Hca Ka for my
fieldwork, I became involved in a curriculum development project for the
reservation schools. The plan was to develop a curriculum for grades three
through eight, focusing on the buffalo. The course would have respected
the school standards and would have ended with a field trip to the buffalo
range. Because the course was to include linguistic aspects, the project leader
tried to work mainly through Lakota language classes.

One of the reasons why I had become interested in the Cheyenne River
bison project in the first place was that the tribal college offered buffalo
management courses in cooperation with the buffalo project. The courses
were part of an effort to build an agricultural science major. James Garrett,
who started those efforts around 1997, tried to work closely with Pte Hca
Ka. The courses, besides providing a scientific and economic basis, had to
be holistic and culturally correct. Among other courses, Garrett taught
"Foundations of Bison Production and Management" and "Philosophy of
Lakota Environmental Belief and Thought." In 2000, Michael Collins was
the head of the program, and it was to include a summer practical course
with Pte Hca Ka. It was with Michael Collins's support that I was able to

participate in that year's Tataka Oyate Conference, where I learned about other buffalo programs at tribal colleges and the Northern Plains Bison Education Network (NPBEN). Both Garrett and Collins have continued these success-ful efforts of teaching ecology and range management, currently at Cankdeska Cikana and at United Tribes Technical College, respectively.

The NPBEN was a consortium of tribal colleges and universities, estab-lished in 1997 with support from the Kellogg Foundation and U.S. Department of Agriculture (USDA) and organized by United Tribes Technical College. Its goals were to link tribal buffalo programs to academics and to promote collaboration and information exchange among the partic-ipants. NPBEN had developed an "Indigenous Homelands Philosophy" that defines bison as "sacred animals and relatives," to be "sustained in a natu-ral, compatible environment with minimal interference," with the humans as "caretakers." The coalition strives "to nurture an authentic understand-ing about American Bison and its evolution, history and unique cultural rela-tionships with the land and people" (Beheler 2001). Some of the most active programs in NPBEN included Oglala Lakota College on Pine Ridge, Cankdeska Cikana Community College in Fort Totten, and Sinte Gleska University on Rosebud.

As a part of the future park, Pte Hca Ka had also planned to build a research station. The vision was to build up Native research on buffalo and also on plains ecology, such as traditional medicinal plant use. Although bison have gotten more into the focus of academics, mostly by virtue of the expanding bison industry, this research is mostly either strictly biological or based on the presumptions of range management. Montana State University and North Dakota State University are two centers for bison research. While many peo-ple involved in tribal buffalo projects generally welcome any research on buffalo, specialized work has led to academic papers that are hard to under-stand for those outside the discipline and unaccustomed to its jargon. Also, because much of the work done is geared toward the bison industry, people who work for the culturally appropriate handling of the buffalo—and I hope it is by now clear that "culture" refers to both Lakota and buffalo culture—would like to have research done along their own lines of interest. Range man-agement as an academic discipline is often seen as emphasizing production returns and optimization and technological solutions (Donahue 1999:114). Production optimization is not what Pte Hca Ka was opposed to, but it was not its sole goal, either, and ideally had to be accomplished through a com-bination of traditional knowledge and scientific inquiry.

In my experience, Pte Hca Ka was open to any kind of buffalo research, although I have heard other experiences from tribal members. There have been several researchers working with the corporation. In summer 2000, I met a Navajo range management student from Montana State University who did a comparative feeding study on cattle and buffalo. Some years before that, another student apparently wanted to do a study on buffalo migration. Although the buffalo managers tried to make her understand that buffalo in an enclosure would not really show any useful migration patterns, they still let her do what she wanted to. The fact that Pte Hca Ka was open for an anthropologist like me to come and write his dissertation on the buffalo operation shows the commitment to "getting the word out," as Fred DuBray used to say. The fact that tribal members experienced a harder time to get access might be explained by the fact that intratribal sharing of information is often coupled with suspicions about political motivations and potential competition from tribal members.

The efforts of buffalo operations to further education on the buffalo culture are efforts in traditional education. It should be clear from what I have said previously about ideological splits concerning the future of the reservation that not all people on Cheyenne River agree that traditional education has a place in the school curricula. This has, in some instances, led to real or perceived pressures by tribal administrations to keep the curricula free of attempts to restore aspects of the culture.

In the eyes of some of traditional people I talked with, this pressure was not just idle words. In the late 1990s, the Takini school had tried to revise the curriculum to center it on the traditional buffalo culture and had even bought six buffalo from Pine Ridge to encourage students in those efforts. When some people had complained to the tribal council about this change in the curriculum, however, the council had disbanded the school board despite a widely signed community petition to leave the new curriculum in place. The council or the new school board—accounts differed between my sources—had also wanted to sell the buffalo. They, however, belonged to the students, not the school, and the students decided to keep them.

Although some people I talked with about the Takini buffalo said those who complained about the new curriculum were mostly white ranchers in the area, others pointed out that many Lakota are afraid of bringing back the old culture. When Lakota language programs were introduced to the reservation schools, some Lakota parents pulled their children from the schools. These attitudes are present not only in parents who are convinced that assimilation is necessary or beneficial for their children but also in people who, out of a reflex, almost, reject anything having to do with traditional culture because they fear either ridicule or some form of punishment from the outside. These notions extend, of course, to the buffalo project. At the beginning of Pte Hca Ka, as Carol Goodstein reports (1995:35), "The elders were afraid, DuBray explain[ed]. They associated the buffalo with the culture that the government had spent years trying to eradicate, through measures such as the reservation system, mandatory boarding schools in which Indian children were forbidden to speak their native languages, and the Dawes Act of 1887."

When I returned to Cheyenne River in 2001, the agricultural courses at the newly formed Si Tanka-Huron University had discontinued the focus on buffalo and Lakota environmental philosophy. The university had also discontinued its role in the NPBEN. The grant under which the buffalo courses had run since 1997 had been limited to four years and because of limited interest from students, the university was now applying for a grant based on a more ranching-focused curriculum. Although the university was always trying to incorporate Lakota culture into every course, administrators said, the new curriculum would place more emphasis on a scientific range management approach; after all, most people involved in agriculture on the reservation are farmers and ranchers not buffalo herders. The lack of interest from students and the effort to serve the needs of the reservation population were, of course, valid reasons to change the curriculum. However, there had also been no great efforts made to recruit people for this innovative program (e.g., advertisement efforts off the reservation or a close cooperation with a major university). This could have attracted interest from wildlife and livestock management students. Whatever the reasons, the decision to discontinue the program in that form constituted a shift of the curriculum from an integration of traditional knowledge to a more purely scientific approach.

It is important to understand that such a change in focus is not without consequences. The kind of knowledge used in ecological interactions is important beyond its direct application to day-to-day management activities and is an expression of social and political values. Kalstad makes that clear in his discussion of similar problems facing the Norwegian Saami reindeer economy, readily applicable to buffalo (1998:243):

The herder's knowledge can be considered as technology for making decisions and resolving problems. However, this knowledge is at the same time embedded in Saami [and Lakota] pastoralism as a way of life. The question is to what extent this traditional knowledge of users will continue to be employed in reindeer [and buffalo] management or to what degree the professional knowledge of biologists, economists, engineers and lawyers will dominate. . . . A [buffalo] industry solely focused on meat production for profit, with a centralized decision-making system strongly committed to biological and economic sciences has little room for traditional user knowledge. . . . Lack of knowledge of [buffalo] . . . result[s]. In that sense choice of knowledge system is a part of managing the pastures, and is a practical as well as a political issue.

The consequences of the shift in approach become much more apparent when they impact not a classroom, but a practical operation. This is exactly what happened in 2001, when the political pressures became so great that the tribe decided to take over the buffalo corporation, not the least to replace the traditional knowledge system that was used for range and animal management with one based on biological and economic sciences.

Not surprisingly, with the expansion of its land base and projected economic and cultural importance through the tribal park and tourism, the corporation became a prized object of attention for a tribal administration that was leaning away from traditional practices to the application of "modern" economics. Based on the experiences with the Takini school that I discussed previously, Pte Hca Ka also knew it was walking a tightrope with the engagement in educational activities and the curriculum project. For several reasons, the curriculum was not developed before the council eventually dismantled Pte Hca Ka, and as far as I know, the idea has not been brought up again.

In summer 2000, the tribal council became actively involved in the corporation, pressing issues like meat marketing, herd counts, and the branding of buffalo, an activity contrary to the hands-off management philosophy of the corporation. The tribal council also decided to use the processing unit for cattle when Pte Hca Ka was not using it for buffalo—a notion that was rejected outright by the corporation. According to several employees, the tribal chairman, looking to enhance the self-sufficiency of tribal enterprises, specifically prohibited the corporation from applying for grants, although grant money made up most of the corporation's income. This coincided with a nationwide collapse of the buffalo market, which substantially diminished the net worth of the corporation. It was already becoming apparent that the corporation would not be able to carry all the direct and indirect costs from the VE purchase by itself. The payments for the land could only be made with the help from philanthropists. The chairman proposed that the tribe buy the land from the corporation. Tribal involvement in the land purchase itself might have been a good idea because the plans for the VE range were to convert this fee land into tribal land anyway. The context in which this discussion took place, however, raised some worries about the tribal council exerting control over this essential part of the corporation.

At the time, I heard from many sources that some cattle ranchers were lobbying for the tribe to take over the VE and make it available for outside leases for cattle. People were criticizing the purchase in general, and some were worried about what they saw as a too traditional approach to the buffalo. Beside the official pressures from the tribal council, rumors were circulating in summer 2000 about financial irresponsibility of the corporation and Fred DuBray personally. These allegations and rumors were persistent and founded on the fact that DuBray had built up his own, private buffalo herd in the meantime and had exchanged some land with the corporation to consolidate his own and the corporation's property. Still in 2002, Chairman Bourland, about to leave office after losing the tribal general election, alleged "collusion in the original purchase [of the VE], saying that 'some people got pretty rich off that deal'" ("CRST Bails Out" 2002:1). The plain fact is that from the purchase of the VE land on, as DuBray pointed out, the corporation was submitted to "a tremendous amount of pressure . . . to focus on the buffalo herd as a 'commercial' ranching operation, which would operate much the same as a cattle ranch" (2000:9).

Old Swiftbird Day School. In November 1999, Pte Hca Ka moved their offices to the Old Swiftbird Day School. The move to the school compound allowed them to expand the gift shop and offices and to host seminars and meetings as well as school field trips and summer language immersion camps. The old school compound was seen as a suitable headquarter for future endeavors, including a research institute and a tribal park. These offices were used until the reorganization of Pte Hca Ka in the fall of 2001.

Lake Oahe and US 212. The damming of Lake Oahe in the 1950s was a severe blow for the Cheyenne River Sioux Tribe (CRST). The lake flooded the tribe's most valuable lands and destroyed several settlements, including the agency, which used to be located to the left of the present-day bridge. During the drought years, starting in 2002, the level of the lake receded about ten to twenty feet, laying bare foundations of the old agency. The view here is from the eastern, off-reservation shore, approaching the Cheyenne River Sioux Reservation. One reason why the now-flooded bottomlands were economically invaluable is that they supported tree stands that provided shelter, building materials, and firewood.

Mobile processing facility. From 1997 until 2002, Pte Hca Ka operated the world's only mobile bison slaughter and processing unit, shown here as it was set up in 2000. A Swedish company, Sandstrom's Transport Producers AB, built this facility based on a model used for reindeer in Lapland. The facility was custom built on two trailers, one for the slaughter unit and one for the processing and packing unit. It featured the latest technology, including electrical generators, water supply, electrical saws, refrigerated storage rooms, lockers, and an inspection and packing station. This facility could handle twelve buffalo in one slaughter event, and all of this equipment was installed in such a way that various parts of the facility could be hydraulically extended from and retracted into the trailers for ease of transportation.

Mobile processing facility. In an effort to secure a commodity food contract with the U.S. Department of Agriculture (USDA), changes were initiated to the mobile processing unit after the reorganization of Pte Hca Ka in winter 2001. The USDA demanded, among other things, that the waste product chutes from the facility had to be covered. The additions to the facility (note the white hut left of center) rendered the facility immobile. After this picture was taken in spring 2002, the facility was put on a concrete slab, reoriented, and today is absolutely immobile. It started to operate under USDA inspection several months later.

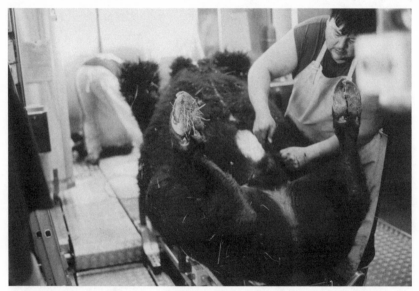

Tim Pickner slaughtering a buffalo. Pickner was the processing facility manager until the reorganization of Pte Hca Ka. In this photo from 2001, he is starting to take the hide off a bison. The dead animal has been loaded into the
slaughter unit, decapitated, and laid on a special bed. After Tim has taken off
the hoofs and separated the hide from the belly, the hide will be hooked to a
stationery mechanism while the animal's body will be lifted onto overhead rails.
In the late nineteenth century, bison hunters used strong horses to pull hides
off dead animals.

Chris Arpan slaughtering a buffalo. Arpan was the designated shooter for Pte Hca Ka before the reorganization. He also helped Tim in the processing facility. In this photo taken in spring 2002, the buffalo has been stripped of his hide, has had its internal organs removed, and is hanging upside down from its hind legs. Chris is using an electrical saw to cut the body in two halves. The platform he is standing on is actually a lift. At the next station, each half will be cut apart, and the quarters will then be stored for fourteen days before they are brought to the connected processing unit.

Field slaughter. In winter 2002, Pte Hca Ka hosted a training workshop for member tribes of the InterTribal Bison Cooperative (ITBC). As part of the training, a buffalo was field slaughtered behind the processing facility (the left edge of the photo). The bison was shot in the pasture and is hanging from the front loader of Pte Hca Ka's tractor, while preparations for the slaughter are underway. In the background, the old Swiftbird Day School compound is visible; by this time, the offices had already been moved to a mobile home next to the slaughter facility.

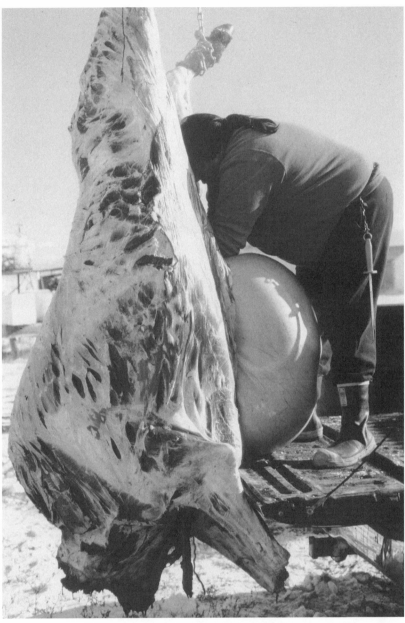

Field slaughter. The head, front hoofs, and the hide of the young bull have been removed. Tim Pickner is standing on the bed of the pickup and is removing the intestines from the bison. A buffalo's internal organs are neatly packed in a large bag, which Tim is removing out of the chest cavity. These bags, and their ability to hold fluids, allegedly sometimes saved early explorers from dehydration. Removing the bag whole is a critical process; when it breaks, it soils the meat.

Corralled buffalo, Custer State Park. The dust settles over the bison destined for sale at the annual Custer State Park auction in winter 2001. A snowstorm hit the Black Hills the day after the auction. The auction, a large event attracting buyers and spectators from all over the United States, provides revenue for the state park and allows the park to manage its herd. Animals over ten years old are usually culled from the park's herd, as are most bulls. This is a contrast to how Pte Hca Ka valued older animals, which were thought to educate the younger buffalo.

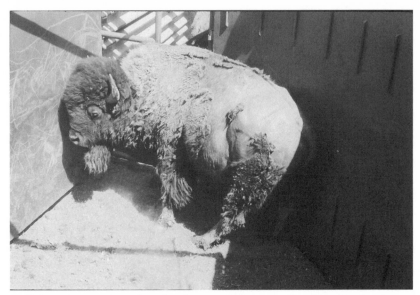

Buffalo bull in new corrals. After the reorganization of Pte Hca Ka, the Game, Fish and Parks Department (GFPD) built new holding and sorting corrals on the VE pasture, next to Blackfoot Road. These new corrals became operational in mid-May 2002, and were used to ship bison to the North American Bison Cooperative's (NABC) slaughter facility in New Rockford, North Dakota. Here, a bull has been cornered during the sorting. The graffiti on the metal wall by his head is actually scraping from stressed animals' horns. During this drive, at least, GFPD employees used electrical prods to herd the bison, in what provided perhaps the strongest contradiction to Pte Hca Ka's previous management values.

CHAPTER 9

Buffalo Ranching

The emphasis on raising meat and economic pressures that force ranchers and farmers to become industrial workers influence the ways animals are seen and treated. According to a U.S. Department of Agriculture (USDA) statistic, 35.4 million cattle and 1.01 million calves were slaughtered commercially in the year 2001 in the United States. Production was slightly down from 2000. Of these 35.4 million cattle, 57 percent were slaughtered in fifteen slaughtering plants (USDA 2002:1). In numbers, that is over 20 million cattle, or about 1,345,000 cattle per plant. This means that as a statistical average, each of these fifteen plants processed some 3,658 cattle per day.

In an industrialized agriculture that uses such things as slaughtering plants, farming is no longer about an ideal cyclical system but becomes an extraction industry, alienated from humans by machines and scientific calculations. More profits demand more machines, more horsepower, more fertilizer, more land, and more water, and the economy demands more profits. The idea that one of the most important functions of farming is to take care of the land is lost in an economically based concept of functionalism. The land becomes a tool for producing the maximum number of animals. I would like to emphasize that this does not necessarily mean that the land is not conserved—a good business owner takes care of his means of production. But the approach is different. In one case, the cattle and the land are integral parts of the cosmological system, and in the other case, they are economic accessories to it. The consequences can perhaps best be seen in places like Dodge City, Kansas, surrounded by masses of cattle waiting for transport or slaughter, awaiting death amassed in feedlots that make their presence known to the traveler miles away by their pungent smell. "Our relation to nature has, so to speak, left the pasture and entered the sophisticated but ungodly realm of urban politics; this is our difficulty," says Langdon Gilkey (1993:171). "Put theologically, the fate of nature—as the Genesis myth intimated—is now subject to the baleful consequences of the historical Fall, and so it shares in the tragedy of an estranged history."

It should not come as a surprise that the social pressures that influence the cattle industry also bear increasingly on the buffalo industry. Although a niche industry can work in alternative ways, one that wants to enter the mainstream markets will come under increasing stresses to adapt to the dominant economic system. That said, the buffalo industry is still much at a numerical disadvantage in comparison to the beef industry—in 2005 there were somewhat over three hundred fifty thousand buffalo in North America—and this is reflected in problems and concerns over marketing the meat.

Although the National Bison Association (NBA) and its predecessors were trying to market buffalo meat, they were never able to develop a good market for it. During the 1990s, bison herds were built up primarily for breeding, in anticipation that a meat market would certainly develop. As more and more people became interested in buffalo ranching, live animals were valued more than slaughter animals, and ranchers made good profits. With the involvement of Ted Turner in the buffalo industry, ranching buffalo became more fashionable and respectable in the 1990s, and a coinciding depression of the beef market got even more people involved. Production in both Canada and the United States grew by as much as 20 percent a year.

With too much inventory and no market, however, prices for buffalo eventually plummeted, and by 2000 and 2001 hit almost bottom. Because the breeding stock had been overprized when many ranchers started their operations, there were no returns. Many people who had bought heifers for three thousand dollars now had to sell heifer calves for three hundred dollars or less. At some auctions in the 2001–2002 season, calves went for sixty dollars. Quite a few producers had waited for prices to go back up and had held back selling their animals for a few years but by 2001 ran out of land and grass for their growing herds and were forced to sell. At many auctions I attended, the auctioneers appealed to the buying public to think of the future of the industry, meaning not to set even lower prices as precedents for future sales. From a commercial standpoint, the industry, it seemed, was in a desperate state.

One part of the problem with marketing buffalo meat for the NBA had been that individual producers had no clout against the powerful beef lobby and were perhaps even competing with each other. Another problem was the relative rarity of slaughter facilities open for buffalo. These problems were targeted with the founding of the North American Bison Cooperative (NABC) in 1993 and its modern slaughter plant in New Rockford, North Dakota, designed exclusively for buffalo. The idea was that under NABC, individual bison ranchers could pool resources to develop a worldwide market for the meat. This notion worked well until the market crash in 2000.

With the market plummeting in 2000, NABC could not sell as much meat as it was processing (North American Bison Journal [NABJ] 2001), and some NABC members had had payments for delivered animals deferred for as many as two years (Bell 2002). Sales picked up in 2002, however, and the cooperative acquired New West Foods to increase market penetration. Ted Turner, a member of the NABC, also began opening his Ted's Montana Grill restaurants in major U.S. cities in 2002, in part to promote and sell buffalo meat in a wider market. As in many other sectors of plains agriculture, the federal government has been lending a hand, too. In 1998, USDA started to buy surplus meat from NABC and the Denver Buffalo Company for distribution in its federal nutrition programs (Brasher 1999). A large part of the nutrition program is the commodity program for American Indian reservations and free school lunches in public schools. The bison meat was targeted primarily for reservation consumers. This was reflected in the legislative language authorizing the purchase of the meat.

In 2001, when congress passed legislation to buy another $3 million worth of buffalo burger from NABC, the InterTribal Bison Cooperative (ITBC) protested. The legislation, cowritten by NABC, provided for USDA to buy buffalo "from Native American producers and cooperative organizations" (Thorne 2001). The inclusion of "Native American" producers was probably meant to alleviate concerns in Congress. However, ITBC, who had by this time built up tribal herds to a point where tribes were ready to enter the market on the one hand and were hurting from the market crash on the other, saw an opportunity and took the language literally. Although NABC had some individual members who were Native Americans, ITBC interpreted the language to mean that buffalo could only be bought from

American Indian producers and American Indian cooperatives. On appeal to the U.S. Comptroller General's office, ITBC won the contract.

Although the live buffalo for the program then had to be purchased from American Indian producers, however, NABC won the contract to process the buffalo; ITBC had scrambled to provide an alternative slaughter facility but could not find any. This was the trigger for ITBC to look for an adequate slaughter plant, which it eventually found in Malta, Montana. After this episode, however, the language in the commodity program legislation was rewritten, striking out the "Native American" in the text, and only referring to "cooperatives." ITBC, being a cooperative itself, once again put in a bid for the 2002 program, but it lost the bid to the intended receiver, NABC. Although some tribes who were not part of ITBC, such as the Three Affiliated Tribes on Fort Berthold Reservation, received part of the contract, most of the buffalo burgers for the commodity program on reservations primarily came from off-reservation ranches. Once again, off-reservation interests profit from reservations, while the reservations, with their own buffalo programs suffering under the market, subsidize the rescue of a direct competitor.

In 2002, the government spent $6 million "to buy bison meat that goes to needy people on Indian reservations," and authorized another $10 million as a meat surplus removal program, subsidizing the troubled industry (Bell 2002). Despite these subsidies and Ted Turner's initiatives, NABC had to declare bankruptcy in 2004. Ironically, though, the bison market seems to have recovered to a certain degree during the same time; prices for animals have stabilized or are actually rising slightly, and the market for bison meat is expanding.

One of the arguments that ITBC used to support the legitimacy of its appeal was that NABC might use beef trim or grain-fed buffalo meat in their buffalo burgers, which would raise the fat content in the meat (Melmer 2001b). Much of the meat was going to be distributed on reservations, and it is the alleged low fat and cholesterol content of buffalo meat that many people hope will help reverse the grim diabetes and heart disease situation on reservations. Because health food or organic food is more expensive than industrial products in the United States, many people on the reservations cannot afford to eat healthy. Government distribution of buffalo meat would be a welcome way of getting healthy food to the people. The change from traditional foods to industrial foods is often seen as a general cause for illnesses that affect American Indians more than other groups in the United States:

I think that all these sicknesses that come today, like diabetes, heart troubles, cancer and arthritis are from the wrong food. A long time ago, our Elders never had diabetes. Now quite a few of them have it. My mother was a diabetic but my grandmother wasn't. It is from the wrong diet, not eating enough traditional food (Horse in Sexsmith 2000:8).

Robert Chasing Hawk, a former Cheyenne River Sioux Tribe chairman, advocates a high protein, low carbohydrates diet (Bell Gease 2003), one, he says, that allows the Lakota to survive without diabetes. Although sometimes, people blame the government for intentionally or unintentionally giving American Indian people food that will make them sick, Chasing Hawk is an advocate for individual responsibility: "Sometimes we call ourselves grass-roots people or traditionalists, but we really enjoy today's carbohydrate lifestyle, but are afraid to return to our traditional nutrition way of life, high protein and limited carbohydrate diet, drink plenty of water, more exercise or physical activities like our ancestors did" (Chasing Hawk 2000). In view of the severe health problems on reservations, especially diabetes and heart disease, and because bison are seen as traditional, buffalo meat has come to be seen by some as a possible contribution to healing. Because it allowed trim in the burgers, the proposed program for bison meat distribution was perceived by some residents as yet another plot by the government to keep American Indians unhealthy and impoverished.

Nutritional benefits of buffalo meat became apparent as early as the late 1960s, especially its high percentage of polyunsaturated fats (Rorabacher 1970:106). Today, buffalo meat is marketed as the "healthy red meat," and its consumption as an alternative to beef has been endorsed by the American Heart Association (AHA). During my fieldwork, doctors as far away as Pennsylvania and New York ordered meat directly from Pte Hca Ka for their heart patients. Many direct buffalo meat retailers have on their websites a chart comparing the cholesterol content of buffalo meat, skinless chicken, and beef, with the buffalo showing the lowest numbers. Although numbers vary in different studies (see NBA 1990:304–20 for a compilation), it has become a truism that buffalo has, indeed, a low cholesterol content—if not lower than chicken, at least much lower than beef. Despite a popular belief that this truism can be translated into nutritional differences between grass-fed and grain-fed bison, that conclusion, just as the difference between bison and beef, is not so clear-cut.

Actual research on buffalo or bison meat has been mainly conducted by Martin Marchello at North Dakota State University and Judy Driskell at University of Nebraska. The first comparison of grain-finished and grass-fed bison was published in 2001. The authors found that the "meat from grass-finished and grain-finished animals had nearly identical profiles for protein . . . and cholesterol," although they recorded small differences in moisture, fat, and calories. There were, however, "considerable differences in fatty acids expressed as a percentage of total fats. Meat from grass-finished bison averaged approximately 5% more saturated fatty acids, 6% more polyunsaturated fatty acids, and 11% less monounsaturated fatty acids than did meat from grain-finished bison" (Marchello and Driskell 2001:68, 69). In another comparison study, funded by the Nature Conservancy, Marchello (n.d.) found that differences in protein, fat, calories, and moisture are variable and "are probably negligible in terms of human consumption because of the individual variability of human metabolism." The differences between fatty acids, however, seem to be consistent. Specific numbers vary, but consistently, grain-fed animals have more monounsaturated fat and less saturated fat.

Research comparing beef and bison meat in terms of health benefits is also direly needed. However in a study testing the buildup of plasma cholesterol in beef-fed, bison-fed, and soy-fed hamsters (Wilson et al. 2000:713), it was found that, "the hamsters that consumed the bison and casein had significantly lower plasma [cholesterol] concentrations compared to hamsters fed the beef with no differences between the casein- and bison-fed hamsters." Because "the relative percentages of saturated, monounsaturated, and polyunsaturated fatty acids are similar for bison and beef," the researchers looked at four individual fatty acids; palmitate, stearate, myristate, and linoleate. Basically, palmitate and myristate raise cholesterol levels, whereas stearate and linoleate are either neutral or lower plasma cholesterol levels. The results of the meat analysis showed that the ground beef "contained 21% palmitate and 17% stearate, whereas the . . . ground bison contained 15% plamitate and 22% stereate." In contrast to the beef, the bison contained no myristate, and the bison had a two and a half times higher linoleate level than the beef. Although beef has an overall higher fat content than bison, which might have contributed to the higher plasma cholesterol level in the beef-fed hamsters, the different levels of fatty acids "may have led to the greater plasma cholesterol concentrations in the beef-fed hamsters" (Wilson et al. 2000:714).

Although these results are only first steps toward a conclusive picture and although it is not clear whether the differences actually result in large health benefits, it seems true that in terms of cholesterol inducing fatty acids, beef is relatively less healthy than grain-fed bison, which is less healthy than grass-fed bison meat. Whether the chemical differences between grain-finished and grass-finished buffalo are of importance for human consumption and health remains to be seen; it does not seem probable. Bison meat is, in any case, an excellent source for vitamin B_{12}, phosphorus, zinc, and selenium, and a good source for vitamin B_6, thiamin, and niacin (Driskell et al. 2004; Marchello and Driskell 2001).

One organization that advocates more buffalo meat in the diet of American Indian people is the Indigenous Diabetes Education Alliance (IDEA), based in Spearfish, South Dakota. The dependence on commodity foods, which are often high in fat and cholesterol, IDEA argues, is at least partially to blame for the high occurrence of diabetes among reservation populations. The organization "works directly with the tribal bison herd managers, diabetes program directors and tribal dieticians in ensuring that nutritional education and food preparation instruction are available, an exercise program is discussed and that bison meat is distributed to the project on a weekly basis" (IDEA 2003). Buffalo meat is primarily purchased from local tribes but if necessary also from neighboring tribal operations. In all cases, however, the buffalo have to be Native raised and grass fed.

Because the people behind IDEA have a background in working for ITBC and tribal buffalo programs, it is not surprising that they focus on buffalo. Their perspective on buffalo falls right in place with that of many others actively involved in ITBC. IDEA president and director of the Fort Belknap tribal buffalo program, Mike Fox, who used to be president of ITBC, says that buffalo meat is not a magical device, but that "it will bring out more spirituality and connectedness to the buffalo and old ways. It has more meaning" (Fox in Franscell 2002:A-01).

In the context of the Gila River Reservation, Carolyn Smith-Morris defines three "major domains of influence" for diabetes: political-economic factors, genetic factors, and cultural factors (2004:39). Although the genetic factors are probably the most debated and the least changeable ones, tribal buffalo programs seem to be made to address politico-economic and cultural factors. Not only this, but as Smith-Morris reports (39), the "most successful examples of diabetic health programs are the ones with a community-based focus

. . . or ones that strive for cultural sensitivity and relevance." Tribal buffalo operations, if run as true community cooperatives, are not only in a position to revive cultural discourses about responsibility, health, nutrition, and world-view, they can also provide the traditional food that might be useful for diabetes patients. Their potential in the fight against diabetes is an as of yet largely untapped resource. I do not want to portray bison meat, or any diet change, as the magic bullet against diabetes. However, if nothing else, the discourse around buffalo cooperatives could generate community awareness that contributes to the life changes needed to fight diabetes.

While many tribes and organizations, such as the Great Plains Bison Cooperative, advocate for purely grass-fed buffalo, the industry as a whole seems to follow a tendency toward grain-fed or grain-finished buffalo meat. It seems, as Hudson says (1998:235), to be "speeding along a road paved by the beef industry." Because many Americans, including many American Indians, have become accustomed to the more fatty beef, buffalo marketing strategists believe that a change of cooking and tasting customs would be too much for consumers and that naturally lean buffalo meat therefore has to be made fattier. Ensuring uniformity and consistency in meat quality and having animals reach "market size" earlier are other concerns leading many producers to feed their animals grain, at least before slaughter (Hudson 1998:236; Knowles, Mitchell, and Fox 1998:245–46). "This particular topic has been a recurring issue within the industry," as Karen Conley says (2000a:138); "There are those who are opposed to the NABC because of their policy of finishing animals on grain." Just how deep the rift goes becomes evident in her comments further along: "Even though many of these naysayers keep their thoughts to themselves, there are enough vocalists out there that are being heard not only by those on the inside, but by the public as well. At a time when the bison industry is poised to jump head-long into the thick of production agriculture, those negative attitudes certainly are a shackle to progress" (138,139). The key words here are "production agriculture." It is true that "if we are going to include the bison in production agriculture" (Conley 2000b:157), "there will be animals in feedlots and in small pastures," but those who argue for purely grass-fed buffalo may not want to have their animals part of production agriculture. The argument goes back to the one mentioned previously: whether or not to keep buffalo as wild as possible.

Although organizations such as ITBC, IDEA, and National Plains Bison Education Network (NPBEN) are trying to get the word out about bene-fits—ecological, economic, physical, and social—that can be gained from buffalo, the preference of many American Indians for beef over buffalo meat shows that there is a lot of work to do. Probably the largest group that propagates buffalo, focusing on the economic and physical aspects, however, is the bison industry through its marketing campaigns. Focusing on the ecological benefits are environmental groups. Because each focus represents a different perspective on the buffalo as an animal and as a resource, or as a nonresource, the different groups involved and their messages compete with each other. This contributes to the difficulties in educating the public about the benefits of eating buffalo meat.

Some people propose that diseases, such as diabetes, are primarily caused by historical trauma or the continued presence of colonial policies (see Ferreira and Lang 2006). Although I see many problems with such a theory, obviously, environmental relations are always a factor in community health. Buffalo ranching is not only directly linked to the health of the community, but also indirectly, through the health of the land. If one talks about the pressures that commercial agriculture is facing, especially on the plains, one cannot avoid the impact that agricultural practices have on the land, and the impact that the land has on agriculture. Buffalo ranching, many of its advocates point out, is a much healthier practice than cattle ranching or farming.

This argument is larger than simply community health: it revolves around ecosystem health. One of the most notorious proposals stemming from this approach came to be known as the "Buffalo Commons" proposal. To evaluate the health of the ecosystem as a whole and to understand outside views of tribal bison enterprises and of buffalo ranching in general, it is necessary to discuss issues from a much broader perspective.

The plains, like any other ecosystem, are not a uniform environment and have never been one. Perhaps more so than most other regions, they are defined by local extremes. For the prehistoric, historic, and contemporary plains, local disruptions have always been common, but because they have been a defining element of the ecosystem, these are internal disruptions, a part of the system:

> Indeed, change shaped the ecosystem. Fires frequently swept across great expanses. Severe winters were momentous and inevitable, even ordinary. Periodic droughts eliminated or reduced species not adapted to the region. Incredible herds of bison grazed waist-high grasses down to the earth and then moved on. Rivers reconstructed their course with

erratic regularity. The great contiguous grasslands were an odd mixture of timeless stability and regular disruption, a thriving, healthy,
and resilient ecosystem that had persisted for thousands of years. That
was about to change (Licht 1997:10).

Before Euro-American settlement, millions of buffalo were an integral part
of the plains ecosystem. They were probably not the most important part of
the system; their symbolic character made people perceive them as such.
That being understood, however, one can say that the plains were a buffalo
ecosystem, keeping in mind that buffalo also adapted to other, different environments, from the eastern woodlands to the subarctic forests. Another essential factor in the ecosystem was of course the human presence, and for about
two hundred years before the Euro-American conquest, the presence of
horses.

On the grounds of disturbances and changes caused by humans, Andrew
Isenberg has rejected the notion of the plains as a stable ecosystem
(2001:11). He proposes that a system is only stable if it does not experience
any disturbances:

> For as long as they have existed, people have inhabited, altered, and
> been affected by the nonhuman natural world. Even such precapital-
> ist societies as the equestrian bison hunters of the Great Plains were
> sometimes given to waste and degradation of the resources upon which
> they depended. To assume an unchanging, harmonious relationship
> between Indians and Great Plains environment classes both Indian
> culture and nature as static (12).

This is, of course, true, but human presence alone does not mean instabil-
ity or degradation. The old ecosystem in its entirety, neither a harmonious
nor a nonhuman world, was changing, but slowly enough that it was stable
while doing so. Whether any given ecosystem is seen as stable is a matter of
how it is defined in space and time. As a whole, one can surely say that the
plains as an ecosystem were more stable before than after Euro-American
settlement, which brought along catastrophic ecological change for many
parts of the old system. Because every ecosystem changes over time, it is
already understood that to say that the plains ecosystem was always stable has
to be a relative statement. The statement also does not take away agency from
the people or any other part of the system. To act within a system does not
necessarily mean to impact the whole negatively. In fact, to stay healthy—

and stable—the system probably needed local disruptions like fire, grazing, and sometimes even excessive hunting. Although local and occasional waste did occur, there is a difference between parts of a system interacting with each other and gradually changing and an outside factor invading and destroying a system. This destruction occurred with the transformation of the buffalo ecosystem to an imported system of agriculture.

The perceived deficiencies in the region's suitability for agriculture led many Anglo-American writers to see the plains as "alien, deficient, and peculiarly hard to love in its natural state" (Flores 1996:7). Early explorers, as Flores (7–8; also Bennett 1996:251–52) points out, saw the plains quite differently and gave the ecosystem glowing reviews; but when people tried to transform it into agricultural landscapes, they changed their minds. Had the settlers been interested in learning from Plains Indians, they would have known that except for the wide river valleys, especially the Missouri, this land was not suited for agriculture. Had the settlers adapted to the special ecological circumstances on the plains, instead of simply trying to impose their ideas about nature on the landscape (Licht 1997:12–16; Manning 1997:275–76), the impact of less intensive farming practices would still not have been as degrading as it turned out to become: "The presence of farming per se has not caused . . . environmental and economic dislocation. The problems have been brought about by the substantial expansion of cultivated acreage beyond the sustainable land base onto marginal agricultural lands and wetlands" (Baydack et al. 1996:249). Bennett finds that the problems were caused mainly by "the illusion that constraints were illusionary," and the general perception that "North American aspirations simply could not tolerate a sense of limits" (1996:252) If the land was not going to be hospitable by itself, it for sure could be forced to become so. Cunfer explains this history from a slightly different perspective (2005:217–25). He argues that the plains were simply the terminal stage for systematic swidden agriculture on a national level, which depended on new farmlands to the west once the old lands were depleted. Once the farmers reached the plains and there were no more farmlands further to the west, farmers adopted a strategy based on artificial soil renewal, namely fertilizer. "When farmers stepped off the westering trail, they stepped onto a treadmill," Cunfer concludes (225). However this was a treadmill that seemingly enabled not simply maintaining the status quo but a continued expansion into marginal lands made fertile by industrial agriculture.

The arid and semiarid lands in the western plains were converted to cattle range, which is more compatible with ecological conditions. But overgrazing has degraded many ranges, and the introduction of cattle has changed the land. Again, it is not ranching per se that causes problems. Many ranchers are concerned about environmental degradation (Russell 1993). But as Strang points out in the similar context of the Australian cattle frontier (1997:129–32), ranchers view the land from an economic, not an ecological, perspective, and to survive economically, sometimes ecological consequences have to be disregarded. *"The crucial element here,"* says Bennett (1996:275, italics original), *"is institutional, not ecological;* that is, in a market and profit-making economy, agriculture is subject to forces outside the control of local resource users, who have to do what the general economic system requires of them, regardless of economic costs." Mostly through fragmentation and monocultures, industrialized agriculture is threatening or has already completely changed plains ecosystems. "Today, no piece of prairie exists that has not been impacted by humans in one way or another. The plant and animal communities that have occupied the Great Plains for thousands of years have been completely restructured by humans in the last two centuries. They have been impacted by such a variety of factors both intentional and unintentional that we will never understand them all" (Benedict, Freeman, and Genoways 1996:149). The early settlers must have had a rather pragmatic view of the region once they got there—less than 20 percent of settlers in the northern plains stayed with their first homesteads (Bennett 1996:261). But the promoters and planners of settlement and the general expectation of technological progress and hegemony saw the plains not as they were but as they wanted them to be. This perspective on the region caused negative consequences not only for the ecosystem but ultimately also for the settlers' own economies (Bennett 1996:261–62).

Only a few years after Frederick Jackson Turner declared the Frontier to be closed in 1890, it opened up again. The Frontier, as defined by Turner and the Census Bureau, was the line between those parts of the country with a population of more than two people per square mile and those with less. "Nearly a century later, however," Frank Popper found that "the declaration looks odd and premature" (1986:104) Applying the criteria of less than two people per square mile to the county level, he found that according to the 1980 census, 143 counties matched the definition of the frontier. All of these counties, but one, lie west of the ninety-eight meridian, and the counties covered a total area of 949,500 square miles, more than a quarter of the United States. Disregarding Alaska, the frontier counties of the contiguous United States "contain thirteen percent of its total land area" (Popper

1986:104). If one applies a definition of the frontier as the area in which the population is less than six people per square mile, the counties, ten of which lie east of the ninety-eighth meridian, cover a third of the contiguous United States (Popper 1986:106).

Popper's diagnosis for the Great Plains was especially dismal (1986:118–19). "Agriculture," he wrote, "is dying throughout much of the plains both for economic reasons and for lack of water. . . . No replacement crops, federal subsidies, or foreseeable irrigation techniques are likely to save plains farming." On the contrary, continued agriculture on the plains might lead to another Dust Bowl, Popper feared. As a consequence, "the nation may conclude that this part of America . . . should never have been farmed or settled in the first place."

This notion was not a new one and neither was the grim diagnosis for the plains. Aldo Leopold had warned against overdevelopment of the land since the 1920s (1991a). Worster's analysis of the 1930s Dust Bowl points to causes that lead directly to the farm crisis of the 1980s (1977:223–30). What drove farmers from their land were not so much natural causes, says Worster, as social ones. Consolidation of the land and advancing agricultural technology led to ecological degradation and directly to the eviction of farmers from the land. "In many ways resembling the English peasants uprooted by the eighteenth-century enclosure acts, these surplus tenants were the victims of America's judgment—perhaps justified—that agriculture must be made to pay a higher return" (225). In other words, industrial capitalism had caught up with the frontier on the plains already in the 1920s, and the decades since have simply been witness to its expansion into the heart of what was supposed to have been a uniquely U.S. yeoman society.

Having diagnosed a trend of population decline in rural plains counties, Frank and Deborah Popper made a "daring proposal for dealing with an inevitable disaster," in what became to be known as the Buffalo Commons proposal:

> We believe that over the next generation the plains will, as a result of the largest, longest-running agricultural and environmental miscalculation in American history, become almost totally depopulated. At that point, a new use for the region will emerge, one that is in fact so old that it predates the American presence. We are suggesting that the region be returned to its original pre-white state, that it be, in effect, deprivatized (1987:12).

After a recount of agricultural disasters on the plains from the 1890s through the 1980s and after asserting that "to the Indians and the early cattlemen, all the plains was a commons," the Poppers suggested that the only alternative to future disasters was for the government to acquire the land that would soon become deserted, anyway. This program would not include those parts of the plains that remained economically viable. On the acquired land, however, "the government will take the newly emptied plains and tear down the fences, replant the shortgrass, and restock the animals, including the buffalo" (Popper and Popper 1987:17). Some of the land might also be used to settle Plains Indians' land claims "by giving or selling the tribes chunks of the new commons." On the whole, the Poppers thought (18), "The federal government's commanding task on the plains for the next century will be to recreate the nineteenth century."

Initial responses from the plains were mostly incredulous (Matthews 1992). People felt that two professors from the East Coast had condemned their future, their way of life and their land and were proposing that the federal government should chase them off (Rocky Mountain News 1991; Shepard 1994; Swisher 1994; Wagoner 2002:8–9). Others evaluated the idea from a more professional or benign perspective (Egan and Whitney 1994; Gauthier 1994). The Poppers, reacting to the initial outcry and professional critique, have since rephrased their proposal, leaving the federal government out of it (Popper and Popper 1994, 1999). People on the plains have come around to acknowledge that the region is facing severe problems and have come to terms with an ongoing debate about its future (Cameron 2002; Donovan 2001; Harlan 2001; Martin 2001; Williams 2001). Resistance to the idea is still strong, however, with people who believe that one of the plan's essential features is to evict them from their homelands. A man in Nebraska told me in summer 2002 that "some Easterners" are trying to get all the people off the land, people who have been on the land for 150 years. He strongly believed, as do others, that the plan calls for all towns to be erased and people chased away. When I explained to him that the Poppers and others want the towns to stay, but their economy to become based on buffalo ranching and ecotourism, he skeptically agreed that that might actually work.

The discussion about the Buffalo Commons has spawned two separate debates. One is focusing on buffalo and ecology, arguing for the environmental restoration of the plains by returning buffalo and other native species. This is a more direct continuation of the Buffalo Commons proposal and sees the economic future of the plains mostly in ecotourism and buffalo ranches (Callenbach 1996; Licht 1994, 1997). One proposal that has come out of this debate is the Million Acre Project, with the involvement of Frank Popper, an attempt to restore at least one million acres of plains ecosystem to their "original" state. This debate can be seen in the context of general calls for a "rewilding" of North America (Foreman 2004). The other debate is one focusing on economics, trying to find a solution for the socioeconomic problems the plains are, indeed, facing. In this debate, buffalo and buffalo ranching play a minor role, simply as one part of a wider economic solution. Recreating the nineteenth century is not an option in this debate, which has accepted the challenges from the Buffalo Commons proposal, but is looking for different answers.

What the Poppers describe to be happening on the plains is basically the disappearance of the rural plains; I use "rural" in this context to denote the presence of functional settlements; their disappearance would give rise to a depopulated not a rural landscape. The rural plains seem to be vanishing both in terms of population outmigration from rural counties and in terms of a change toward an ever more urbanized, industrialized agriculture, which cuts jobs. The balance between town and country, which is the foundation for the well-being of both, has been and is upset by the industrial or postindustrial economy. As Karl Marx and Friedrich Engels point out, the bourgeoisie, by its necessary industrialization, subjects the country to the rule of the towns, in the same way, to use modern terminology, that it has made the South dependent on the North, or in more useful terms of world-system theories, the Peripheries on the Centers or Core (1990:63) This is even more true for regions like the plains, where towns are just intermediaries between the country and the larger centers, and thus are limited in autonomous decision making.

Frederic Jameson points out that the completion of modernization implies "the effacement of Nature, and its precapitalist agricultures, from the postmodern, the essential homogenization of a social space and experience now uniformly modernized and mechanized" (1997:366). On completion, postmodernity reaches the point where this capitalist uniformity is no longer a problem for "the people successfully molded by it (and who can no longer even recognize or thematize it as such)." In the same vein, Danbom notes that (1997:17), "[u]rban, industrial, capitalist culture is so pervasive and hegemonic that it has largely overwhelmed the rural society that has traditionally been viewed as its antidote." This is a national process,

but the plains might be more affected by it because their settlement coincided with the beginning of the national trend toward urbanization; their
rural areas never had time to find a balance of their own. The census first
showed in 1920 that urban areas accounted for more than 50 percent of the
national population. By 1990, however, suburban populations exceeded 50
percent, and the other half was almost evenly split between urban and rural
areas (Howarth 1997:8, 9). In less than a century, in other words, the nation
had moved through modernity to postmodernity and so had the con-
stituencies supporting its policies. Rural regions have changed, too; only 10
percent of rural populations still produce resources. These are mostly large
commercial farms, which are stunningly efficient, but as a consequence,
the "reality of American rural life no longer favors that old agrarian dream"
(Howarth 1997:9). On the plains, the population of metro counties grew by
152 percent between 1950 and 1996, and urban nonmetro counties (those
with a city of at least twenty thousand people) grew by 39 percent. Those
with a city of between twenty-five hundred and twenty thousand people did
not grow, and rural nonmetro counties lost more than a third of their population (Rathge and Highman 1998:19). Although population loss as such
might not be a negative trend, what happens on the plains is an "outmigration of youth and mid-level professionals" leaving an older population that
stays (Northern Great Plains Rural Development Commission [NGPRDC]
1997b:2). At least for the present and the next few decades, this will create
problems for the region, which will lose civic and social capacity. Eroding
tax bases will also strain public services in many regions on the plains (Sheaff
2001:3).

   Although advances in technology and a postmodern economy influence
patterns of living on the rural plains by eliminating jobs in a now industrial
agriculture and promoting the consolidation of lands, a process that is often
decried, some analysts also see new opportunities created. Many Americans
would prefer to live in rural areas, given that they can take advantage of
improved transportation and communication technology to commute or
work from their homes (Rowley 1998:3). Others want to take advantage of
rural regions for rest and relaxation. Many rural areas are becoming play-
grounds for the suburban populations whose homes are more and more
urbanized. Judging from planned and advertised subdivisions around towns
like Pierre, people in central South Dakota are hoping for this process, too.
There is a big problem for northern plains states in this, however: they are
perceived to not have many scenic, natural amenities, such as mountains,

lakes, or mild climate (Rowley 1998:4; Sheaff 2001:3). Whereas regions like the Black Hills are growing in business opportunities and population, areas on the plains proper are still looking for ways to attract people. Communities are investing in communication technologies, but a lack of transportation infrastructure and scenic amenities is harder to overcome. And although the northern Great Plains are a hunter's paradise and the hunting and fishing economy brings in resources, family tourism would do more for the economy than rugged, single men out hunting.

If the plains in general are increasingly ruled by the "towns," American Indian Reservations on the plains have always been a step ahead. Most have been kept in dependency until the economic infrastructure around them had been built by others, and to compete with established business in a limited market during the process of building one's own business is not easy. Doing so in a retracting market is even more difficult because nobody will give loans to such a venture. Most economic models assume that people depart from a ground zero and make either gains or losses. But the reality of the reservations is that this ground of departure is already much in the negative. Any efforts, therefore, to solve economic problems on American Indian reservations in the northern plains will have to focus on how to get people to neutral first. With a model that rewards those who already have and punishes those who have not, that is extremely difficult. As Cornell and Kalt point out (1992:43), "Chicago can afford a few politicized contracts and burned investors. Indian tribes cannot."

Plains Indian reservations are located in rural areas and are affected by some of the same issues as the surrounding rural regions: "Many reservation lands are in agricultural areas and many of these lands are used in farming and ranching. Whether American Indian or not, these farmers and ranchers will be impacted by the changes affecting all of agriculture" (NGPRDC 1997a:16). As Humphrey notes (2001b), a "shift in rural identity may mean sweeping changes in rural programs including those that fund agricultural and rural development programs tribes used to help build infrastructure, education and economic development." Keeping in mind what Bennett says of how farmers on the plains have to follow the general economic system regardless of local costs, Indian reservations on the plains are doubly "subject to forces outside the control of local resource users" (1996:275). On the one hand, they also partake in the same economy as other ranchers. On the other, they are in many cases directly under federal control.

There is one other big difference, though, between plains reservations and surrounding rural counties: reservation populations are growing. Considering the economic problems on northern plains reservations, this seems to defy the notion that depopulation is fueled by economic hardships. Some researchers in fact point to reservation community ties as models for other communities on the plains. Still, the adverse social climate and a lack of recreation opportunities that seem to be some of the main reasons why young people leave rural areas are also present on reservations (Humphrey 2001b). Rural counties in which minorities account for the majority of the population are generally poorer than other rural counties in the United States. Yet, they saw a growing population trend in the 1990s, many as a result of inmigration (Cook 1999). I think there are a few factors contributing to this on the reservations.

One is that while the surrounding counties are experiencing an economic downturn, reservations, although their economy is worse off than their neighbors', are actually experiencing an economic upturn. This perception is installing hope in a future on the homeland, which brings me to the second important factor. Reservations are the only land that remains as a homeland to northern Plains Indians. Not only is the relationship to land traditionally different from the U.S. one, but land is all they have left, and it thus acquires a much higher importance, both economically and symbolically. For many American Indians, living in an environment they see as hostile, reservations are a refuge, a place where one can be oneself, a home in the true sense of the word. Although many young people go out for periods of time—over the summer, or for a few years—to find work, they do so mostly not to build themselves a future off the reservation, but on the contrary to be able to return and live on the reservation as soon as possible.

Although for many people today, with the Buffalo Commons proposal and Ted Turner getting national media attention, buffalo ranching might be a symbol of ecological awareness, the people who started to promote the business were not necessarily environmentalists. "Restoration" was "a concept specifically opposed" by pioneers of buffalo reintroduction to the Big Open in Montana (e.g., Scott 1998:362). Although these people tried to base the local economy on a more sustainable footing by introducing native grazers, their goals were guided by economic and not ecological concerns. The fact that many ranchers feel the need to make this distinction speaks volumes about how threatened they feel by what they, Indian and non-Indian alike, see as "extreme" environmental advocates. The Million Acre Project and the people who work for it are specifically put into that category by quite a few buffalo ranchers who I know are striving to conserve and restore native plants and ecosystems themselves. The larger social context of the environmental movement, and the fact that many Western ranchers feel misunderstood by it, has created some deep divisions between people who probably agree on many practical issues.

Matthews reports how Vine Deloria Jr. tells the Poppers that "most of the Great Plains' original tenants" are supporting the Buffalo Commons and that they "have all the young Indians politicized" (1992:158–63). The idea in the abstract might have at first looked appealing to Plains Indians but mostly for political reasons. As mentioned previously, the Poppers did include some cautious remarks about the government using the newly created Commons to settle some American Indian land claims. But in a 1991 response to an editorial that saw the Buffalo Commons as an extremist ecological pro-Indian campaign against ranching, Deloria pointed out that the Poppers "could care less whether it is Indians or Neil Bush who lives on this land" (1991). Without taking anything away from the Buffalo Commons vision, this was probably true, especially from an American Indian perspective because the proposal seems primarily concerned with what happens with the land and not with who owns it. Although the proposal stems from an overall concern for what will happen with the rural plains, for politically active American Indians, the priorities were somewhat off the mark.

Deloria's statement can, however, also be seen as an expression of Indian and non-Indian ranchers' concerns over environmental agendas. The reason why many people on the plains become cautious when dealing with outside planners has a lot to do with their perception that these people could care less about the inhabitants of the region; what they are concerned with is the environment, the economy, or some other overarching agenda. Human interests, it seems, are often overlooked, especially when dealing with sparsely populated regions that do not have much lobbying power. This is of course true for the perspective of residents of almost any regions coming under scrutiny from (almost always nonindigenous or at least exiled) planners. Visionaries, on the other hand, cannot help but throw a macro-theory into the arena of public discussion. Ranchers, who are often caught between environmental concerns and the need to be more and more profitable to survive economically, might have enough of a spiritual connection to the land that they do not want to leave, but without real economic alternatives, ecological alternatives also seem to be unrealistic. Despite being conscious of what is happening with the land, a primary, short-term concern for the people prevent ranchers from changing because of a shortage of economic resources. Together with a normal rural conservative perspective, this can make people defensive and lead them to group any interfering outsiders together.

Some environmentalists, in line with Deep Ecology theories, really do want to abolish anthropocentrism in ecological interactions and values, and therefore put ecological restoration above concerns for the people who live on the land. To a rancher, however, no matter how ecologically conscious, this is obviously just not going to work. In this context, I would maintain that no matter how ecologically minded Indians were, are, or are perceived to be, their relationship with the land was never non-anthropocentric. The luxury to demand a non-anthropocentric ecological relationship belongs to people who usually do not have a deep working relationship with the land but rather an aesthetic, romantic vision of how things should work in the ideal. As mentioned previously, the mere presence of buffalo on the land is not an improvement for the ecosystem per se. Well-managed cattle can have less of a negative impact on the ecosystem than overcrowded buffalo. Conserving the environment is not just a matter of a perceived spiritual connection to the land, no matter how deeply people might feel that goes; it is a matter of hard work and practical compromises. A deep connection to the land usually also does not stem from a romantic vision of harmonic beauty but from living through droughts, storms, and other manifestations of natural forces, while still recognizing and appreciating them as part of the natural process.

However, the requirement that American Indians be non-anthropocentric has allowed authors to condemn them for being so. This tearing down of a straw man is playing out all over American Indian country, but a focal point has been the near extinction of the bison on the plains. Ever since the buffalo have been hunted to the brink of extinction, people have suggested that American Indian peoples of the plains had a greater hand in the destruction of the buffalo than generally acknowledged (Braun 2007). In view of what I have said previously, I cannot help but to place such arguments in the context of what can be seen as a backlash against the notion of indigenous ecological practices and as such in the context of an ongoing debate about traditions and sovereignty.

Ever since their first encounters, buffalo have gained symbolic significance for the settler culture. Although I do not want to give a comprehensive review—

Dary gives a general overview from buffalo nickels to state flags (1989:279–85)—one persistent aspect of the symbolic relevance of buffalo in U.S. culture is that the value of buffalo rests almost always on the large, powerful, free animal as an incorporation and representation of U.S. character. On the brink of the extinction of the animals, Hornaday (2002:398–399) valued the buffalo because, as he assured his readers, "the American bison is the grandest of . . . all the larger ruminants of the world," the bull possessing "a grandeur and nobility of presence which are beyond all comparison amongst ruminants" (2002:398–99). This, and the association of the buffalo "with untrammeled lands and uncivilized nature," can be linked, as Shell says (2002:xiii), to nostalgia for what Hornaday and his hunter and sportsman friends "perceived as vanishing wilderness." But there is more to it than just nostalgia.

The buffalo became a symbol for the frontier and wilderness. At least since Frederick Jackson Turner, the Frontier has been seen as a formative event for the building of a unique American character (Worster 1977:218–19). The argument that it would be valuable to conserve wild game for hunting—and wilderness as such for an ongoing contest of man against nature—as a character building activity was widely used for conservation efforts, not only by Hornaday. Aldo Leopold (1991b:137), one of the earliest and most prominent conservationists, picks up the argument, assuming that "physical combat between men and beasts" needs to be preserved for the betterment of mankind. "Hunting for sport in its highest form," he says, "is an improvement on hunting for food in that there has been added, to the test of skill, an ethical code which the hunter formulates himself and must often execute without the moral support of bystanders." As it is the wilderness and the struggle of man and beast that formed "the indigenous part of our Americanism," the wilderness needs to be preserved, Leopold asserts (1991b:138), "as a means for allowing the more virile and primitive forms of outdoor recreation to survive the receding economic fact of pioneering." Note how Hornaday defends hunters (2002:497–98): "A sportsman is not supposed to kill game wantonly, when it can be of no possible use to himself or any one else." The examples he gives of sportsmen who might have possibly broken this rule are all (decadent) Englishmen; this is in line with the notion at the time that the Frontier, that wilderness would be the phenomenon to save America from becoming effeminate and decadent like Europe.

This line of argument might be dismissed as historical; alas, it is quite alive. Supporters of wilderness and conservation still use these arguments. As a proponent of a Buffalo Commons-like plains, for example, Callenbach describes buffalo as "a memorable symbol of fierce American pride in survival with freedom," and thinks that "[s]trength, endurance, adaptability, and cooperation in the face of danger make the bison a striking emblem of America" (1996:2). "Bison," he says (9–11), "are quintessentially American animals: stalwart, noble symbols of wildness, freedom, and self-sufficiency," and the "implicit motto of the bison rings with a determination we remember well from our history: Live Free or Die!" This is Turner's Frontier thesis without the American Indians. Instead, the buffalo have replaced them as the agents that formed the U.S. character.

To fulfill their symbolic role in this argument, buffalo have to be valued for their male characteristics. A simple list of Callenbach's adjectives supports this. The emphasis on the male sphere contrasts strongly with what I see as a Lakota emphasis on the female sphere. The meanings of buffalo are contested between the two cultures, in other words, because the symbol itself is only superficially shared, if at all. Through the continuous transmission of values between the dominant society and the marginalized, but appealingly alternative cultures, symbolic meanings have been diffused across cultural differences. Because U.S. culture places value on buffalo bulls, the idea that the Lakota word for buffalo is tatanka has become popular knowledge, for example. However tatanka is the Lakota term for the strongest herd bulls—buffalo in general are pte. This term includes both smaller and younger bulls and cows. However, the leadership in the herd clearly belongs to the experienced cows. DeMallie points out that according to traditional Lakota values the "Lakota people, the buffalo, and the land were one" (1987:32). It makes sense that the buffalo played a central role in the coming of age ceremony for girls (St. Pierre and Long Soldier 1995:67–75).

As a historical note, Müller (1970:235–46), in a comparative study, points out that Siouan people to the east of the Lakota, although hunting buffalo, conceive not of a buffalo-earth connection but of an elk-earth relationship. Because the Lakota migrated onto the plains from the east, he concludes that the buffalo has come to its prominence in Lakota culture relatively recently, replacing the elk in this position. He also emphasizes that the buffalo, identified with the earth, is structurally positioned in the female half of the cosmos (240–42). One potential problem with Müller's theory is that the elk, at least in the Oglala context, seems to have been a male symbol (Brown 1997:16–19). However, the now more important buffalo could have replaced the elk as the female power, bound with the earth, and pushed the elk into the male sphere.

Buffalo have become, through the values that have been attached to them, a strong cultural symbol of Western wildlife in general. In a society that operates predominantly on economic value systems, symbolic values are not sufficient for conservation, though, and in addition, wildlife has to be assigned economic values. "An important step in sustaining these conventionally non-valuated resources," Edwards and Abivardi state (1997:333), "is to define them as goods and services which can be quantified in economic terms." Hunting and tourism are the primary ways in which wild animals are not only assigned symbolic but also economic values (Gray 1993:134–49). "Of particular interest here," as Harrod says (2000:xxiii), "is the massive recreation industry and its pervasive infrastructure. Animals are projected in this industry either as exotic occupants of national parks, ready to provide the sensitive tourist with a unique aesthetic experience, or as 'sport' animals whose existence provides enjoyment for recreational hunters."

When buffalo are seen as providing aesthetic pleasure, people tend to forget that they are real animals. This can have serious consequences, as when tourists in Yellowstone kick a bull because they want to take his picture standing up or just walk closer and closer, seeing buffalo only through their viewfinder, in which they tend to appear rather small and cute, just like the plush animals back at the store. On the other hand, wildlife as game animals provides a wilderness experience to people who are looking for a taste of the "physical combat between men and beasts," although their equipment usually leaves no questions as to the outcome of this supposedly epic struggle. On private farms and some tribal buffalo operations, buffalo are increasingly offered as trophy animals for anybody who can climb in a pickup and pull a trigger. Admittedly, other packages on buffalo farms include black powder rifle or bow hunting, for a taste of the frontier experience. In all of these instances, however, buffalo are "cultural artifacts" (Harrod 2000:xxiii), valued for their use in providing human satisfaction. Appreciation of buffalo stems not from the buffalo themselves but from what they can provide to the human experience and is measured by how much people are willing to pay to have that experience.

Cultural and symbolic values of buffalo are not just lofty ideas. Whether they are translated directly into economic values or whether they govern how people treat animals, like all aspects of our ecological perspectives, they do translate into real actions. Whether to raise buffalo for tourism, for meat, or as a contribution to ecological or cultural restoration is an important decision based on different values held by the society around the particular rancher and a decision that most likely will determine most of the details of the operation. A rancher who raises buffalo to provide aesthetic pleasure or for trophy animals probably wants to breed big bulls because it is those animals that most of society values as typical buffalo. A rancher raising buffalo for meat probably will cull all bulls over two years except for one or two breeding bulls. To people who regard buffalo in a mostly utilitarian way, it does not matter whether buffalo spend their lives in a feedlot. People who value buffalo for their own ways, however, might take care not to disrupt their family units and to treat them with however much respect they think the animals deserve. Raising buffalo because people will learn behavioral values from them, on the other hand, most likely will lead to a hands-off management because in this case, the value of the buffalo rests in their being buffalo, not a specific type of buffalo.

Once economic concerns begin to outweigh ecological ones, if the latter ever precede the former, operations that take care of land or animals begin to change. This was just as true for Cheyenne River. The process of change came to a climax in the fall of 2001, when the tribe decided to reorganize Pte Hca Ka.

CHAPTER 10

Pte Hca Ka, Inc.
Reorganization

By 2001, with the added obligation of paying for the VE land, Pte Hca Ka had to find a way to turn a large economic profit. The chairman, as I have mentioned, did not want to see the operation running on grants. Many of Pte Hca Ka's economic hopes had been pinned on the U.S. Department of Agriculture (USDA) commodity food contract and being able to process the meat for this contract in the mobile unit. These hopes collapsed when the contract did not go through as expected, partly because of the conflicts between InterTribal Bison Cooperative (ITBC) and North American Bison Cooperative (NABC) and partly because the processing unit was not yet operational under USDA inspection. With no money from grants, the corporation could not make the payments on the VE land. At that point, the tribe decided that they could not help the buffalo program with the payments. Although the tribal administration had supported the land purchase and had actually told Pte Hca Ka to buy the land or get rid of some buffalo, they now said that the corporation had paid too much for the land. As a consequence, the tribal council dispersed the board of Pte Hca Ka and installed its own Parks Commission as the board, so that the buffalo program was now intricately linked to, and even controlled by, tribal politics. The board then wanted to refinance the VE land deal, but the banks had been counting on the USDA contract all along. When that did not materialize, they backed out. With the buffalo market in a depression, investing in a buffalo herd—tribal or not—probably did not seem to be the most prudent business decision.

161

Finally, the tribe decided to shut the buffalo program down, and all employees were let go at the end of October 2001. This decision was taken without anybody coming to the office and inquiring of the employees what was going on with the corporation. The tribe simply decided that the financial problems were the responsibilities of the program and did not take into account that structural issues and the actions—and inactions—of the council itself had contributed to the problems. The tribal Game, Fish, and Parks Department (GFPD) was given the job of caring for the buffalo, but its budget was not increased and no additional personnel hired. Pte Hca Ka's office was dissolved; the gift shop items and a giant stuffed buffalo head were moved to Eagle Butte (one can admire the buffalo head in the lobby of the new GFPD building on the east side of town). We moved the corporation's files to the old office, which I now rented for my home, because the secretary was supposed to close the program down. GFPD also took all the stored meat out of the freezer units to give it to the nutrition program in Eagle Butte.

Over the next few weeks, GFPD tried to figure out what to do with the buffalo. Without anybody riding the fences everyday, buffalo got out of the pastures more often, and whenever that happened, game wardens had to scramble from their other duties on the reservation to chase them back. In addition to the buffalo, they now also had to take care of the wild horses that had been released on the VE land in October and fence the southern half of the VE range, which had been rested to recover from the previous overgrazing. The USDA inspection process was essentially aborted, and meat orders were not getting through. Nobody took care of the old day school building that had been the office, and eventually the pipes in the building froze and burst. In mid-November, the tribal council decided to hire the secretary and the processing unit manager back part-time or as needed. That way, at least meat orders and requests for donations of by-products could get through, and there was somebody at hand who knew how to operate the unit. Technically, Pte Hca Ka remained an independent corporation, with a separate budget. The administration still insisted that the corporation had to make the land payments on its own, without help from the tribe. During this time, the marketing director of the corporation was still kept on at full pay, a heavy toll on a budget with no income other than my monthly rent for the trailer and occasional meat orders of loyal customers.

When I asked Fred DuBray, who had also been fired as the director of Pte Hca Ka, what he thought of all the changes, he said that they could work out for the better. Part of the problem as he had seen it for some time was that although the tribe wanted the corporation to operate on a purely economic base, it also had come to regard it as a truly separate business. This was the danger of removing the corporation as far as possible from tribal politics: a disconnection between the corporation and the administration had occurred. As the corporation became integrated into GFPD, he hoped, the buffalo would also again become more integrated into the tribe as a whole. As far as the cultural agenda was concerned, he said the program had always rested on the support of the grassroots people, not so much the tribal politicians. These people would eventually exert pressure to run the buffalo in a culturally correct manner. For the time being, however, DuBray also saw the change to an operation that focused more on economics as an opportunity for the corporation. From his perspective, the change was part of a necessary balance, and although the buffalo program had emphasized culture, it might be time for the pendulum to swing the other way for a while to allow Pte Hca Ka to grow as a business. These changes in business management practices were not of primary importance to him, perhaps partly because he assumed that the simple presence of buffalo would help the reservation. In the debates of tribal politics, locked in a dialectics of adaptation and resistance, between people who see buffalo as just another commodity and others who do not want them associated with any kind of market economy at all, management would balance out in the end. Of prime importance, DuBray said, was that the buffalo program had grown too large for anybody to dispose of it.

Even after the secretary and the unit manager had been hired back part time, GFPD still lacked the budget and manpower to run the corporation. The tribe, although having made the decision to keep the buffalo program running for the time being, was still debating its future. In the meantime, problems developed because there was only scarce direct communication between the new leadership and the old employees. GFPD was under political and financial pressure to run the corporation efficiently, and this, together with the fact that Pte Hca Ka's office was an hour's drive away and in practice in another time zone and running on a separate budget led to a lot of control being exerted on the work in the office and the slaughter unit. At the same time, the new leadership did not know what was involved in running the buffalo operation.

After an ITBC workshop on buffalo slaughter and processing practices, for example, GFPD employees came to the office to "cut the buffalo meat."

When the secretary and I assured them that the meat had been cut, they said they had to load it up to send it out. The telephone for the office had been redirected to the GFPD in Eagle Butte, and meat orders had bypassed the corporation. It was standing practice of Pte Hca Ka to let meat hang for two weeks in a special process to make it more tender, of which practice the person who took the order was not aware. The corporation, on the other hand, was not aware of any meat order, and there was no meat in storage because the tribe tried to cut expenses to a minimum and did not allow Pte Hca Ka to slaughter animals in advance. Only on December 10 did we set up an office again, this time in the trailer, and reconnected the office telephone.

In a Park Committee meeting on December 16, 2001, the leadership heard plans for the future of the corporation. The marketing director had plans to have the slaughter unit not only inspected by the USDA, but also certified for organic products, and to sell meat to Europe and Japan. He also wanted to market buffalo hunts and eco-tourism tours in the future park. He estimated that USDA certification could be received within a month. When the unit manager, who had worked closely with the USDA inspector for months, tried to explain what needed to be done with the slaughter unit that had been agreed on and tried to explain that the USDA had presented a long list of requirements, the committee did not want to hear him out. He was barely allowed to explain that what was most needed was a concrete slab to park the units on, and the GFPD director promised to look into that. Satisfied that certification was basically secured, the committee focused on marketing, and criticized ITBC for not doing enough in that direction. DuBray, who had become ITBC president, tried to explain the complexities of a weak market coupled with competition against the powerful beef marketing lobby.

In the course of the meeting, some members of the committee also raised the possibility of moving a part of the buffalo herd to the western portion of the reservation to create jobs there. The buffalo program, they said, profited only the East End right now, but if the buffalo belonged to the people, they should profit everybody, and the West End needed jobs. With a program that was all but dissolved, with no money and a huge land payment to make, and in a year leading up to tribal elections in summer 2002, it became obvious why the corporation needed to be separate from the political process to function properly and succeed. When I drove to Gettysburg with a friend ten days later, I asked him what he wanted me to emphasize in my writing. He thought about it and said, "That politics is the worst thing ever." I had to laugh, but he was probably thinking about not getting paid and trying to support a family.

After this meeting, communication improved, especially with the director of the GFPD. Still, miscommunication and control issues resulted in a waste of energy and time. But GFPD at least recognized the need to have some meat on hand and allowed the slaughter of two or three buffalo a month. They also helped Pte Hca Ka out with payments on the operating budget. GFPD bought fifteen buffalo from the corporation for eighteen thousand dollars. Although on the one hand GFPD tried to help Pte Hca Ka, on the other, there were quite a few conflicts of interest that became apparent in treating the two organizations separately, yet under the leadership of one. Nominally, Pte Hca Ka owned the buffalo and the VE—indeed, the tribe insisted on Pte Hca Ka being solely responsible for paying off the land—and yet, GFPD was responsible for looking after the animals, ran wild horses on the VE land, and made decisions about how to use the range, whereas the tribe was counting on future economic development through the tribal park (i.e., the VE land).

The changes in business management, which, as I discussed previously, could be seen in a positive light, brought with them changes in range and animal management. It was clear that GFPD operated much more on a scientific base than on traditional ecological knowledge and that there would not be as much room for input from traditional perspectives. It became clear that "choice of knowledge system is a part of managing the pastures, and is a practical as well as a political issue," as Kalstad says (1998:243).

After GFPD took charge, the plans for a research center were off the table. This made sense in terms of economic investment that could be spared; however, it also made sense because from the perspective of GFPD, there was no need for a research center because the knowledge base to operate a bison operation could be directly lifted from cattle operations and thus already existed. With the change in management and management philosophy, therefore, also came a change in interests on research and knowledge. Following Kalstad, the "traditional knowledge of users" was discontinued and replaced with "the professional knowledge of biologists, economists, engineers and lawyers" (1998:243) As he lays out for reindeer production, an "industry solely focused on meat production for profit, with a centralized decision-making system strongly committed to biological and economic sciences has little room for traditional user knowledge" (243).

In January 2002, the marketing director quit. GFPD took over the process for the USDA certification of the processing unit, and some men from GFPD were designated as the new herd managers, so they could devote themselves to the buffalo full-time. Still, however, they stayed based in Eagle Butte and had to commute to the pastures every day. GFPD also decided to build new buffalo corrals on the northern VE pasture next to the Blackfoot Road and began to regularly feed the buffalo hay. This was contrary to earlier practices: although hay feeding makes the buffalo stay inside a pasture, it also makes them rely on being fed.

The new corrals became operational in mid-May 2002, just in time for a shipment of buffalo to NABC in New Rockford under the commodity program agreement. A previous shipment had gone from the old corrals on the Swiftbird pasture. One of the buffalo had to be shot at that time because it became too stressed, and the handlers could not leave it alone to cool down. During the sorting of the buffalo from the VE, the animals were so stressed that they barely reacted to the men, even though the wardens used an electrical prod—something that would have been unimaginable under the old management. Quite a few buffalo were injured, and I heard later that two of them died on the way to North Dakota. Although the men who sorted them had a lot of experience with cattle, as noted previously, buffalo react differently to stress than cattle. During the sorting, I noticed three bulls with red ear tags. Those were buffalo which had been brought in from Wind Cave especially to enhance the genetics of the herd: they were not supposed to be slaughtered because they could not fulfill their role that way. The handlers, however, said they did not know anything about this, and the bulls were sent to slaughter with the others. This incident supports Kalstad's argument that a lack of true knowledge results from a centralized decision-making system based on biological and economic science. Although one might argue that the knowledge that should have been applied emanates from biological science, the decision to send the bulls to slaughter anyway was made in deference to economic pressure and because no centralized, political decision maker was on the spot. Practical knowledge, even if present, could not have been applied in this system.

Another incident showed how biological knowledge might lead to different actions than traditional knowledge. In the first few days after taking over the herd, GFPD shot a buffalo because it was severely limping. The staff biologist that was consulted thought it had a broken leg. Once it had been shot, however, it was discovered that what made it limp was not a broken leg but mud that had accumulated in one of its hooves. Traditional knowledge—based on experience and long-term observance—might have diagnosed the limp in a different way, taking into account possible answers that were outside the biologist's realm of experience.

Traditional user knowledge does not discount or ignore biological science or economics but puts them into a larger framework, in which "knowing buffalo," or reindeer, includes nonbiological and noneconomic categories. These categories, however, were cut from the management practices under the new leadership; they were cut by design because the goal was exactly to make Pte Hca Ka economically more efficient.

Although more than three hundred buffalo ended up being shipped to New Rockford, the money from these sales did not cover the amount needed by the corporation for the land taxes and payments and the operating line. In a last minute deal, the tribe finally made the land payment in May 2002, taking out a $630,000 loan. An *Eagle Butte News* article reported that a "series of irregularities within the buffalo corporation resulted in the tribe removing its semi-independent status and placing it under the auspices of the CRST Game, Fish and Parks Department, as well as obtaining a $403,000 loan to make last year's payment" (Webb 2002:1). Several people assured me that the previous payment had been made without any help from the tribe. The article referred to the land, the buffalo, and the processing unit as "formerly owned by Pte Hca Ka, the tribal buffalo operation." Here was the dilemma in a nutshell: if Pte Hca Ka did not own the land, anymore, but rather the tribe, then why would the buffalo program have to make the payments? One councilman was quoted as advocating the position of some tribal members ever since the VE had been purchased: "If we use realistic figures, and run outside cattle [on the VE land], we can probably make it."

Already in February, some people had been calculating how much money an outside cattle leasing of the VE land would bring. Some said that the southern half of the VE was not used, anyway, and rather than letting it lay empty, cattle would at least bring in some money. They did not understand that the land had been overgrazed, and the corporation, concerned not only with buffalo, but also with the restoration of the total ecosystem, let it rest deliberately. The perception that the same people who had been advocating against the buffalo program for years now were trying to dissolve it to make money because they had control caused more traditional people to feel disenfranchised.

Besides the increased sale of buffalo, and if possible buffalo meat, the new board came up with another plan: to produce and sell buffalo jerky. Jerky sells for higher prices than meat, and although the buffalo meat market had become somewhat crowded, there were not many buffalo jerky producers. Several jerky makers on the reservation were commissioned to produce some trial buffalo jerky samples, and in March 2002, the board decided to build a jerky plant. For a while, the now empty old Swiftbird Day School building was considered, but eventually they settled on building a facility from the ground up. This building was to be built according to USDA specifications. A grant proposal for the plant was submitted in spring 2003.

In late 2001, the tribe proposed a $30 million bond issue, primarily to pay off the acquisition of Huron University and its merger with the tribal college to form Si Tanka-Huron University. Several other projects, including the buffalo program, were also planned beneficiaries, however. "The tribe is considering using [the bond issue] to pay off the debts of the university, repay a loan for the tribally operated Super 8 motel, refinance an outstanding bond issue for a tribal buffalo ranch and construction of a new 60-bed nursing home facility" (Humphrey 2001c). From the start, people made a connection between this planned bond issue and the Joint Tribal Advisory Committee (JTAC) settlement for the Oahe Dam. In an *Eagle Butte News* article, Chairman Gregg Bourland denied that the bond issue was dependent on JTAC money: "'JTAC is not the primary repayment source for these bonds,' said Bourland, who added that even if it were, JTAC will provide over $200 million in matured interest over the next 10 years, with these projects representing only about 11% of that amount" ("Tribe Seeks" 2002:20). Preparing for a referendum on the issue, the tribe failed to put people's fears at ease. Different accounts talked about a $25 or $30 million bond issue, about a forty-bed or sixty-bed nursing home, and the situation at the university, plagued by several changes in administration and law suits, was not clear. Many voters were already upset about the JTAC deal, and others felt that the tribe was going to spend money that it did not yet have. After the tribe lost the referendum in April, Chairman Bourland (2002) stated that "the resolution had nothing to do with the Buffalo Corporation, SiTanka/Huron University, or any other program. It was simply to build an elderly village . . .". Such changes in professed policies could only reassure voters that the issue had not been defined enough.

From February 2002 on, when it became clear that some major refinancing had to be effected to save the corporation, some tribal councilmen on the board were looking to secure a $6.5 million loan. This would have paid off the VE land, which had been bought for $4 million in 1999. After tribal elections and a change of administrations, this refinancing was still in the air in January 2003. Eventually, however, GFPD ended up with the brunt of Pte Hca Ka's debts, about $6 million.

One of the problems the USDA inspector had with certifying the processing facility was the waste disposal. The waste products were flushed out of the facility through chutes and were collected in plastic containers placed under these closable openings. This, of course, was in line with the mobility of the processing units. USDA, however, insisted that this process had to occur in closed spaces. To comply with this request, GFPD decided to build wooden shacks that would then be attached to the mobile slaughter unit to cover the containers receiving the waste products. Two men built the enclosures and attached them to the unit with glue, in fact demobilizing it.

When the inspectors came back in April 2002, however, they insisted, as the unit manager had told GFPD from the beginning, that the units also be parked on a concrete pad. That would not only prevent the facility from sinking into the mud but also make it much easier to clean around the unit. GFPD therefore had to tear the enclosures off again, and the concrete was poured in summer 2002. As a consequence, the unit was parked on the slabs, and its wheels were removed, thus ending the mobility of the unit. By January 2003, the processing facility was ready for inspection, except for a problem with the waste disposal from the vicinity of the unit. In previous years, all the waste products had been hauled to a nearby coulee, where the coyotes and other grassland inhabitants disposed of them in an extremely natural way, which, however, did not find the approval of the federal bureaucracy. Finally, the inspection was scheduled for June 2004. With new enclosures attached to the unit and an additional building covering the entrance for the animals, USDA certification was obtained.

The process, although delivering a new asset to the operation, effectively made the facility stationary. One could argue that this was not a great loss because the units had never moved, anyway. The loss might therefore have been symbolic—the innovative idea of a mobile processing unit, itself, and future possibilities of renting the facility to other tribes—but nevertheless still important. The USDA's insistence on covered waste chutes obviously presented a problem for mobility, but mobile slaughter units approved by the USDA are a possibility. The Lopez Community Land Trust (LCLT) on Lopez

Island, Washington, for example, operates a mobile slaughter unit designed for cattle, hogs, sheep, and goats that is approved by the USDA (LCLT 2002; Mapes 2001). The problem with the waste chutes might have primarily existed with the processing unit, and a solution for the slaughter unit alone would probably have been possible. The abandonment of the idea of a mobile slaughter unit, and the concepts this idea stood for, in favor of a stationary, ordered, conventional, and business-like unit was more than a practical solution toward USDA approval, however; it was also symbolic of the changes in management overall. The constant struggle to incorporate traditional culture and modern technology in a coherent, yet undeniably somewhat self-contradictory whole was replaced by a clean-cut, no-nonsense business approach. As often happens in cases when new management suspects the old of chaotic, ill-fated practices, control became one of the main issues.

In telling some of the history of the program, I do not want to lay blame on anybody. I am convinced that everybody involved made their decisions in good faith, wanting only the best for the buffalo program and the tribe as a whole. Debate and conflict are normal in every society. If some accounts emphasize conflicts on reservations, that might say more about the outside society's view on the reservation than about the reservation society itself—for many authors, indigenous people should not debate anything, but walk along beautifully and peacefully as "noble savages" forever. What the history of Pte Hca Ka shows is how a society is trying to resolve outside influences and traditional culture in a positive way and how much this resolution is a part of every decision taken.

Pte Hca Ka is a work in progress, and despite the changes and challenges that I tried to recount, that progress continues. By summer 2003, the new administration was trying to reestablish the corporation as a more independent organization. With Fred DuBray leaving as the director of the program and Gregg Bourland losing his reelection, there was a chance for a clean new start. In summer 2003, the schools began to buy buffalo meat from the corporation. The buffalo program, with over 2,200 animals in 2001, really had grown so large that its size ensured its survival.

A new director for Pte Hca Ka was appointed in fall 2003, and under Roy Lemmon's leadership, business started to improve. With experience from the agriculture department at Si Tanka, he turned the program into a joint cattle and buffalo meat operation. This change would have been unthinkable under the old management; although it had been discussed as an option to bring in more revenue, the management philosophy in place precluded it. Pte Hca Ka entered into contracts with reservation schools, with the Lakota Thrifty Mart in Eagle Butte and also delivered to several restaurants as far away as Arizona. With almost full-time slaughtering, about twenty jobs had been created by July 2004. Pte Hca Ka now focused on the slaughtering, while GFPD still took care of the buffalo. At the time the concrete pads for the then mobile slaughter unit were poured, some people had voiced the possibility of pouring two pads, one by the Swiftbird pasture, and another by the new corrals. The plant—if still mobile—would then have been able to travel back and forth. With the operation being switched to the VE land, most buffalo to be slaughtered would come from there, and transportation of buffalo carcasses to the processing facility takes a long time. This problem was solved in a conventional way by the new administration, by building holding pens and chutes behind the slaughter unit. Buffalo and cattle bought from local operations, including feedlots, can be held in these pens until they are slaughtered.

In 2005, the tribe broke new ground for an expansion of the slaughter plant that would allow it to increase production from around forty animals a week to three hundred animals. Pte Hca Ka had sold around one million dollars' worth of buffalo and beef in 2004, and this addition is likely to increase that sum to between two and five million dollars. James Garrett, who had been one of the visionaries behind the original project, was voicing opposition to the new management strategies, and in an Argus Leader article (Shouse 2005) celebrating the success of Pte Hca Ka, he criticized the new philosophy.

In the article, Shouse (2005) gives voice again to the key arguments that have evolved around the operation ever since its inception. Garrett argued that the bison are now managed just like cattle and that Pte Hca Ka "really changed the focus of the buffalo herd from a cultural-ecological preservation program to a totally buffalo-ranching situation." Dennis Rousseau, the GFPD director, says he would like to give more emphasis to traditional management practices, but that this would not bring in enough revenue. Lemmon, the new director, is quoted as maintaining that an alternative management philosophy would not make much difference. Fred DuBray, finally, is keeping to his views, in arguing that if "we can keep the spiritual part intact, then the economic part will follow." He also, however, in his role as leader of ITBC, keeps to the organization's principles and argues for tribal self-determination. This will ensure, he is quoted as saying, "the proper balance of commerce and preserving the buffalo's return to Great Plains cultures and ecosystems. 'There is a natural need for them to complement each other, but how the tribe goes about that is up to each and every tribe'" (Shouse 2005).

The changes implemented under the new management are significant and go to the heart of the operation's philosophy. Holding corrals for buffalo before slaughter, the expansion to cattle processing, and the immobilization of the plant, while all making economic sense, would have been diametrically opposed to the cultural mission Pte Hca Ka was pursuing. The changes represented not only a stronger focus on economic revenues but also an adaptation to the management philosophies of the dominant society. What becomes evident, then, is how buffalo have become symbols of much larger issues and how strategic political decisions on general future economic development reflect back on practical ecological management. In 1944, Davis noted that "[t]he Indian's whole cultural background was alien to tending stock" (58). Although I do not agree with Davis's statement and therefore do not see a total culture change from American Indians to cowboys, so to speak (see Iverson 1994), what becomes evident through the history of Pte Hca Ka is how much American Indian culture on the plains, or at least on Cheyenne River, has changed to a ranching culture, and how traditional perspectives of buffalo and of holistic approaches to reservation revitalization, have, for the time being, been pushed to the background.

In early summer 2002, I had a conversation with two of the people from GFPD, who were now looking after the buffalo, which can serve to exemplify this process. They argued that the program needed to be run strictly as a business, as "dead buffalo don't pay wages," alluding to rumors of mismanagement by previous herd managers. I agreed with the statement but pointed out that the philosophy of Pte Hca Ka was exactly that buffalo were not here to make money but to bring back aspects of the culture and physical and psychological health by changing abusive habits and diets. They replied that, "to change people—that's communism," and charged that the program, by actively trying to distance itself from tribal politics, had snubbed the people who, in the end, could save it financially. Pte Hca Ka, they argued, should have sold buffalo when the market was still running high, and when I noted that the goal had been to build a herd and not to make money, they answered that the buffalo sold could have been replaced by donations of surplus animals from the National Park System (NPS). In other words, they suggested that one way to create profits is to get free surplus animals and then to sell those animals or their meat. I argued that what the buffalo could contribute to the reservation communities—other than direct economic value—could be worth all the money invested in them and that the program had specifically been set up not simply as an economic one, but as a nonprofit corporation, emphasizing cultural and ecological goals, too. The management philosophy had been not to run buffalo strictly as a business because that would have meant to run them like cattle. They said that it did not matter whether buffalo were run like cattle because in this world, "everything is about the money." This last statement directed my attention to the values we all had just expressed in this conversation.

One of the charges against the Euro-American worldview I have most often heard from Lakota and other indigenous peoples is that "whites" think that "everything is about money," and neglect, or cannot see, the spiritual aspects of the world. This conversation, then, put us in a kind of role-reversal. By saying this I do not mean that I was "more Lakota" than these two tribal members, but it occurred to me that we were each arguing for the "culturally appropriate"—or what we thought was such—perspective of the "other." Just as I had become convinced that the only way for the Lakota to gain true sovereignty was to reclaim some of their cultural traditions in everyday life, an approach that is also influenced by my European upbringing, because it is actually feasible in Europe that governments subsidize cultural and not only economic projects, these two Lakota had become convinced that the only way for them to survive in the dominant society was to adapt to its economic values. They were still the Lakota and I was still the "Westerner," but perhaps the way in which that was expressed most clearly was in our mutual critical view of our own societies and not terribly critical view of each others', or what we, in our own perspectives, took for that.

What I would like to argue, then, is that my own experience as a European of the "Western" approach to development and ecology brought me to criticize a purely economic approach. I suspect it was the experience of traditional Lakota with the ranching "Lakota" culture that brought them to the same conclusion. The point is that in this conversation I was still Swiss and they were still Lakota, and we were arguing according to our own cultural values, but our experiences with the specific problem of economic development led us to different positions. From this perspective, the management changes at Pte Hca Ka are not leading it away from a Lakota philosophy but are simply expressive of another school of thought within Lakota culture.

I have to agree that the reservation needs money. Perhaps it needs money more than a cultural revival to ensure the physical survival of the people. On the other hand, I had been fascinated by Pte Hca Ka's long-term, holistic approach to reservation development, something that was seemingly missing under the new management. I cannot argue that the right "Lakota way" is to think in holistic, long-term goals; obviously, the buffalo program is still managed by Lakota for Lakota, even if the management philosophy has changed. What I will argue, however, is that a purely economic approach to development might ensure the physical survival but not the spiritual and cultural survival of any people and that it will deepen dependency, not build toward sovereignty. I will say more about this in the following chapters.

As I mentioned previously, Lakota culture on Cheyenne River, but not only here, might have changed to the extent that buffalo are predominantly seen like cattle. The people who are trying to restore buffalo to their traditional place in Lakota culture would then be up against a dominant Lakota culture that is resistant to that very idea. I do not mean that Lakota culture has become homogenous with Western culture. But certain aspects of it may have become so, especially those seemingly tied to the survival of the people. If I have argued before that the buffalo had not simply been of essential importance for traditional Lakota culture because of their economic value, then cattle, which have replaced buffalo in many ways, can also be of importance in more ways than simply economics. I cannot discard the notion that in places where the cattle industry has become of prime importance to reservation communities, the Lakota culture has changed from a buffalo culture to a cattle culture, with all the values a ranching culture brings with it. Judith Graham (2002) reports the director of the National Wildlife Federation's (NWF) Rocky Mountain Natural Resource Center to have said, "The Indians are light-years ahead of the rest of our society in seeing the importance of these prairies. The rest of us have forgotten that the buffaloes are wildlife that belong there, like the elk, the eagles and the wild horses. They're the only group that over all these years has remembered these are animals that should be respected, and allowed to roam free and wild" (8). In the same article, she cites Pte Hca Ka's buffalo manager saying, "Many of the tribe's members farm cattle and will accept the buffalo only if they're enclosed by barbed wire fences and kept away from the range land where the cattle feed."

The juxtaposition of these quotations is rather striking in terms of environmental values expressed. The paradoxes that are opened between outside expectations and stereotyping and actual political and social discourse and decision making by the reservation community show that cultures are never homogenous and essentialism will not do them justice, especially not essentialism that is based on a period in the past. On the other hand, it would be a mistake to think that traditions have disappeared just because a society has changed or adapted its values in one aspect of its culture.

Pte Hca Ka was founded as a culturally and ecologically sustainable economic development project; its goals were to grow the tribal economy but only so far it was compatible with Lakota culture and the environment, both biologically and as perceived from traditional symbolic animal-human relations. This approach to economic development was chosen because it was seen to eventually break the dependency on not only outside investment but also outside management practices and cultural hegemony and would therefore lead to a holistic and not simply a narrow political or economic concept of sovereignty.

With the changes in management practices, the cultural and ecological aspects of this approach have changed. With increased production, the herd has also been diminished in size. In 2004, the tribe slaughtered around four hundred animals itself and sold about three hundred bison to other operations; this reduced the herd size to around seventeen hundred (Shouse 2005). With the proposed expansion of the slaughter plant and production, the numbers of slaughtered animals are charted to go up, and there is little doubt that these kinds of numbers are not locally sustainable.

In the following chapters, I will put Pte Hca Ka in a wider context of ecology and sustainability on the plains and of sustainable economic development on American Indian reservations.

CHAPTER 11

Culture and Sustainable Development

As Stanford Zent writes (1999:92), "It has become abundantly evident that the indiscriminate diffusion of Western technology and economics to developing world settings has failed to alleviate human poverty and overpopulation, and it may be responsible for worsening ecological problems such as loss of biodiversity and global warming." Even if one can dispute whether the plains reservations fulfill all criteria of "developing world settings," it is clear that they are part of a region that has economic and social difficulties, stemming in large part from disturbances of the ecological and cultural balances brought about by the indiscriminate application of technology to the landscape:

> In our time, the realities of large-scale disturbance, large-scale production, and bio-chemical imbalance, for example, remind us that we must construct conditions of sustainability as part of the cultural construction of the landscape. Rural regions cannot be sustained unless we learn that this kind of transformation requires extending resources, inventorying and building on native environmental assets, adopting a conservation ethic, and developing the political will to generate local solutions to national and global problems (Gottfried 1997:13).

Technology never applies itself, however; it is always a tool for social ideas and practices, in this case the capitalist market. Capitalism has changed and is still changing the land. "The market is not only the place of economic exchange now," says Rasmussen (2000:522–23), "it is a model of society itself and a logic for it, a determiner of relationships of all kinds. In that form it continues to do what colonization and development did; namely, further modernity's assault on intact local community and transformation of the land. People are largely shorn of 'their self-organizing, self-governing, and self-provisioning capacities' in the places they live and on the terms and with the resources indigenous to those places, peoples, and traditions." This is not to say that capitalist market forces cannot be made to work positively for indigenous communities: my argument here is not so much strictly economic as geared toward the broader implications that the prevailing economic ideology has on its social and cultural context. Rasmussen himself proposes that the "way to go is 'sustainable community'. Its basic question is how we wrap both economy and environment around healthy local and regional communities. The proper goal of an economy is not increased production and consumption as such. It is materially healthy communities, for the long haul" (2000:525). I would add to this that the proper goal for a contextualized economy is not only materially healthy communities but also spiritually, ecologically, and physically healthy communities.

The economic development of rural regions, which has come to the foreground in the late twentieth century, together with the realization that capitalist, industrial development, although potentially economically positive, is having a negative impact on ecological and cultural resources, has brought about the concept of sustainable development. "Sustainability" seems to have invaded the discourse of economic development on many levels, of which many are paradoxical, if not contradictory. What it meant at the time of its popularization (by the 1987 Brundtland United Nations Report) was that economic development should leave enough resources for current and projected future needs. For example, this means that ecological resources should not be that much affected by economic development that they become extinct. "Although natural resources such as soil fertility and air may not be tradable," say Edwards and Abivardi (1997:325), "they are essential for human survival, and conventional economic activity is increasingly harming them." With this concept in mind and worried that economically developing countries, to become "developed," might commit the same mistakes that the "West" has, a new validation system for ecological resources was invented. This is a system that tries to expand capitalism directly into the environment and thus negate the conflict between the market and its social, ecological, and cultural context.

For people to protect ecological resources and not destroy them for economic gain (e.g., clear-cutting forests for industrial agriculture) and yet to allow people hope for an economically better future, conservationists set out to attach economic value to undeveloped ecological resources. "If we can achieve an effective fusion of ecological and economic understanding," Edwards and Abivardi suggest (1997:348), "our efforts at ecological restoration will be seen less as an expensive luxury which can be applied by the affluent developed world, and more as an essential part of reversing global environmental degradation and achieving sustainability." Ecological resources in their natural state are thus awarded monetary values (Williams and Diebel 1996:20–21). This has led, among other developments, to the fact that air *is* actually tradable today because factories and countries can buy clean air from other factories and nonindustrialized countries to be allowed to keep up their levels of pollution. In relation to buffalo, this valuation system concerns particularly the value of wildlife and the value of the plains as an undeveloped resource.

Gray explains the valuation of wildlife in terms of "use" and "nonuse" values (1993:135–36). Use values stem from activities "that affect the satisfaction people get from current uses of wildlife, including consumptive activities, such as hunting and trapping; nonconsumptive recreation, such as wildlife photography and observation; and indirect use values, personal enjoyment of wildlife without direct contact." Nonuse values, on the other hand, refer to "the satisfaction individuals derive just from knowing that wildlife exists" (existence value), future possible benefits of species, in the absence of present use or contemplation of use (option value), "the willingness to pay in order to ensure that future generations . . . will have the chance to see or benefit from a species" (bequest value), and "the value of preserving our options, given the expectation of growth in knowledge" (quasi-option value). Edwards and Abivardi discuss these values under the concept of "ecosystem services" (1997:333–44). Williams and Diebel attempt to list the values of the undeveloped prairie ecosystem (1996:25–27). Consumptive use values in this case are grazing, harvesting plants, and hunting, whereas nonconsumptive use values extend to recreational, educational, and research activities and ecosystem services, such as erosion control and water quality enhancement. Nonuse values include "existence and option," "aesthetics," "cultural-historical and sociological significance," "ecological or biological mechanisms," and "biodiversity."

Although the assignment of monetary value to undeveloped resources can undoubtedly be an incentive toward sustainability or even conservation, what some economists overlook is that the decision to accept this system is still based on ethics and thus based on decisively noneconomic values. In other words, as long as the people in control over the resources do not resolve to accept the argument behind these values, which are essentially based on a conservation ethic, the values themselves have little significance. While some nonconsumptive use values have practical potential, especially in the tourism industry, the nonuse values are only valuable as long as their economic potential is not exploited. To assign value to a buffalo herd that is not used for slaughter can make economic sense if this herd draws income from other sources or saves money in other expenses (e.g., in health or social programs). As soon as one tries to convert nonuse values, such as value put on the existence of buffalo for purely aesthetic reasons, into practical, monetary value, however, the value is lost. Nonuse values are then, despite all rhetoric to the contrary, still essentially ideological, not economic values, and a luxury that few economically depressed societies can afford. I would also argue that they do not fit the inherent pragmatism of most indigenous cultures.

Critics of sustainable development say that the term "is an oxymoron" (Boff 1997:67; see also Churchill 1997:348; Tinker 2004). Leonardo Boff emphasizes "that ecodevelopment represents an advance over unlimited growth heedless of the ecological costs" but sees development fundamentally based on "plundering Earth and exploiting the labor force" (1997:66, 67, 129). As long as development is inherently associated with economic growth, accumulation, and growing productivity, he argues, "the real causes of poverty and environmental degradation are not being examined," and critical decisions will always go toward economic growth (66). This assumption thus directly negates any possibility of resolving the conflict between market and environment or culture and advocates a radical shifting of paradigms away from the market.

As Boff writes (1997:111), "It no longer suffices merely to adjust technologies or to reform society while keeping the same basic logic, although such things should always be done; the more important thing is to overcome such logic and the sense of being that human beings have held for at least the last three centuries." In other words, the fundamental issue of human-environment interaction is not the efficiency of the technology used but the values associated with that usage. Because Euro-American economic values have become globally dominating, and most economic analysts have been raised in this value system, the cultural hegemony can sometimes be mistaken for biological determinism. Aldo Leopold made this clear in regard to ecological behaviors (1991c:259): "Sometimes I think that ideas, like men, can become dictators. We Americans have so far escaped regimentation by our rulers, but have we escaped regimentation by our own ideas? I doubt if there exists today a more complete regimentation of the human mind than that accomplished by our self-imposed doctrine of ruthless utilitarianism."

Not only has utilitarianism become a hegemonic concept but also has economic growth. "The economic sustainability of an enterprise or a house-hold," argue Brogden and Greenberg (2003:289), "requires that income exceed expenditures by a sufficient margin to meet its needs over time." However, to be sustainable, why would there need to be a continuous profit? The "needs over time" are exactly what expenditures are for and to be sus-tainable, all that is needed is a balance over time. Similarly, official propo-nents of sustainable development do not so much argue for a change in underlying assumptions or a reduced industrialism as for the development of technologies that could produce more with fewer resources. In this argu-ment, as Kay Milton points out (1996:185), "The expressed need to change production and consumption patterns in the North is not intended to imply that less wealth should be created, since more wealth, overall (albeit more evenly distributed), is needed to eradicate poverty." It is easy to see that this approach—more wealth equals less poverty—is based on and leads not to sustainability but to growth. It is this fundamental assumption of necessary constant economic growth that authors like Boff are critiquing.

Pushing toward a fundamental change, the critics want a revolution at the basis of the ideology, not just an adaptation of superficial policies that they regard as more or less merely rhetorical. As long as people and envi-ronment are measured in monetary values, in other words, decisions will be made based on economics. Rather than providing a path toward conserva-tion, application of nonuse values brings ecological domains into the realm of economics, which is, from the perspective of the critics, inherently bad; on the contrary, economics should be subsumed under ecological or social paradigms. As Arturo Escobar puts it (1995:197):

Liberal ecologists and ecodevelopmentalists do not seem to perceive the cultural character of the commercialization of nature and life that is integral to the Western economy, nor do they seriously account for the cultural limits that many societies posed to unchecked production. It is not surprising, then, that their policies are restricted to promoting the 'rational' management of resources. As long as environmentalists accept this presupposition, they also accept the imperatives for capital accumulation, material growth, and the disciplining of labor and nature.

This line of argumentation, as much as it makes a valid point about the fundamental values of the discussion, is in danger of opposing any "rationality" and of falling into the noble savage trap. It would be a serious mistake to think that only Western culture and society employs rational management of resources or that such rationality always leads to ecological degradation. Every society relies on resource management, whatever form this takes, and to deny traditional societies rationality in such decisions serves only to mystify them as mythological eco-saints or to deny them the same intelligence "Western" societies are supposed to operate under.

The argument also disregards actual ecological decision making by contemporary indigenous communities. Access to technology does not constitute, as some critics of Western society seem to believe, an automatic infection with industrial cultural values. Choices made by people who use technology at any level reflect their own values, not those of the society that originated the technological inventions. If, therefore, indigenous communities choose to use new or old technologies to harvest timber, sell furs, exploit oil reserves, hunt whales, protect caribou, or irrigate the desert, they can make the choice to follow their own rationality, and often that rationality is influenced by their own economic goals. To assume that all indigenous peoples are close to nature (the original meaning of "primitive") and therefore beautiful and innocent (like children) until they become infected by Western rationality is just another expression of intercultural arrogance.

Escobar suggests that (1995:201), "Struggles against poverty and exploitation can be ecological struggles to the extent that the poor attempt to keep natural resources under communal, not market, control, and resist the crematistic valorization of nature. The rural poor in particular, because of their different culture, practice a certain 'ecologism,' contributing to the conservation of resources." Although the first part of this statement, concerning the attempt to keep resources out of the market and under communal control, is important in the case of buffalo programs and many other indigenously controlled development projects, the association of this with resistance against valorization seems to me to spring more from ideological wishes than from reality. Many indigenous societies have long since—and in fact long before contacts with the West—comprehended that communal resources are only valuable (i.e., worth the struggle to keep under control) if they carry value. Whether or not the rural poor have different ecological values than urban poor, rural rich, or any other subgroup of their society, or whether they just do not have the means to engage in large-scale activities with great ecological impact, is also debatable. The two issues, communal control and ecological conservationism, are different, and there is, as far as I can see, no inherent relation between them, direct or indirect.

Arguments for the inclusion of culture into sustainable development usually leave one critical question to be answered: what culture? Many authors have argued that development projects need to be compatible with and supportive of traditional culture, and, indeed, this was the assumption under which I started this study. It has become increasingly unclear, however, what traditional culture is and who its representatives are. Ironically, it seems to be the case that just as anthropology is recovering from a long debate over the essentialization of cultures, indigenous cultures are once again essentialized but this time by the critics of the anthropological approach in a movement that might be called "indigenous nationalism." An effort to "decolonize" the social sciences (e.g., Harrison 1991; Tuhiwai Smith 1999) has led to what Garroutte calls "Radical Indigenism" (2003:113–39). Although this position is based on cultural relativism, it basically holds that ontological differences between cultures are so great that interpretation of culture is only possible from the inside and by using the specific cultures' philosophical approaches "as tools for the discovery and generation of knowledge" (113). This is in stark contrast to the anthropological—and scientific—approach, which holds that cultural systems or grammars are compatible enough that outside observers can, with enough patience and insight, understand, describe and translate such systems (e.g., Sahlins 1995). The position also raises extremely fundamental questions of intercultural and interpersonal communication and of cultural authenticity as represented by individuals.

It is not necessary, or possible, to discuss this complex discourse on authenticity here; I have already attempted to briefly sketch some of it, and in a way, the discourse on Cheyenne River shows an example of how this complex dialogue is played out on the ground. I do believe that for truly sustainable development to work, cultural differences have to be included in the equation. These, however, have to based on careful analysis. People have the right to be themselves and the right to be grown-ups, who know what they are doing at least as well as we know what we are doing. As Wuttunee (2004:189), in an extremely valuable study of development practices in Canadian Aboriginal communities, points out: "[t]o expect systematic application of Aboriginal wisdom even within Aboriginal societies is unrealistic and would not respect the diversity inherent in Aboriginal communities; yet its contribution to the continued survival of Aboriginal peoples cannot be underestimated."

Instead of emphasizing economics or ecology, one always to the exclusion of the other, what we could learn from indigenous peoples on all continents, even those in Europe, is that economics and ecology are always integrated in a systemic whole, and that for real sustainability, a truly systemic outlook might need to be adapted (see also Beach 1981:16–38; Harries-Jones 1995), one that includes culture as a third criterion for value. I need to reemphasize here that to emphasize economic profits over cultural preservation or restoration in one sector does not mean that traditional cultural values are not present in the society as a whole anymore. Economics are always cultural choices, as a broader look at cultural values of the ecology on Cheyenne River shows.

Joseph Epes Brown suggests that for traditional Indian value systems to survive (1998:63, 64), two factors must be in place: the ability to live "in an area of as-yet-unspoiled nature," which at least gives a potential access to transcendent values, and the possession of "the traditional metaphysic of nature." In other words, the survival of traditional values is linked to the survival of place and knowledge, which then can both be translated into practice. On Cheyenne River, there can be no doubt that wide areas have survived, if not unspoiled, at least sufficiently intact to provide access to the forces and values of the land. Practical ecological behavior, however, differs widely on the reservation, as it does in other societies.

Blanket statements about either ecological wastefulness, as sometimes made by people referring to piles of abandoned cars and other machinery surrounding reservation houses, or heightened ecological awareness, as assumed in noble savage myths projected onto contemporary indigenous peoples, make no sense in everyday reality on Cheyenne River. On my first visit, I was appalled by heaps of trash left behind by the side of the road or in bushes at popular gathering spots, such as the Forest City recreation area. Quickly, however, I learned that many people from the communities close to the area were just as upset about the state of things. Several of my friends made a point of cleaning up not only their own trash but also that of other people. One young woman from Blackfoot told me that whenever she goes to Forest City, she takes some big trash bags along and spends some time cleaning up the area.

One of the complaints from game wardens, who are also responsible for the tribal park areas, was that some people destroyed their efforts at providing nice facilities. After they had built shades and toilets for the Rousseau Creek area, for example, somebody burned them down. This could well be directly related to the absence of communities close to some of the recreation areas. Local, and mostly rural, people tend to feel responsible for "their" areas, but visitors from farther away might feel both anonymous and disconnected from the specific environment. In this context, it might be fruitful to emphasize that acts of random destruction are not limited to reservation settings but occur all over the plains and other regions. Shooting at abandoned houses or road signs seems to have become a favorite Saturday night entertainment activity all over the country, which often also leaves behind traces in the form of beer cans and other trash. A lack of alternative recreational activities and progressive general alienation are most likely responsible for this. The fact that American Indians are not immune from such general social trends should not make them a favorite target for blame.

Of main interest to me here, in the narrower context of values placed on buffalo, is the general interaction with animals. Brown (1997) describes the traditional Lakota culture's respect for the forces and powers of animals. Without trying to make direct comparisons to historical perspectives, I have had people on Cheyenne River talking to me about similar values in regard to animals. Most of my information comes from the Tribal Game, Fish and Parks Department's (GFPD) game wardens, who became responsible for the buffalo during my stay. Some of these wardens were traditional people, mostly from the Red Scaffold and Cherry Creek area, whereas others were not involved in the traditional value system.

Before GFPD was put in charge of the program, Pte Hca Ka had an assigned shooter for hunting buffalo. It quickly became apparent to me that being the shooter involved more than being able to fell a buffalo with one shot. For example, he did not drink the night before and did not eat breakfast that morning. In general, whereas otherwise an outgoing person, he was very introspective and quiet before going out to shoot a buffalo. Once, when a friend of his teased him about having shot so many animals as he is an experienced hunter, he became very serious and made a point of stating that he has never shot an animal for sport and that he only shoots animals for the meat or for skins—in other words, only when it was necessary and useful to do so.

One day, one of the wardens really wanted to shoot a buffalo. He talked about it a great deal before we set out for the hunt. The buffalo were spread out in small herds and ran away on our approach, so the wardens stopped to discuss the situation. As we sat in the pickups, parked side by side and looking out over the scenery, the warden began to feel sick. For days and weeks now, he had wanted to shoot a buffalo and had talked about this wish. Finally, he had seen an opportunity to make his long-standing wish come true. He approached the task the same way a big game hunter would approach a safari; he had boasted about one day shooting a buffalo every time the wardens had come down to the compound. The longer we sat in the pickups to let the bison calm down, however, the sicker he felt. Finally, he asked one of the more traditional wardens to shoot. That man accepted, and gradually, the original shooter started to feel better again. When we set out to continue the hunt, he was back to his usual self. Nobody made any comments about this, and yet everybody knew what had caused this sudden change.

Once a buffalo was shot, there always was a small ceremony. This did not include drums or long prayers, but at the minimum a cigarette was broken open and tobacco sprinkled on the buffalo. To a passer-by, these prayers might have been obscure and actually not noticeable, but this is in accordance with Lakota and other American Indian spiritual values, in which ceremonies are not defined by circumstantial symbols but rather by the symbolic acts themselves. It would be a misconception to disregard or downplay these ceremonies, for example, because they involved a commercial cigarette crumpled by a guy in coveralls and not a pompous public smoking by a "traditionally" clothed spiritual leader surrounded by officious markers of spiritual power. Such markers are simply not necessary to lend power and significance to the act itself. This follows the same necessary carefulness in the measurement of values that I have discussed previously in the context of people's presence during slaughter.

Besides buffalo, other animals hold powers and require respect from hunters. Cheyenne River is excellent deer hunting territory. Because the reservation has regulations that differ from those of the state, because residents rely on hunting for subsistence, and because people hunt for trophies, there are problems with poaching. The game wardens often discussed the issue with me while they were stopping by for coffee. Some poachers took only the heads of animals, presumably because all they were interested in were the antlers and left the bodies to rot. These people, the wardens said, "don't respect the deer people." Even when one cannot use the meat, one should give it to an elderly person, or somebody else who has use for it. Once, one of the people from GFPD mentioned a warden who left poached deer meat to rot instead of taking pictures of the poached animal and then distributing the meat; they said this would get back at him. The big white tail bucks were too powerful to be treated disrespectfully.

Deer are not the only animals that have power; Cheyenne River also has quite a large bobcat population. One warden told me that he knew a man who hunted bobcats and cut off their paws to use for decorations. After a while, he lost control of both his hands. So when the warden shot a bobcat in his youth, he gave it away because they have too much power.

Many middle-aged people on Cheyenne River grew up without electricity or water and with their families subsisting by hunting. Except in spring, there are always animals around to be hunted for food. People who grew up with this intimate knowledge of nature and the ways of hunting respectfully usually still keep traditional perspectives alive. Some residents also still maintain trap lines. One man who had a trap line thirty miles long died during a winter in the 1990s. He became lost and froze to death. Because he always walked his trap line and camped out when night fell, nobody could understand why he got lost. A warden said it must have been the work of the *yu'iktomi*, who make people lose their paths.

Habitat restoration is extremely important on Cheyenne River; beside grassland and wetland restoration, this means primarily riparian restoration and upland tree planting. As Pte Hca Ka tried to restore not only the bison but also their whole ecosystem; values placed on habitat are also important to note.

In its Terrestrial Wildlife Habitat Restoration Plan for Lake Oahe (GPFD 1999:21), the CRST Game, Fish and Parks Department points out that "[w]oody draws constitute 1% of the northern Great Plains and 70% of the region's wildlife rely on woody draws as critical winter survival habitat." Because Lake Oahe destroyed the wooded areas along the Missouri, the tribe decided to restore habitat by planting trees, either along other, smaller rivers and creeks, or in upland areas. Along small creeks, trees can help prevent erosion, which in many places is an obvious process, eating into the grassy hills. Creeks without trees also run dry faster during the summer. On Cheyenne River, Clarence Mortenson has won national recognition for his efforts to restore riparian habitats. He concluded from oral histories and the numbers of beaver pelts shipped out from the region that in the 1830s all creeks west of the Missouri must have had trees on them and set out to restore that habitat (Askren 2002). Although restoring or creating riparian habitats and wooded areas certainly benefits some species, planting trees on the plains can also be problematic. The CRST Habitat Restoration Plan recognizes that planting shelterbelts, for example, contributes to prairie fragmentation and may have negative impacts on native species (GFPD 1999:23, 24). Efforts to restore wooded areas are therefore concentrated on riparian habitats, where trees are supposed to have less impact on the native ecosystem.

While settlers harvested trees—for houses, fence posts, tools, and as fire wood—they also planted them; trees gave emotional shelter from endless grasslands, practical shelter from winds, snow, and sun, bore fruit, and protected against erosion (Licht 1997:59). From 1873 on, the Timber Culture Act provided free land for anybody who grew small forests on it. "To the credit of Congress be it said that it did not require the prairie dogs to climb the trees or to live in the forests," as Webb (1981:500) remarks. The Dust Bowl era killed off many of these tree plantings, but it also sparked a renewed interest in tree planting. About two hundred million trees are planted annually on the Great Plains (Licht 1997:59). "Although oak-hickory forests and their associated fauna have decreased," Benedict, Freeman, and Genoways point out (1996:159), "fast-growing woody plants, both native and non-native, have increased in abundance on the Great Plains because of the control of prairie fire, decreased flooding, and intentional planting." This has led to the situation that "trees are now much more prevalent than they were historically" (Licht 1997:60). The result is the creation of woodland corridors through the plains, especially along rivers and streams. These corridors, and the prevalence of wooded edge ecosystems throughout the region, have led to hybridization of western and eastern species that now can travel through the plains along tree habitats. The expansion of woodlands has also led to the expansion of such predators as the red fox and the raccoon onto the plains (Benedict, Freeman, and Genoways 1996:158–60; Licht 1997:60–67).

Ecological restoration projects in general and in specific cases, as with tribal buffalo programs, lead to hard choices: On one hand, the building of Lake Oahe undoubtedly has destroyed thousands of acres of wooded areas. Yet, on the other hand, the creation of wooded habitat on the plains could have adverse impacts on that ecosystem. In determining what kind of ecosystem to restore, the same limits apply as in cultural restoration; the question is what time limit one uses to determine what needs to be restored.

The discussion of cultural ecology shows that decisions on ecological issues are still informed by the presence of traditional ecological knowledge, even though in some sectors, especially those controlled by the tribal government, capitalist economics or scientific ecological knowledge may seem to override this. What is most important in all decisions, however, is a pragmatic approach. Pragmatism relies on a system of symbolic values, both projected from the outside and interpreted from the inside, and this adds a significant level to the discussion.

American Indians have been symbols of European social and political dreams and nightmares ever since interaction between the two continents began (Bitterli 1982; Ellingson 2001; Rodenberg 1994). While Puritans saw them as personifications of the devil, a notion that goes hand in hand with that wider secular concept of "savagery," others saw them as models of democracy and a free civil society. From Baron Lahontan and the ideological preludes to the French revolution on, North American Indians, or rather their perception in certain quarters, became models of what European society was not but could or should have been. These counterimages were based on ethnographic information, but as they were used in and produced for political purposes, it was their abstract usefulness as political alternatives that became most important and not their historical or ethnographic accuracy. It should be no surprise that the environmental movement—evolving in the 1960s from another social movement yearning for democracy, a free civil society, and a more harmonious relation with the environment—continued this tradition. What is ironic, perhaps, is that this movement rebelled against what it saw as the sins of the enlightenment (Horkheimer and Adorno 1994), and yet gave rise to almost the same images of indigenous peoples as models for the counterculture as had its predecessors in the eighteenth century, the founders of the enlightenment. Given the ahistorical, and sometimes antihistorical nature of the movement and its political imagery, however, this might not be surprising.

American Indians—and other non-European peoples—became icons of a supposed unison between humans and nature (again an interesting repetition of positive notions of the primitive, originally an expression indicating the immediacy of perceptions of nature). They were seen as the "first ecologists," knowing nothing about "turning the sod-cover over," living directly with nature, without a "mind-body dichotomy," in a "nonrational, mystical way, considering themselves part of nature" (Fertig 1970; Kidwell 1973). While some of these notions are easily proven wrong by pointing, for example, to the sophisticated agricultural techniques and technologies of American Indians in the Southwest and Southeast, notions of an essential indigenous philosophical unity with nature persist in New Age and Deep Ecology movements. As a consequence, Vine Deloria Jr. points out (1997:213), "a self-righteous piety has swept Indian country, and it threatens to pollute the remaining pockets of traditionalism and produce a mawkish unreal sentimentalism that commissions everyone to be 'spiritual' whether they understand it or not." Many American Indian people are reacting to pressure from the outside, along the notion that everybody in American Indian country has to be deeply connected with the environment in exactly the romantic way that the outsiders, many times from urban settings, envision. On first meeting me, some people on Cheyenne River offered to show me "all the Sun Dance places" around, probably because most people who come to Cheyenne River are in search of some "spirituality."

It would be incredibly naive to assume that contemporary indigenous communities are not active participants in the shaping of perceptions about their philosophies. As Brosius points out (1999:281), "historically marginalized communities have begun to recognize the political potency of strategically deployed essentialisms." This is especially important in the content of the radical indigenism and other concepts briefly mentioned previously. Indigenous peoples are using the same strategies of building group political and cultural identity as Benedict Anderson presents for nation states (1991). These strategies include the construction (literal) of museums, parks, and other unifying projects—for example, bison herds—and the construction (metaphorical) of distinctive group characteristics against those seen to define their historic oppressors. As the sociologist Ian Nederveen Pieterse says (2004:33, 57), "Growing awareness of cultural differences is a function of globalization," which has led to an "age of ethnicity."

It should come as no surprise then, that Martinez (1994:91), in one of many examples, perpetuates such notions of special indigenous ecological awareness by saying that "indigenous peoples learned to work with Nature in a positive way," whereas "Westerners view humans as separate from Nature." Although these notions might rest on a misunderstanding of the meaning of "the sacred" for indigenous peoples (Brosius 2001), they have become a mainstream hegemony, against which anthropological responses (e.g., Ellen 1986) can barely be heard. Krech (1999), writing on the myth and history of "the Ecological Indian" and the historic relationships between Plains Indians and buffalo, consequentially became mired from the beginning in a debate that was more political than academic, and his arguments were appropriated by both supporters of the notion of ecological indigenous peoples and those supporting a growing backlash (Harkin and Lewis 2007).

The post-neofunctionalist, post-equilibrium-homeostasis anthropological argument (see Krupnik 1993:20–21; Milton 1999:109–41) targets the fact that "the traditions are read from either a New Age or an uncritically romantic perspective; they are seldom, if ever put into their historical context" (Harrod 2000:122). The New Age meets the romantic in the Deep Ecology movements, which seek to overcome anthropocentrism in human ecological perspectives. Continuing a long tradition, perceptions of American Indian and Asian philosophies serve as models for an "ecological" future. Writing specifically about buffalo, for example, Ernest Callenbach finds that "Western peoples often consider themselves a special part of creation, separate from and above other living elements of the world. Whereas Indians and Buddhists regard all living beings as kin, we distance ourselves from other animals, treating them as subservient living machines" (1996:145–46). This is not the place to point out the differences between American Indian and Buddhist or Daoist traditions, or even among American Indian traditions themselves (see Barnhill and Gottlieb 2001). Nor do I want to list the many historic Western traditions calling for what today we might call an ecological understanding of the environment. Neither is it the place to argue that as humans relating to our environment, anthropocentrism can hardly be avoided in human thought, even if, as Eric Katz suggests (2000:39), we can "deemphasize human-centered categories of value." Because it is relevant to the symbolic meaning and status of buffalo, however, I would like to point again to another issue, already mentioned, that intersects with notions of "ecological Indians": the at times massive and continuing appropriation of indigenous, and here specifically Lakota values, by New Age groups (Grim 2001:47–48; Kurkiala 1997:212–15).

As John Grim writes (2001:36), "the insights of indigenous peoples have been taken for granted as environmentally sensitive, but those appreciative often show little understanding of the thought and practice of indigenous communities." I agree with Val Plumwood in seeing such appropriations as "oppressive projects of unity" and "hegemonic relationships of colonization";

Some of those who adopt these oppressive projects of unity lay claim to Aboriginal identity, culture, and knowledge on the basis of alleged empathy, while others appear to regard indigenous culture as a free good, available to all, and others still are clearly intent upon harm. But even where the motivation is sympathetic, the oppressive and transgressive character of these projects of unity is fully evident to the indigenous people concerned (2000:67).

Such appropriations are "insensitive to the other's independence and boundaries, denying the other's right to define their own reality, name their own history, and establish their own identity," whereas respect for others would require "recognizing their difference and boundaries—not claiming to be them or to encompass them" (Plumwood 2000:67). Grim reports that "indigenous scholars have objected to an overly facile identification of environmentalism and traditional native life" and suggests that such "moments of discord present opportunities to consider the difference and resistance that indigenous peoples present to dominant societies" (2001:36). The debate about buffalo management practices, knowledge, and symbolic meanings is a perfect example of the usage of markers of cultural difference and resistance, as is, as I will argue further on, the introduction of buffalo as such.

At the same time that the academic debate about the ecological Indian certainly is an opportunity to explore cultural and personal reactions to colonial encroachments, it must also be aware of "the politically sensitive character of religious lifeways" (Grim 2001:47). In knowledge of the history of reinterpretations and appropriations of indigenous ecological traditions and practices, this must be a cautious debate, and its arguments have to based on careful examinations. There are enough interest groups ready to appropriate any argument against perfect indigenous ecological records and turn them around to attack Native peoples as ecological sinners. Ironically, these also include the very same environmental interest groups that appropriate and reinterpret Native practices for their own spiritual enlightenment. This opens the door to interest groups using "indigenous" philosophy to argue against Native sovereignty and practices of indigenous people, even if these are undoubtedly traditional practices. Academia cannot control the interpretation and misinterpretation of its products, but it can make sure that they are based on as careful an argument as is possible. Contemporary arguments about sovereignty and tradition that are based to a large part on the debate about ecological Indians range from Makah whale hunting to oil drilling in Alaska.

On the plains, as in other places, this same basic question underlying the debate about the ecological Indian is brought up again and again: were the traditional hunting practices in strict accord with the supposed ecological worldview and rituals? If not, say people who argue most strongly against the notion of Native peoples having been ecological, then the whole purported environmental consciousness of indigenous nations is a sham. This has become then, an essentialist argument, applying standards that would deny any and all ecological consciousness to our own, and, indeed, any society. On the other hand, to ignore the practices and only look at purported worldview ignores a real aspect of indigenous life and culture and is just as essentialist an argument. Were one to pass judgment based on only looking at the political ecological rhetoric in industrial and postindustrial societies, for example, they would probably be the most ecological of any culture, contemporary and historic.

As Igor Krupnik points out (1993:238, italics in original), "in analyzing the role of the traditional hunter in the . . . ecosystem, we must distinguish his *ecological experience* from his actual *ecological behavior*." Both are always dependent on the local environmental situation. Thus, different environments, both social and natural, not only give rise to different ecological experiences, each valid in its own area, but different states of the environment also give rise to different ecological behavior. It is the ecological experience that gets encoded in myths, folklore, and worldview, whereas the ecological behavior as the "actual resource management practices" is "multifaceted, sometimes contradictory, and . . . in many cases downright destructive" (239).

Ecological resource management is always contradictory or paradoxical at best, and even more so if the survival of people is directly hinged on it. Cases of destructive behavior do not take away from ecological traditions because they were the exception, or part of an overall stable cultural ecosystem that encompassed such excesses. Cultural rules are never and cannot be followed in fundamentalist ways; they prescribe, however, general guidelines that are followed more often than not. Unfortunately, affluent societies that can afford to apply moral judgments on others (and put up moral screens that prevent the same judgments from being applied to themselves) often do not take into account complexities underlying day-to-day decision making in other circumstances. This is especially true if moral, essentialist arguments can be used to reach political goals, as is true with the debate about ecological Americans Indians in the American West.

Ever since conflicts over land rights, water rights, and sovereignty have taken on a moral argumentation—the historic fact of conquest can hardly be contested—taking care of the land has become a crucial issue. The assumption in the moral argumentation is that whoever speaks with the voice of the land becomes indigenous, in the sense that they have now become the real stewards of the land. And as its stewards, they claim its ownership. This argument is not so much directed against plains nations as it is used in debates over the spoils of the conquest. In their state as colonized peoples, American Indians are dependent on federal policy, and the battles over the future of the plains can safely be played out on a field that to the most part ignores contemporary American Indians but uses their ecological traditions as political tools (see Braun 2007).

Tribal buffalo are of necessity economic and not simply cultural assets. What Peter Suzuki says of the Winnebago is true for all tribal bison projects (1999:145): "Notwithstanding the nascent character of the Winnebago Bison Project and the Winnebago cultural values associated with this animal, the commodification of bisons [sic] by means of the Project puts the effort squarely in the realm of a business enterprise, a point that needs reiteration." Depending on the management direction and on the tribal government's willingness and ability to subsidize cultural projects, this is true to a greater or lesser degree, but even when bison are not held for primarily economic purposes, in the context of contemporary political and economic situations, the animals will become, to a certain degree, an economic and political commodity.

With about fifteen thousand bison held by the member tribes of the InterTribal Bison Cooperative (ITBC), and more by tribes that are not members of ITBC, tribal buffalo operations are already a great success. In fact, as the events on Fort Berthold show, some tribes are now faced with having too many animals. On the Crow reservation in Montana, the herd should be culled at several hundred animals fewer than the eleven hundred present in 2004 (Stark 2004). On Lower Brule, the tribal bison herd approached the pasture's carrying capacity in 2006 (Harriman 2006), and the same was true for other herds that either had reached or surpassed the carrying capacity of their pastures. When Montana opened a hunting season for bison that leave Yellowstone National Park in 2006, the Crow Tribe rejected its share of hunting licenses, pointing at its own herd that needs to be reduced. Simultaneous to the state-run hunt that included Montana Indian tribes, Nez Perce from Idaho killed five bison under treaty provisions allowing the tribe to hunt buffalo near the park. The Nez Perce emphasized that they saw this hunt as an opportunity to revitalize cultural traditions.

Although Ken Zontek gives an overview of some of the existing bison operations on reservations and reserves in his dissertation (2003), I want to point out some parallels between Cheyenne River and a few other bison operations. The relative worth of generating economic revenues versus providing an environment for cultural and social revitalization has been brought up in the context of many tribal bison operations. In personal discussions, even people who are active in traditional culture acknowledged that from an economic standpoint it might be a luxury to subsidize cultural projects rather than seeking revenues. They did not question the necessity for cultural retention and revitalization, but economic realities are such an overwhelming presence on many reservations that they cannot be ignored.

In 2001, the Ho-Chunk Nation of Wisconsin decided to keep their buffalo operation running, although it was not producing revenues. The bison project there had been started in 1997, and the buffalo were used for educational and health purposes and in the diabetes program. In June 2001, when the tribal government faced budgetary problems, legislators voted to close the project. Some of them argued that it was cheaper to buy buffalo meat than to subsidize the tribal bison project to produce meat that then could be donated to tribal events. Only a few days later, however, on appeals from supporters, the tribal legislature reversed its vote, recognizing the cultural and social importance of the bison project, and in fact valuing that higher than economic revenues. However, the staff for the project was cut (Kozlowicz 2001).

Tribal bison projects are not only in the crosshairs of budget-conscious tribal councils, however. When, to the contrary, they are run as economic enterprises, it seems that allegations over management issues arise. In 2003 and 2004, both the *Bismarck Tribune* and the *Billings Gazette* reported on such allegations from the Fort Berthold Indian Reservation in North Dakota. For two years in a row, tribal members called in outside authorities from the National Park Service (NPS) and from the state Board of Animal Health because, they said, the bison on the reservation were starving. The Three Affiliated Tribes, in turn, called the concerned people "troublemakers" and asserted that the dead animals simply represented a normal winter attrition rate and not neglect on part of the tribe. In 2004, some people asked that a committee of elders be installed to monitor the bison management, but the tribal chairman thought that the complaints had been politically motivated. Whatever caused the death of these bison and whether the allegations were founded or not, it becomes evident that buffalo had become important political and social symbols and were used as such in discussions that probably had much more to do with the general political direction of the tribe than narrowly with buffalo management. In a similar chain of events, bison on the Pelican Lake First Nation in Saskatchewan were dying in 2003, and some people on the reserve looked for charges of neglect against the tribal buffalo management.

The ability of tribes to manage bison underwent public and governmental scrutiny and initially held up against stereotypes and doubts in the case of the National Bison Range (NBR) in Montana. Since 1994, the Confederated Salish and Kootenai Tribes, on whose reservation the NBR had been established in 1908, have sought an agreement that the tribe take over the management of the NBR and the Ninepipe and Pablo National Wildlife Refuges (Devlin 2003). It is evident from interviews conducted mostly in the 1920s that people on the Flathead Indian Reservation—both Indians and local non-Indians—had vibrant memories of the Pablo-Allard bison herd (Whealdon and Bigart 2002). It is also clear that, although the connection to the animals had changed, tribal members kept the oral history concerning buffalo behavior and buffalo hunts alive; this knowledge, and the cultural connection is still present (Brown 2005). In the case of the Confederated Salish and Kootenai Tribes, the cultural connection to the bison and the reassertion of sovereignty over tribal lands led to a 2004 agreement between the tribal government and the U.S. Fish and Wildlife Service for shared management responsibilities of the NBR. Although the agreement underwent much scrutiny and resistance from non-Indian interests, and although it did not provide the tribes with broad authority over the management of the range, it represented a first step toward an acknowledgement that American Indian tribes have the expertise—from both traditional knowledge and scientific training—to effectively manage an ecosystem. The agreement was contested and abandoned in 2006. The future will have to tell whether the cooperation can be restored, and whether it is a first step to true comanagement of protected areas (see Stevens 1997), but it is symbolically fitting that the agreement concerned buffalo.

CHAPTER 12

Culture, Ecology, and Economics

Freeman and others begin a recent study on Arctic whale hunting by noting that "Inuit hunt whales to fulfill a number of social, economic, cultural, and nutritional needs" (1998:29). The same can be said of European peasant farming, Amazonian horticulture, and Lakota buffalo hunting. With the onset of industrial alienation and economic and ecological theories heavily grounded on material culture, this notion was often overlooked in the past, but with a growing awareness of systemic interactions and reports about the central cultural and social components of development projects (i.e., Ferguson 1994; Lansing 1991), it seems to be trickling back into the consciousness of mainstream academia and institutions.

Some societies have developed a largely objectified sense of their environment. In this perspective, the environment is not a willful actor but is made up of purely reacting factors: the dominant scientific perspective of what is sometimes called Western culture is often accused of this. I would argue, though, that good scientists know the limitations of their approach and know that other entities are not simply objects. As Gregory Bateson explains (2000:229):

> If I kick a stone, the movement of the stone is energized by the act, but if I kick a dog, the behavior of the dog may indeed be partly conservative—he may travel along a Newtonian trajectory if kicked hard enough, but this is mere physics. What is important is that he may

exhibit responses which are energized not by the kick but by his metabolism; he may turn and bite.

I do not think there is a single physicist who would deny that kicking a
dog could get such a reaction. There is a difference between admitting that
a dog can turn and bite or a bison can turn and horn and assuming that
dogs or bison have their own culture and social organization that parallels
that of humans. However the difference between these two assumptions
seems to be smaller than between the assumption that other beings are simply entities with no ability to take decisions and the assumption that they
have some decision-making abilities that is independent of their direct reactions to outside input. Also, while there are indeed people who kick buffalo because they want to take their picture standing up, such stupidity,
besides usually being punished swiftly, might better be explained by a general ignorance of basic manners, respect, and a constant exposure to tales
of power and arrogance. There is a definite relation between objectification, alienation, and arrogance, but this objectification does not stem from
the presence of "science."

Some approaches to ecological anthropology in the past have been misled by an overemphasis of objective data as the only relevant component of
ecological systems. A focus on such "scientific" data has lead to a functional
approach: the goal of a study is to find how ecological relations "really" function to have a society survive. Whether the primary interest in this lies in
adaptation or in systemic function, what characterizes most of these studies
is that although culture is theoretically acknowledged to play a role, it seems
not to be scientific enough (i.e., not easily defined in workable subunits) to
be a useful category for the analysis. Roy Rappaport (1968:224), one of the
most influential early ecological anthropologists, thinks that in studying ecological relations, people should be regarded as "a population in the animal
ecologist's sense." This can be interpreted at first as a rejection of anthropocentrism, which might lead to a less objectified perspective on ecological relations. However, Rappaport does not create an equal basis for
judgment by giving the "environment" a certain sense of intentionality but
by taking that away from humans: "My belief [is] that it is not only possible
but preferable to examine man's ecological relations in terms that also apply
to noncultural species" (241). Thus, ecological relations can best be studied if we look at interacting species after having eliminated culture. This
also eliminates the "acting" from "interaction" and creates a new analytical

problem by flattening out a crucial difference between the actors, namely that some of them have culture and some do not.

There are generally three possible perspectives that inform thoughts about the interaction of humans and animals in an ecological framework: that both humans and animals have culture, society, and independent thought and are therefore "actors"; that humans are actors because they have independent thought and thus culture, whereas animals are subject to natural laws; and that human and animal cultures are nonexistent or negligible vis-à-vis ecological and natural laws. The first view can be attributed to societies that see animals as potential equals and for which the boundaries between human and animal form are fluent because humans can be transformed into animals and vice versa. It is important that in Western societies, such beliefs have survived the "age of reason" in the form of folktales, for example, in which both humans and animals speak and reason with each other. Many people also treat animals as if they were children or even adults. The second perspective is one that draws a definite boundary line between humans and animals. This does not necessarily mean that animals are seen as worthless. Farm animals can be respected, for example, but they are obviously not in charge of their own destiny, and in the eyes of the farmer, should not be. According to this perspective, there exists a certain hierarchy in this world, with humans standing above animals because we have culture and they do not. The third view can be characterized as a purely biological perspective.

Because I have laid weight on cultural explanations of how Plains Indians treat bison and why buffalo ranching can lead to a restoration of societies and health on reservations, I must first deal with the third perspective. I agree with Keith Basso's argument on the tendency to interpret ecological interactions on a biological basis:

> Conventional ecological studies proceed on the tacit premise that what people think about the environment—how they perceive it, how they conceptualize it, or, to borrow a phrase from the ethnomethodologists, how they 'actively construct' it—is basically irrelevant to an understanding of man-land relationships. To accept this premise is to conclude that cultural meanings are similarly irrelevant and that the layers of significance with which human beings blanket the environment have little bearing on how they live their lives. But the premise is not correct, for American Indians or anyone else, and to suppose otherwise would be a serious mistake (1996:67).

The premise is simply wrong because cultural meanings influence all human interactions; in fact, to intentionally interact with something else, be that an animal, a plant, or another person, any being must first differentiate the Other, and for cultural beings, differences are always based on cultural perceptions. "Human beings," as Bennett puts it (1996:353), "create values out of their needs and desires, while the other animals have only needs."

Tim Ingold draws the boundary between the "social" and the "ecological" as corresponding "to that between the intentional and the behavioural components of action" (1987:127). For a willful interaction (i.e., one that is not based on reflexes) people always act a certain way because they attach specific meanings to the Other. For Nikolai Bukharin, "the ultimate basis for materialism was to be found in ecology" because he saw human beings as a product of nature (Foster 2000:227). But as Ingold points out (127), "[h]uman beings are, of necessity, simultaneously involved in systems of both social and ecological relations, constituting them respectively as conscious persons and as individual organisms." However much weight one wants to put on the biological component of action, then, to disregard the cultural component means to forfeit a useful, corrective analysis (see also Krupnik 1993:20, 21). By extension, the same goes for a purely formalistic economic analysis of ecological interactions, one that assumes that all human beings act according to the same, supposedly inherited or inbred economic values and rationality, and thus is really biological for all intents and purposes. Bronislaw Malinowski's examination of economic values should have taken care of that assumption (1992).

If the importance of cultural values is not brought to the forefront, or if they are dismissed a priori, the mistakes of the past are seen as correctable biological processes—in contrast to historical processes, which include an analysis of human actions and values—and the underlying fundamental choices are not questioned. This can have grave consequences, as can readily be seen on the plains. The Great Plains Committee, in its 1936 report to President Roosevelt, identified as the sources of the Dust Bowl disaster "not only an ignorance of natural science but more importantly a cluster of traditional American attitudes" (Worster 1977:231). I would argue that the results and forewarnings of natural science were ignored exactly because they contradicted fundamental cultural values, and a look at the list of cultural values identified by the committee as having fundamentally contributed to the Dust Bowl is enlightening by itself:

According to the committee, these included the assumption that the corporate farm was more desirable than a smaller family operation, that markets would expand indefinitely, that the pursuit of self-interest and unregulated competition made for social harmony, that humid-land farming practices could be followed on the plains. There was also the pioneering view that America's vast natural resources could never be exhausted.... But at the very top of their list for fundamental causes for the Dust Bowl, they placed the misguided notion that man thrives by conquering nature (Worster 1977:231).

A quick overview of these values shows that few of them have been changed since the 1930s, a fact that contributed heavily to the farm crisis of the 1980s and to behaviors creating ecological problems well into the twenty-first century.

Once the idea that culture plays an important part in human-environmental interactions is accepted, another problem appears, one that a purely biological perspective elegantly avoids: what if different cultures do not accept the same rationales toward their environment? How can one compare ecological interactions if they do not agree on basic parameters? This problem becomes especially important if one tries to find better ways to structure ecological interactions, as a growing movement in the industrial world has been doing since the 1960s. If other societies are to be models of environmental behavior for one's own society, then they have to act on comparable premises. In the context of Plains Indians and buffalo ranching, this problem becomes acute when one talks about buffalo as sacred animals, as relatives to humans, and especially in certain ecological beliefs of Plains Indian and Euro-American cultures. Krech sums up the problem as follows (1999:149):

Were these [buffalo hunting Plains] Indians ecologists or conservationists? To call them ecologists, one must allow for the presence, in some of their ecological systems, of lakes under which buffaloes disappeared. And to brand them conservationists is to accept that what might have been most important to conserve was not a herd, or an entire buffalo, or even buffalo parts, but one's economically vital, culturally defined, historically contingent, and ritually expressed relationship with the buffalo.

The second point becomes important in disputes over whether animals should be conserved per se or because they fulfill a certain role. In the strict sense of conservation, this dispute is no longer problematic in regard to buffalo, but it can be clearly followed in arguments between environmentalists and indigenous communities over fur trapping, oil exploration, or traditional whale and seal hunting (e.g., Freeman et al. 1998; Huntington 1992; Sullivan 2000). If the environmentalists involved have taken supposedly indigenous ecological interactions as models, the indigenous communities are often accused to be traitors of their own cause or acting in a nonindigenous way.

The first point raises a fundamental issue, namely whether indigenous societies can actually be taken as models of ecological interaction by our own culture. If historic Plains Indian societies are to be models for Euro-American ecological reform, we have to know, for example, what the Lakota in the 1700s would have done with a bulldozer. Would they have used it to build bigger, more efficient buffalo surrounds to kill more animals? Or would they have used it to restore wetlands, degraded by huge herds of ponies? The question alone shows how absolutely ridiculous the idea is. We do not know because there were no bulldozers in the 1700s, and even if some society in, say, Africa might have had them, there is no way to know how another culture would have incorporated them into their own ecological system.

Although nobody I have met on the plains still believed that buffalo disappeared into caves or lakes in the fall to emerge replenished in numbers in the spring, it is true that this was an integral part of the traditional belief system. Anybody living within a Western knowledge system has to reject that idea: buffalo have been observed throughout the seasons, and no instance has been recorded when they went underground. From a natural science standpoint, the idea is humbug, and one can make the point that the Lakota ecological system thus cannot work. Some people have argued that it is for this reason that the Lakota and other tribes were not concerned about the looming extinction of the buffalo.

I think we should be careful not to jump to conclusions, however. We cannot analyze the indigenous system with an external, scientific framework, which made no sense for believers in the traditional culture. The possibility of slaughtering all the buffalo was not one that existed or mattered in the parameters of Lakota culture because there was no place for it in the ecology. Such fundamental values are hard to change in the few years it took to make this impossibility actual, especially if the culture itself is faced with an existential crisis that contributes to a hardening of traditional values and beliefs.

There are two other points to keep in mind before engaging in an argument about how traditional peoples are blinded by superstitions from seeing what is going on in the "real" world. The first one is that Western societies overlook and ignore empirical data for cultural reasons, too. The warnings about and lessons unlearned from the Dust Bowl are a good example for this. The second, and perhaps more important, reason is that we cannot take all cultural knowledge literally. By this, I do not just mean that metaphors abound in descriptions of ecological processes, but also that ideas, which people know are empirically unsound, persist nonetheless. For example, people in medieval Europe knew all along that the earth was not flat (Enterline 2002:75), yet the official doctrine held on to the idea. Practical interactions with the environment do not necessarily follow available data sets or ideologies (Krupnik 1993:237–40). Bennett notes that among historic societies "there was no doctrine of conservation in the modern sense: Nature was being managed at a modest de facto level of intervention, not consciously conserved or preserved. Ideologically based conservationism arises in societies who have contributed to environmental degradation and are trying to make up for it" (1996:364). Notice that it is not the system of environmental interaction that fails to contribute to conservation: there is simply no conscious effort toward that goal because the system already avoids degradation to a large extent. The system as a whole, however, can only work in conjunction with the culture in which it exists and whose values support it. Thus, the belief that buffalo go underground to have their numbers replenished can be seen as one part of that cultural ecological system. Once the buffalo became extinct, the whole system (i.e., the culture and the ecosystem together) necessarily changed.

Rather than denying culture in ecological interactions, there is a need to take it seriously. I do not simply mean that Traditional Ecological Knowledge (TEK) should be used as additional data for scientific eco-management. Dorothee Schreiber makes an excellent point when she describes how Ahousaht people on the Northwest Coast resist the isolation and extraction of knowledge as TEK from its cultural setting because they understand that "[w]hen knowledge becomes recontextualized into systems of [ecological] management, relations of power shift, and what may seem to be a harmless case of cultural appropriation can make local people experience a loss of control over decisions that affect their lives" (2002:374). To take the cultural component of TEK seriously, one needs to incorporate the total values and beliefs of the system. If these are incompatible with the scientific view of the environment, rather than simply including raw TEK data in the scientific framework, a new system should be developed, one that is compatible with the new culture that is simultaneously developing from culture contacts between traditional and scientific cultures.

Besides the issue of cultural appropriation, a focus on indigenous knowledge as purely scientific data also poses an analytical problem. Over time, TEK data, as an abstraction, can stay the same but may be used in a different way under new cultural or ecological parameters. An analysis focusing only on isolated data may thus be misled to assume a cultural continuity. The relations of Plains Indians to buffalo can serve as a case in point. Although there are conscious efforts to preserve traditional TEK about buffalo and to continue ceremonies associated with killing or slaughter, the overall relationship to the animals has changed and in fact been reversed. Ingold draws on historic cultures to point out that "[t]he rationality of conservation is totally alien to a predatory subsistence economy, which rests on the fundamental premise that the herds are responsible for the existence of Man, rather than men—individually or collectively—for the perpetuation of the herds" (1980:71). Many people involved with buffalo herding on the plains have pointed out to me similar ideas (and I do not think they have read Ingold), expressing a shift in responsibilities. The buffalo, they said, have taken care of us for a long time while we were dependent on them to survive. Now that the buffalo are dependent on us to survive, we have the responsibility to take care of them. Not only can one see the appearance of a rationale of conservation in this, but, as has been pointed out to me, this shift in responsibility is also one cause of the rift between some tribal buffalo operations and tribal councils. To argue with conservation and responsibility means to assume financial burdens even if the investment cannot be returned. Councils, even when they are supporting the conservation of tribal culture, have been shocked by the costs for buffalo programs and demand if not profits, at least self-sufficient operations.

This debate stems from a long use of economic values as pertaining to consumptive use values only, and in this case, an extension of economic values to nonconsumptive use values and to nonuse values might show how education, recreation, and existence per se can hold and create economic values, too. However, I can see two difficulties with this argument on reservations and generally in developing economic situations. One is that regardless of future or even only potential economic value, reservation governments and societies need money—cash—right now. This is especially true if they want to hold on to control over their lands; the option to sell the nonuse resources to environmental groups that would preserve or restore them is not available. The other difficulty I see is that people who have consciously decided to change cultural values are often those who afterward cannot see a middle ground between the values they have newly adapted and those they have abandoned. This is not only generally true for religious but also for political and cultural converts. To consciously change one's identity often leads to a combative stance toward the old values. In other words, if one abandons the values that defined the traditional holistic Plains Indian economic-ecological-kinship sphere and adopts the Euro-American separated economic values, these are often embraced so vehemently that a seeming reapproach becomes impossible.

While most people on any reservation probably agree that their traditional ecological knowledge should be preserved in some ways, the general value change to a "rationality of conservation" has not taken place, perhaps exactly because of the imposition of the new politico-economic model, which in its U.S. incarnation seems not to allow financial government subsidies to cultural or ecological practices. In other words, the change to the new politico-economic system requires the abandonment of the holistic kinship structure as connected to economics but does not require a change in the economic rationale itself. Conservation, be it cultural or ecological, is not of importance under the new value system. It is the contemporary counterculture in both Lakota and Euro-American culture and not the mainstream that argues for a "rationality of conservation." Ironically, in this context, those Lakota who argue for conservation are seen as traditionalists, although they are really the ones who have reversed the cultural parameters for ecological interaction.

The change to conservationist practices and ideology also necessitates the surrender of some TEK. Specifically, in this instance, assuming responsibility for conservation of the buffalo demands giving up beliefs about the supernatural replenishment of the buffalo herds, at least temporarily, until ecological and cultural conditions allow a return to a predatory ideology. Obligations to show respect for hunted animals, however, can stay the same as before because they may not be tied so much to reproduction, but to animals presenting themselves to the hunter (Berkes 1999:83–87). This represents a different approach to buffalo, perceived as "wild," from cattle, perceived as "domestic." Buffalo demand more respect as long as they have to be hunted because humans are not their masters (see Ingold 1987:245–65). In many versions of the pte san win story, the White Buffalo Woman promises to the Lakota that she will present them with the animals necessary for their survival (e.g., Densmore 1992:66). I think there is enough room for an argument that she is here ideologically filling the role of an animal master or guardian, who "owns" the buffalo. This argument gains in attraction with Werner Müller's discussion of the northern origins of Lakota and Dakota ecological ideology (1970:235–46, 347–57). If one could see this aspect of the White Buffalo Woman as an animal master, it becomes clear that this part of the hunting ideology needs to be preserved as long as buffalo are wild; the new ecological system is a mixture of predatory economy and conservation ideology. People who consider buffalo as cattle, however, do not need to hunt them because they are the masters of their animals. This explains the rift between the more traditional American Indian buffalo ranchers and the buffalo industry.

If the difference between hunters and pastoralists is that hunters "aim to *intercept* migrating herds," whereas pastoralists follow them (Ingold 1980:189), one could argue that the ranchers and cowboys of the American West are actually more hunters than pastoralists, of course without extensive herd movement. Their system is also not based on a special religious bond or responsibility between the two species but on economic reason; it therefore presents different realizations than that of the Plains Indian hunters. As Ingold shows (261), the common bond between hunters and ranchers is predation, and the common bond between ranchers and pastoralists is accumulation. Ingold describes the evolution of "predatory pastoralism" and "subsistence ranching" (261–62), and along his lines, I would describe ranching in the American West as "accumulative hunting": the concept of predation is certainly alive in the methods—cowboys go out, drive otherwise mostly wild cattle into surrounds and send them off to be slaughtered—but the concept of a market economy brings in accumulation, control, and limited care-taking. It also takes away the religious aspects of the hunt and makes the people masters of the animals. It is clear that the cattle exist to support the ranchers. Thus, predation alone is not enough, and conservation becomes an issue. Traditional ranchers often adopted an attitude of minimal interference with nature (Bennett 1969:88–89).

It is debatable whether, or how much, that translates into a conservationist attitude, but Ingold is right to point out that "modern ranchers are

of necessity more concerned with the optimum use and conservation of natural resources than hunters and pastoralists have ever been" (1980:262).
Optimum use and management methods do not by themselves translate
into conservation and neither does minimal interference with nature. As I
have tried to show, the introduction of cattle itself can be seen as destructive to the environment (e.g., Crosby 1986; Donahue 1999; Licht 1997;
Russell 1993). In many places, a conservationist ideology translates into
active attempts at restoration, while minimal interference with nature,
which now includes cattle, might allow (further) degradation of the ecosystem. Restoration is expensive, even under the most ideal circumstances,
and depending on the time frame adopted for the restoration goal, might
be directed against ranching interests (i.e., might demand the removal of
cattle from the ecosystem).

With the industrialization of ranching and its economic pressures, there is
also less and less room for thoughts on the conservation of the ecosystem by
the ranchers themselves. Energy and resources have to be spent on the accumulation of greater numbers of animals to obtain a better harvest—greater
numbers to prey on. The conservationist ideology (i.e., to preserve for the pure
pleasure of conserving) thus has to fall by the economic wayside. In these
issues, it is important to recognize that the "new" ideologies, if one can call
them that, do not represent a split between Indian and non-Indian societies.
As I have said, divisions between those contemporary buffalo (and cattle)
ranchers who have adopted or not adopted a conservation ideology do not follow ethnic lines. Some American Indians are trying to maintain a hunting
ideology but have adopted an overall conservationist superstructure, whereas
others have traded their hunting economy for a ranching economy that can
still be characterized as predatory but have not adopted, or are less and less
able to adopt, a conservationist ideology. Some non-Indians are maintaining
their ranching economics without adopting a general conservationist ideology, whereas others have changed their general goals to include non-economic
conservation. It is because of the ideological proximity between indigenous
hunting and western ranching that shifts between the two economic pursuits
do not present many difficulties or differences.

This attempt at a general discussion shows how confusing categories such
as conservation can become when used indiscriminately. A valid argument
can be made that those ranchers who have not adopted a conservationist
perspective are trying just as hard to conserve their own culture as those
American Indians who are trying to conserve theirs by adopting the same.

In a social environment that tends to separate economics from other cultural phenomena and accord economic issues an essential role in social and cultural changes, it is important to keep in mind that economics may carry less weight than symbolism, even in what we might call economic development. This is especially visible in trade patterns, perhaps because in industrial and postindustrial society, including academia, trade (and exchange) seems to be such a fundamental and essential economic activity. As Colin Renfrew points out (1993:14), though, "far more often the exchange system as we most immediately interpret it in terms of displaced goods is merely the material relic of patterns of interaction which had symbolic dimensions of a much wider kind." Although this statement pertains to prehistoric Europe, the reduction of contemporary "economic" patterns to pure economics is just as misleading as the interpretation of material evidence of exchange in purely economic terms. This is particularly true for symbolically central aspects of the culture.

Economics do not always carry precedence over symbolism; in other words, symbolically important items, even if they are a main part of subsistence activities—the cultural sphere that one might assume to be the most economic—are not necessarily important cultural symbols simply because they are central to a society's economics. In fact, the reverse can be just as true. I have tried to argue that buffalo are not only important cultural symbols for Plains Indians because they figured prominently in the economic survival of each of those groups. One subsistence item that can serve to exemplify this is corn. Corn replaced native plants in North American indigenous horticulture, and one could assume that its higher harvest profits and greater storage potential played a major role in its dissemination. Corn also played, and still plays, a central symbolic role in many agricultural American Indian societies, and from an economic or functionalistic perspective, the ceremonial and symbolic aspects of corn in American Indian societies stem from its prominence in their subsistence. However as Christine Hastorf and Sissel Johannessen point out (1994:434), it might well be that the causality played the opposite way and that corn fits into models "in which early crop production and food exchange occurs based on social needs and symbolic values." Corn could have been traded from one American Indian nation to another not for its economic or nutritional value but, like tobacco, for its symbolic significance:

All crops and foods have their economic aspect of course, but to understand innovations in food systems we must look for the shifts in social and cultural dynamics that accompany changes in production and consumption. Social identity, both individual and group, is closely bound to food preferences and changes in food entail an alteration in self-definition (Hastorf and Johannessen 1994:435).

Many societies began to plant small amounts of corn and changed to primarily corn-based agriculture hundreds of years after corn had already been introduced. "[C]orn," Hastorf and Johannessen argue (441), "was mobilized as a sign and symbol in the process of expansive social transformation." The statement can be applied, almost directly, to contemporary tribal buffalo ranching on the plains. One of the goals of tribal buffalo operation was to bring about a change in self-definition by reintroducing buffalo to the reservations, and buffalo were and are used as symbols in a "process of expansive social transformation." That much is true not only for American Indian reservations; the Buffalo Commons proposal also tried to employ the same animals (but under a different symbolic paradigm) to effect social, cultural, ecological, and economic transformations.

To give economic factors precedence in ecological decisions means to forego alternative explanations that might be just as important, if not more so. This is why tribal buffalo projects, and I would argue, any social, political, or economic development program, can only be understood if cultural values are taken into account. Culture, as Kalstad says (1998:245), "should not only be seen as a by-product of economic, market-driven development, but as a basic premise in the socio-economic planning process." With this in mind, I propose another look at the economic, political, and ecological history of Cheyenne River.

CHAPTER 13

Sovereignty, Land, and Development on Cheyenne River

Reservations are forced to participate in the same market as the economically and politically dominant society. Independent states have some space to maneuver with customs and taxes; this avenue is lost for reservations. Administered by the federal government, there is no room to carve out a protective domestic niche. For example, having their land in trust, on the one hand, offers a layer of protection and, on the other, makes it almost impossible to get a loan from a bank. Reservations do not have the resources necessary to participate in this New World order other than as consumers, and they do not have the resources to participate as consumers other than by going into debt. In other words, they add to their political dependency by succumbing to economic dependency. As Brown observes (1998:48–49):

> The reevaluation by Native American peoples of their own conditions involves an assessment of their relationships to the materially dominant society. Frequently, when sincere attempts are made by Native Americans to adjust to or acculturate within the dominant society, they become involved in a process of diminishing returns, or reach dead ends with regard to acquiring a meaningful quality of life.

In other words, successful participation in the dominant economic system—which is a condition of successful participation in the dominant social, cultural, and political system—is of necessity leading to conflict with traditional values. Because culture is always a system, cultural concerns influence economic relationships and choices and vice versa.

As a result of acts and supportive court cases, Stephen Cornell and Joseph Kalt see a fundamental policy change having taken place over the last thirty years (1990:96): "Since 1975 reservation development has moved progressively into Native American hands. Development programs on many reservations are beginning to follow Indian agendas, and success and failure are beginning to be measured in Indian terms." However, as I have pointed out previously, what American Indian terms mean is a function of history and not simply an essentialist revitalization of historic cultural values. American Indian nations, involved in the current world system since its inception (Dussel 1998), have influenced, reacted to, and adapted to outside economic, military, cultural, and political forces for hundreds of years. In the final analysis, contemporary cultural values cannot be understood, therefore, without a look at the historical context in which they evolved: the history of capitalism on the plains and its application to Plains Indian societies.

The history of settler countries is a history of conquest—some people come and take away the land of others. Whether they legitimize it with a doctrine of *terra nullius*, Manifest Destiny, or a Lockean land-use argument, such are the facts. The history of settler countries thus starts with a history of land appropriation, and unless steps are consciously taken by the new ruling majority to right the wrongs, mitigate the consequences, or at least consciously apologize, the problems caused by this will dominate the history of all peoples in the country. It has become a powerful image in U.S. culture to have a father, preferably from a hill behind the ranch, next to a lone tree silhouetted against the setting sun, show his son the land, encompassing everything they can see, to be his one day. Imagine what it means to see the same land and know that all of it is rightfully yours. And at the same instance, you know the same government that guaranteed it to you once upon a time is keeping it from you because legitimate and even legal rights are obliterated by a colonial *Realpolitik* of resource appropriation.

The land appropriation on the Great Plains, or to say it differently, the conquest of the plains, was motivated not only by the supposedly Manifest Destiny but also by Jeffersonian ideas about parcellization of the land to build a society of yeoman farmers. This Jeffersonian ideal saw the yeoman society as the backbone of an intentionally precapitalist—or rather, to avoid false evolutionary implications, noncapitalist—society (Limerick 1987:56, 94).

It is not so surprising then, if somewhat ironic, that the Jeffersonian model has many parallels to the Marxian postulate that the division between town and country must be overcome. Like Frederick Jackson Turner almost a century later in his Frontier thesis, Thomas Jefferson's goal was to avoid what many Americans saw as the downfalls of Europe, alienated from nature by capitalist technology and therefore weak and decadent. In practice, however, the yeoman society got off to a bad start from the beginning and not the least because capitalism was already in the plan.

Foster describes how from the seventeenth to the nineteenth century, the capitalist drive to abolish the commons in the United Kingdom spelled the end of yeomanry (2000:171–72). "All of this meant," he says, "that it became possible to 'incorporate the soil into capital', while creating the necessary army of surplus labor to feed urban industry." Terry Eagleton points out that "the English landowning elite had itself long been a capitalist class proper, already accustomed to wage labor and commodity production as early as the sixteenth century" (1997:31). The same was true for the English landowning elite in the North American colonies, the people who would become the leaders of the revolution against England—a revolution not so much from the masses but from the elites—and dominate politics in the newly founded United States. Equal distribution of the land, "to seize upon a landscape and flatten it out, reorganize it into a grid of identical parcels," as Frederic Jameson puts it (1998:66), would only have prevented a capitalist society if at the same time the forces of a capitalist market would have been outlawed. But as the environment for the Jeffersonian ideal was already a society deeply engaged in capitalist market practices, this was impossible. His yeoman society was designed as a way to avoid the problems that came with an army of surplus labor, so clearly seen at the time in England, but the project was already based on hindsight. The western frontier was, from its beginnings, driven by capitalism, and parcellization of the land could not stop that. Consequently, as Jameson points out, capitalism saw to a most uneven distribution of the values inherent in the parcels of land, until, "sheer speculation . . . now reigns supreme and devastates the very cities and countrysides it created in the process of its earlier development. But all such later forms of abstract violence and homogeneity derive from the initial parcellization, which translates the money form and the logic of commodity production for a market back on to space itself" (66).

By the time the northern grasslands became the target for conquest, it had become exceedingly clear that the parcellization of the region was not

the beginning of a development of capitalism but was rather one consequence of an already highly developed capitalism being applied to new land.
The initial parcellization had taken place earlier and somewhere else: now,
the ideology was expanded as a package. This was not an expansion for small,
independent farmers but for, and of, industrial capitalism. Fur trading had
led the way, followed by mining, the original buffalo industry (i.e., the slaughter of the buffalo) and ranching, and all needed the railroads. The federal
government supplied protection and the land for these operations. All in all,
it was one of the finest examples ever of a military-industrial complex at work.

It is no accident that the grasslands of the West were the last lands in the
United States to be conquered, after the mining districts of Montana and
the Black Hills had long been settled and "civilized." Yellowstone National
Park was founded in 1872, not the least for reasons of corporate profits from
the future tourist industry (Sellars 1997:8–10). Although Wyoming and
Montana were not yet fully settled at that time, the founding of a national
park in the region shows how much the land had already been mentally
appropriated and functionally divided. At that time, the last wars with the
Lakota were still to come.

Patricia Nelson Limerick points out that in many cases, farming, or "getting crops in and out could become something close to an extractive industry—another way of mining the soil" (1987:124–25). But from the beginning,
there was a split between farming and mining and also between farming
and ranching: early farmers lived on the land they tried to cultivate and lived
on that soil in mostly horrible conditions. In contrast, early ranching on the
plains was defined not by small ranching operations but by huge cattle companies that raised not cattle, but beef; those were meat operations, producing for the cities in the East. "[The] early split between stockgrowers and
agriculturalists was enhanced by the public's perception of ranchers, particularly cattlemen, not as settlers, but as wealthy businessmen. . . . The distinction was evident as early as the 1860s. Stockraising was touted not as a
way of life, but as an 'adventure' or get-rich-quick scheme" (Donahue
1999:23). Many owners of the big ranches did not live on the range but in
cities like Cheyenne, Wyoming, which was around 1880 one of the wealth-
iest cities in the world.

While in other words the ranching industry was a part of the capitalist
extension into the West, farming followed mining and ranching into the newly
conquered territories almost as an afterthought. The conquest of the northern plains was not a drive to new resources but a consolidation of territory.

To the small, independent farmers and the homesteaders who were not (yet) part of the capitalist industry fell the spoils of war (i.e., the land that was of no interest to industrialism) and the role of anchoring the conquest after the fact. Somebody had to settle the land, and with the right public relations schemes and the transportation infrastructure provided by the rapidly expanding railroads, it was not difficult to attract people who wanted to farm it.

The conquest of the West can be seen as the culmination of a struggle of two doctrines developed in the eighteenth century for the future of the United States: yeoman peasantry versus capitalist industrialism. It cleared the way for the capitalist elite by providing the necessary "opiate for the people": the myth of unlimited possibilities for the masses, supported in itself by the growing myth of unlimited possibilities by technological progress. Perhaps what is the most amazing in the outcome is how clearly capitalist industrialism won, although the public could be made to believe the yeoman democracy had.

However, the failure to build a U.S. yeoman society was not only a result of political and economic decisions. Parcellization itself created ecological problems that caused direct harm to the homesteaders; as I have shown previously, it was ecologically not possible to operate economically sustainable farms on these plots. Official policies, however, stayed rooted in the myth and caused much harm to the now subjugated American Indian nations.

People around the world realized throughout history that successful economics in marginal environments necessitate some form of cooperation, not competition, and more often than not, this led to some form of communal land tenure. The "tragedy of the commons" is not an issue for people who have lived and flourished with commons for centuries. As Fikret Berkes points out (1999:142), it is not communal ownership, but an open-access regime that leads to a tragedy of the commons. Traditionally, access to the resources of commons was limited to people with a vested interest in the community. Commons have played a huge role in European history and culture and are alive and well. They are and were also common on the plains, and values of communal cooperation and reciprocal help are alive and well with plains farmers and ranchers as they form a security network that is necessary for survival (see Bennett 1968). This is structurally not too different from, say, American Indian concepts. What is different, though, is that Plains Indians have been actively forced to abandon these traditional values, which did not agree with the puritan form of U.S. capitalism.

The conquest of the West, as should be clear, did not just change own-ership of the land and concepts of land ownership as such. Along with a change to capitalist ideology came a change in how the land was viewed, a change in ecological values. Veronica Strang makes this connection clear for the Australian context (1997:110–11): "This was not merely an exten-sion of an economic mode of production: they came with a set of ideas about the environment, what it was, what it was for, how it should be dealt with. Their settlement of the country was, and still is, a process of colonisation, of taking over the land and shaping it in the form of European cultural pre-cepts and values." Alienation is a philosophical and not just an economic problem because economic alienation is "inseparable from the alienation of human beings from nature, from both their own internal nature and exter-nal nature" (Foster 2000:72). Implicit in the process of modernization and postmodernization "is the thud of the second shoe, namely, the effacement of Nature, and its precapitalist agricultures, from the postmodern, the essen-tial homogeneization of a social space and experience now uniformly mod-ernized and mechanized" (Jameson 1997:366). In the context of historical change from peasant societies to capitalism, then, "the relationship between peasant agriculture and traditional culture has become only too clear: the latter follows the former into extinction" (Jameson 1998:67).

As Rebecca Bateman (1996) shows, the conquerors clearly saw the link between systems of land tenure and cultural values. "Communal use of land, cooperative labor practices, the sharing of farm machinery and capital—these were all things that needed to be eradicated before Indians could hope to be truly civilized" (215). Unfortunately for the Native peoples, this strat-egy not only attempted to destroy their cultures but it was also a policy dis-astrously maladapted to the plains environment. Those same cooperative and communal practices that they had to give up "were also the very attrib-utes that enabled Indian peoples to achieve any measure of success in farm-ing whatsoever" (215). Plains Indians were not left a choice to retain their cultural values of communal cooperation, and so the same values that made some people "savages" made others successful.

It is no accident that, as Klose puts it (1964:191), "There has been more advocacy of socialism in the plains states than in any other agricultural region of the United States." The way to achieve success on the ecologically harsh and economically peripheral rural plains is through forms of communitar-ian land tenure and cooperation. Hutterite colonies, for example, are among the economically and ecologically most successful settlements on the plains:

In general, [the Hutterite settlement] is also the most successful in terms of combining high productivity with a conservationist program for resources—Hutterites usually take good care of their land and water. The Brethren are efficient farmers not only because of their skilled management and intensive use of machinery, but also because of their ability to control consumption in order to fulfill their ideal of austerity, which incidentally provides them with substantial investment capital (Bennett 1969:247).

Not all Hutterite colonies fare extremely well, and living in and with a capitalist system has impacts on the colonies, whose members see disparities between their self-sufficient lifestyle and the collective wealth or want to participate in the dominant system to improve their personal economic situation (Bennett 1996:182–87). The point is, however, that the success of the Hutterite colonies rests on their cultural and political separation from and simultaneous limited economic cooperation with the dominant society (Bennett 1969:272; Braroe 1975:40). This has important consequences for the debate over formalist versus substantivist economic development approaches on Plains Indian reservations. The consequences are especially related to local decision-making processes, or sovereignty, as can easily be seen from a little excursion into history.

On Cheyenne River and on other plains reservations and reserves, cattle economies were established, often as a compromise between government policies pushing for the "civilization" of American Indians through agriculture, the ecology of the land that was not suited for farming, and the symbolic links between hunting and ranching cultures that enabled an easier transition to ranching than to farming. The history of these cattle economies clearly shows that as long as they were allowed sovereignty, they were successful; when the government interfered, they proved to be costly.

In 1877, the agency for Cheyenne River gave out the first live cattle to the people living around it. By 1879, those initial 450 heifers and four bulls had become almost two thousand head. This was the "inauguration for the Cheyenne River cattle industry" (Iverson 1994:66), which continued to grow in the following twenty years with the support of the agents, who knew that the land was not suited for farming. Even after the record harvest year of 1885, Indian Agent Charles E. McChesney in 1887 "advised the government to focus its effort completely on cattle ranching. A little subsistence farming would be fine. He cited the traditional laundry list: the hot winds of July and August dried and burned up the crops, too little rain, irrigation too costly, and frequent wind- and hailstorms" (Iverson 1994:67). By the turn of the century, Lakota ranchers, often mixed bloods, had established themselves as big operators. Fred Dupris, Felix Benoist, Fred LaPlant, Basil Claymore, and Narcisse Narcelle all had successful ranches on the reservation (Iverson 1994:67; Kougl and Cudmore 1984:34).

"Unfortunately," as Iverson puts it (1994:67), "federal wisdom intervened at the expense of native ranching." In 1902, Cheyenne River Reservation, together with Standing Rock to the north, was opened for lease. The Matador Land and Cattle Company from Texas leased almost all of the eastern half of the reservation for three and a half cents an acre (67). Although Iverson puts the number of Matador cattle at sixteen thousand, Kougl and Cudmore put it at fifteen thousand (1984:35). Their deal with the Bureau of Indian Affairs (BIA) "was that each Indian be allowed to run 100 head of stock on Matador range, free of charge, but must pay a fee of a dollar a head per year for all numbers above one hundred" (Kougl and Cudmore 1984:35). There were several smaller companies leasing land, but the other big company on Cheyenne River was the Turkey Track, purchased in 1907 by the Diamond A Cattle Company under Cap Mossman (Kougl and Cudmore 1984:38–39).

Fouberg writes that "the economies of the reservations west of the Missouri River were in relatively good shape in the early twentieth century. Cattle prices boomed during World War I, so ranchers, including Indian ranchers, did well" (2000:47). This might have been indeed true of American Indian ranchers still operating, but the problem was that the land policies of the government had barely left any American Indians in the position to ranch successfully. Cattle and grain prices went up in the war years: "At the urging of the government agents, Indians began to lease their reservation lands to whites, who plowed them, and planted field crops. . . . The Indian cattlemen were urged to sell their cattle and horses to the army. Soon the Indian cattle were gone. Some of the Indian range was now stocked with white-owned cattle but thousands of acres were plowed under" (Cushman and Macgregor 1948:59).

With the droughts, dust storms, and economic depressions of the 1930s, many had to sell or lease even the small allotments they still owned (Ziebach County Historical Society [ZCHS] 1982:6). Hoover points out that many residents on Cheyenne River continued to hunt and fish for subsistence, although official policies discouraged these activities (1992:49–53). All over the northern plains, the reservation cattle economies took bad downward turns during the early depression years (Iverson 1994:76–79, 138–42). Allotment and leasing policies created huge problems for Indian ranching (Parman 1994:5–10), and official policies did not help (Dawson 2002). On Cheyenne River, American Indian ranchers, who complained in 1920 that the leasing of the land to outside interests robbed them of a chance to succeed economically, were told that it would not be long before the reservation would be entirely disbanded anyway (Iverson 1994:69).

Only with the Meriam Report of 1928, the New Deal, and the appointment of John Collier as commissioner of Indian Affairs in 1933 did policies change. Collier "hoped to achieve Indian self-sufficiency through improvement and conservation of remaining Indian land, ending allotment and the constant loss of holdings, replacing white lessees with Indian farmers and ranchers, consolidating checkerboard allotments into larger and more manageable units, and providing credit for economic development" (Parman 1994:93). A separate Civilian Conservation Corps (CCC) program for Indians was built up (Parman 1994:93–94), and in May 1933, a Cheyenne River Reservation Camp could give work to about two hundred men, mostly employed in range improvement activities (ZCHS 1982:245).

One of the mainstays of Collier's reforms was to be the Indian Reorganization Act (IRA) of 1934, the same year that the Taylor Grazing Act was passed. The Taylor Grazing Act was a reaction to the dust storms and range degradations in the West, which put public grazing lands under federal management and in that process withdrew initially 80 million acres, and subsequently, from 1936 on, 142 million acres from the homesteading process (Donahue 1999:35–41; Worster 1977:230). I see the two acts as institutional responses to similar land problems: encouraging improvement, conservation and consolidation, damming the adverse effects of homesteading and the exploitation of the public domain. Both acts worked toward initially paradoxical goals, namely an increase of local sovereignty and at the same time an attempt to expand federal control and management in the West. Because the federal government acted as the protector of the public domain and American Indian lands, however, both acts in effect helped to bring about direct control over resources by the people who were rightfully entitled to them: American Indians over their reservations and the public at large over federal lands. Both acts, therefore, can be seen as a reaction to one central issue: that sustainability has to be based on sovereignty.

On Cheyenne River, the late 1930s and 1940s indeed seem to mark considerable economic progress toward self-sustainability. In 1936, a community garden program was started, the objective of which was, according to Lawrence Davis (1944:165), "to encourage the Indians to raise enough vegetables for canning and drying to last him [sic] throughout the winter months rather than to sell garden products." Under a tribal cattle program, from 1935 to 1944, "the number of cattle on the reservation owned by individual Indians . . . increased from 2,900 to 11,667" (163). The 1940s also saw improvement in the land situation, under a program started in 1942, "to exchange poorly located tribal lands for county and state owned lands in order to consolidate Indian holdings into economic units suitable for grazing" (161). More than 210,000 acres had changed hands until 1944: "The state and county have been generous, sometimes exchanging whole sections of grazing lands for a quarter section of good farm land" (161). These programs lead Davis to conclude that "the economic rehabilitation program on the Cheyenne River Reservation has shown exceptional progress in the short period of nine years. Many families have become self-supporting, and the general standard of living has materially improved. This whole program is the direct result of the new policies inaugurated by the Reorganization Act of 1934" (166).

The success of the 1940s was severely curtailed by the flooding of the Missouri River to build Lake Oahe. To alleviate the impact of the Oahe Dam, rehabilitation programs were started on the reservation (BIA 1957, 1958; Lawson 1982:80–124).

I first learned about the Rehabilitation Program in 2001, when a businessman in the border town of Gettysburg explained to me quite matter-of-factly that all economic projects fail on the reservation. To illustrate this, he told me about the program, under which, according to him, each eligible Lakota received one hundred heifers, ten thousand dollars, farm machinery, and fencing material. From his estimation, about 120 farms got started under the program, and most did not last long. "They gave it away," he said, "they sold it, but most of it went straight over there," and he pointed at the local bar. His implication, besides the one pertaining to alcoholism, was that American Indians do not know how to take care of anything valuable. There were other reasons, however, why some saw the rehabilitation program as a failure (see also St. Pierre 1991:142–57). One Lakota man told me that he had just come back from the Navy when the program started, and although he had no land at all, people wanted him to sign on: "Just go to Gettysburg and get the equipment." He did not get on the program because he knew others who were on it, and whenever they needed anything or wanted to make a management decision about their cattle, they had to go to the foreman who lived in La Plant. This was a full day's return journey for many people, and when they got there, the foreman might be out, so they would have to return another day, with no decisions made in the meantime. Eventually, the Rehabilitation Program enrolled over two hundred cattle operators and worked to establish twenty to twenty-five cattle operators in the former Armstrong County area (Cudmore 1984; ZCHS 1982:38).

In 1965, the BIA conducted a ten-year evaluation of the project. The report acknowledges that measurement of success is difficult and that "other factors such as social and cultural values would play an important part in measurement of success," but relies on economics (1968:4, 21). It finds that "60 percent of the 218 who at one time have been in the program are still in the program" (2). One tribal official interviewed sets the standard of success as measured by the program enabling 40 percent of those enrolled to "develop a livestock operation that would support him and his family" (21). About 53 percent of the remaining operators in 1965 had achieved a net worth increase; in total percentage, that is about 30 percent of all enrolled. Not all of these people showed a net ranch income.

The 1968 report gives some advice on how to improve the program. The first advice is that the program must be carried through: "Program administrators must be willing to support the program against political and social pressures" (BIA 1968:4). In fact, it would be advisable, the report finds, to have some non-Indian technical staff take the hard decisions. The second advice seems to take the reader back to the establishment of the reservation: "The less progressive operators should be closed out and their resources should be used to expand the ranch size of the more progressive operators" (4). Whereas these suggestions indicate the degree to which the program was accepted by the tribal population, and the political and social domination under which the program was conducted, the real crux of the program lies with the building of dependency.

Although one of the goals of the program was "to promote Indian use of Indian resources" (BIA 1968:11), operators, the report suggests, have to be encouraged to "go to outside non-tribal lenders and receive financing" (5). The report finds that "Indebtedness had increased substantially for the program operators since the time they made application to come into the program" (19). The tribe worked out a loan guarantee program with banks, but many operators subsequently left the tribe with their debts (5). Encouragement to go to outside lenders would alleviate the burden of the tribe but would not work toward sovereignty; to the contrary, one can see at the hand of this example how reservations were included into the dominant world system and became more and more dependent. Again, the American Indian Policy Review Commission (AIPRC) stated this problem clearly only a few years later: "It is impossible to attain economic self-sufficiency and political self-determination in a system which perpetuates economic dependence" (AIPRC 1976:2).

Dependency means on one hand federal protection, but on the other it means federal intervention in tribal affairs. Although reservations and land bases exist because of federal protection (compare, for example, to the Baswara in Young 1995:13–17), many projects fail on reservations because there are too many institutional controls. These are open invitations for politicians to get involved in programs, something that most people working on projects understandably resent. The controls are not only a constant paternalistic reminder implying that American Indians cannot deal with money but are also a waste of time for people who have better things to do. As then tribal council chairman Frank Ducheneaux put it (1956:29): "We believe that many of our problems could be eliminated by the elimination of some of the outmoded rules and regulations of the Indian Bureau that restrict the individual in the conduct of his own affairs."

What is clearly visible, however, whether the Rehabilitation Program is deemed a success or not, is how a cattle economy was established on Cheyenne River and how this cattle economy came to put pressure on ranchers to become dependent on outside forces. In 1974, 28 percent of all families on Cheyenne River owned livestock (AIPRC 1976:41). Although the Lakota reservations, such as Cheyenne River, Standing Rock, and Rosebud, showed a trend to larger operations than other reservations, the majority of ranches still operated with fewer than two hundred cattle (42). It is easy to see why a historical analysis of these processes would entice the building of a tribally controlled, large bison herd, with the means of production owned and controlled by the tribe. The only way to reduce dependency is to enter the capitalist world system as a sustainable self-sufficient entity.

As I said previously, reservations have to participate in the market economy, and what I have said so far notwithstanding, some reservations have built viable capitalist economies. After all, the practice is never as purely capitalistic as the theory. The Flathead, White Mountain, and Mescalero Apache Reservations, among others, are successful models for such an approach (Cornell 2000:109; Cornell and Kalt 1990). Reservations on the northern plains, however, have not been able to generate much economic momentum. Stephen Cornell (114–15), in a comparison of Apache and Lakota situations, thinks that different tribal leadership traditions have much to do with this. While, according to Cornell, Apaches can build on a history of firm leadership—"the traditional Apache leader was something of an autocrat"—the Lakota "have been stuck with a set of contemporary governing institutions . . . that are at significant odds with indigenous ideas about how authority ought to be organized and exercised." However the comparison with Apache leadership plays out—"autocrat" might not be the first term coming to mind when talking about traditional Apache leadership—the important message for the Lakota situation is that tribal governments need to be legitimate in accordance with the culture to be effective. The conflict about the legitimacy of IRA governments, for example, takes away from the effectiveness of reservation governments because some people do not recognize these elected officials as their legitimate leaders.

My criticism against capitalist economical approaches in the context of rural or (post)colonial economies should not be taken to mean that I would simply favor a socialist or Marxist opposite. I contend that such a solution does not represent a "radical, structural change" (Gardner and Lewis 1996:17). "For neither Marx or Lenin," as Frederic Jameson rightly points out (1997:50), "was socialism a matter of returning to smaller (and thereby less repressive and comprehensive) systems of social organization; rather, the dimensions attained by capital in their own times were grasped as the promise, the framework, and the precondition for the achievement of some new and more comprehensive socialism." Thus, Marx, growing up and thinking within an industrial, capitalist system, could not question the fundaments of this culture, only the internal economic distribution of power over resources. Socialism, although its critique of the system allows a beginning of further dialectics, cannot be the alternative to industrialism because it is still operating within the same framework.

The alternative to the industrial capitalist economy of the dominant and encroaching "global" society is the traditional way of handling things. "Traditional" as I use it here does not mean a reinvention of historical culture or a nonmonetary gift economy to the exclusion of established economic practices. The alternative to capitalism as industrialization, and in the context of the "Third World," its dependencies, is to consciously reverse political, economic, and cultural alienation and choose the concept of community and kinship. As Don Roman Loayza states (2000:19), "the cultures imposed on us have so far brought us nothing but problems: first poverty, then division, and now individualism. But with our own culture, we will regain strength. . . . It is our firm belief that we are not mistaken and that development must be based on local cultures!" Over the last years, attempts to achieve this have increased in numbers, and the tribal buffalo programs are but one example of this trend.

It is important to remember in this context that, as Strang points out (1997:95), "Although the traditional economy is the basis for communal values, there is no real dividing line between this and the 'multiple enterprise economy' that has evolved through adaptation to introduced cultural forms." In the Aboriginal communities she describes, this process "has involved the resurrection of traditional leadership structures (a Counsel of Elders) alongside European-style management structures (an elected Community Council), and land management techniques and economic operations borrowed from the white mainstream but adopted to meet Aboriginal needs" (96). In this way, traditional concerns have been preserved, and even though "people are keen to manage the cattle business . . . , the objective is not primarily to make money—although the advantages of economic independence are certainly appreciated—but rather to reframe it as a communal activity containing multiple social and cultural concerns" (100). The cattle operation that the people from Kowanyama, Australia, intend to build seems strikingly parallel in goals to those set for Pte Hca Ka: not only to run an economic business, but also to pass on cultural traditions, resume communal life, and alleviate alcohol and violence problems.

There are numerous examples from North American indigenous communities in which the goal is economic independence "but mainly so that the community can fully restore cultural continuity and a holistic interaction with the land" (Strang 1997:106). Makah, Inupiaq, and Inuit whale hunting are examples of cases in which societies are trying to rebuild communities based on traditional relations to animals. Whaling is explicitly linked to religious activities, and the hunt is portrayed as a spiritual and not only a subsistence relationship (Freeman et al. 1998:53–56). This relationship, like the one of Plains Indian groups to buffalo, is not dependent on whether or not whales were overhunted indigenously (Krupnik 1993:75–85, 216–40). Whaling is a contemporary expression of social organization, historical respect, spiritual observance, and nutritional health—community and culture (Freeman et al. 1998:29–56). In the Makah case, where whaling was reinstituted after seventy years against the protests of environmental activists (Sullivan 2000), it is also the reification of treaty rights and thus a visible reminder of sovereignty. The whale hunt here grew out of a conscious dialogue with the past that started with the building of the museum (Erikson 2002:200–14).

Schreiber discusses salmon fishing on the Northwest Coast as central to First Nations' social structures (2002). Some of these "salmon people" are using the distinction between wild salmon fishing and fish farming as indicative of their resistance to cultural assimilation. "Resistance to changes in the traditional relationship with the land," Schreiber points out in expanding her thesis to include the James Bay Cree, "is associated with individual well-being and notions of health and prosperity" (375). Salmon have become a symbol of cultural affirmation and fill a similar role to that of buffalo on the plains. The similarities include, for example, the assertion that farmed salmon is nutritionally inferior and that through the introduction of such industrial foods, the health of First Nation people has been damaged (365–67).

Whereas buffalo, reindeer, whales, and even salmon to a certain extent are easily understood to be "powerful" because they, or at least the places in which they are found naturally, seem exotic to Euro-Americans, animals that are symbolically powerful to a community also include such a "normal" animal as sheep. Navajos began to acquire flocks of sheep from the Spanish and Pueblo settlements and during the seventeenth century started to raise their own herds. Over time, these sheep became distinguished as Navajo-Churro, noted for their long, coarse wool and four-horned rams. In 1863, Kit Carson "began a systematic campaign of destroying all Navajo means of livelihood. His soldiers tore up cornfields, burned peach orchards wherever they found them and slaughtered sheep by the thousands, leaving them in piles to rot" (McNeal 1997). The surviving Navajo were starved into surrender and shipped off to Bosque Redondo. After 1868, when the Navajos were allowed to return, American Indian Bureau agents encouraged them "to increase their flocks, and efforts were made to develop a market." Navajo blankets became a widely sold commodity in the late nineteenth century, and the Navajo "became more integrated into the general American economy than any other group" (2).

By the 1920s, however, it became apparent that the numbers of sheep on New Mexico rangelands, including the reservation, were degrading the land. Sheep grazing had been a problematic issue before, and conservationists, "both within and outside government, urged the ouster of sheep from public ranges" (Donahue 1999:33). The sheep grazers, on the other hand, argued that the range erosion was not caused by their animals but had always been evident. At that time, the Navajo herders were already increasingly limited in their range by encroaching white grazers, with land and grazing rights conflicts dating back to at least 1905 (Parman 1994:20). With increasing flocks but receding range available, the impact of the sheep on the remaining range would have undoubtedly increased. Apparently, however, the Soil Conservation Service was worried not only about the tribal range conditions as such but also about the silt washing into the Colorado River threatening the newly constructed Hoover Dam (Limerick 1987:207). With the Dust Bowl raising awareness and urgency about erosion problems, Collier of the BIA and the Soil Conservation Service jumpstarted a herd reduction program on the Navajo reservation, carried out largely by force, and destroying thousands of sheep. There had been no consultations with the Navajo herders themselves, who felt that the range problems were primarily caused by previous range reduction, and especially by insufficient access rights to water sources (Iverson 1998:89; Limerick 1987:207–208). Between two hundred fifty and seven hundred thousand sheep were destroyed; in 1952, the Navajo held only about 36 percent of their 1930 livestock holdings.

Other than rendering the previously thriving Navajo sheep economy marginal and primarily subsistence oriented, the Churro breed was left with about four hundred survivors by the late 1970s. The breed was regarded as not valuable and was therefore a primary target for destruction; subsequently, "improved" breeds had been introduced to the reservation. The short fleeces of other breeds, together with their less coarse, oilier wool, were not as useful to Navajo weavers, however, and the sheep could not adapt as well to the ecological conditions.

So far, the history of the Navajo sheep might seem to be just another story of the disappearance of ancient breeds under the pressures of industrial agriculture and colonial politics. The sheep, however, also hold cultural, symbolic significance to the Navajo people. A Navajo weaver, on seeing Churros from the Navajo Sheep Project, exclaimed, "These are the real sheep!" McNeal (personal communication) compares the status of the sheep in

Navajo culture to that of horses and buffalo for Plains Indians, namely a key element of the culture. Navajo culture is a "sheep culture," and sheep are integral parts of the world in balance. From the perspective of Plains Indian culture, I would argue, the recent history of the breed is closer in parallel to the buffalo than the horse. Like the buffalo, the sheep were almost wiped out, and like the buffalo, the return of the Churros is seen as part of a potential solution for social problems, such as alcoholism, domestic violence, and economic problems. The well-adapted Churros are also hoped to restore the range ecology by helping to drive out invasive species and woody plants.

The Navajo Sheep Project hopes to restore health to Navajo culture, society, economy, and ecology by restoring the bond between the people and the sheep. Although range management, animal breeding, nutrition, and marketing are important parts of the project, as one Navajo said in an article in the *Deseret News* ("Navajo Tradition" 1994), the meaning is deeper: "It is not about making money. Raising animals is about disciplining children, teaching them responsibility and planning for the future. . . . Without animals there is no sense in teaching our children about their culture and teaching them about values." To do so, according to all these projects, one needs not just any animal but the culturally right animal, one that has established a bond with the people over a long time. Whether that means buffalo, reindeer, salmon, or churro sheep, such bonds and their cultural significance can help restore balance to the world, and on that balance, communities can grow.

Thomas Davis shows that symbols used for cultural resistance and sustainability do not need to center on animals (2000). In the case of the Menominee Indian Tribe, the focus is the forest. Sustainability is again defined through community participation: "One tenet of Menominee sustainable development stresses the importance of maintaining communal ownership of the forest and the Menominee environment" (53). Because this tenet remains fundamental, the Menominee have to find ways through dissent to reach consensus (89–95). It is directly through the process of dissent, which sometimes can be played out in hurtful and brutal ways, that the community finds togetherness. As I said in the beginning, I see the history of Pte Hca Ka as a process of community building and dialogue.

Bringing this community, or gemeinschaft, together on the basic fundamentals that everybody agrees on—namely the very roots of their identity and history—is such an essential necessity that people whose history, identity, and traditions were never challenged often overlook it because they take it for granted. Even though it might not contribute to direct subsistence or economic gain, however, it is the basis for all other activities because it shows people, or at least makes them reflect on, who they are as a community. Reinstating pride in one's culture and a feeling of self-worth and knowledge that one can achieve complex tasks is fundamental to community health. Symbolically powerful animals, such as reindeer, whales, salmon, or buffalo, or symbolically powerful plants, such as trees or corn, can be a catalyst on which the community can build.

Sustainable development projects are not dependent on the presence of big, strong, famous, or exotic species. Assuming that such projects as I have mentioned previously have good chances to be successful, they can serve as models for other regions of the world, where local or regional communities can strengthen bonds with traditionally significant parts of their environment. I do think that although these projects, just like the tribal buffalo programs, show that restoring balance to a particular corner of the world will take a long time and is a continuous and conscious process, they also show that community development is not dependent on technologies and economic theories but on bringing the community together around a purposeful and symbolically important project. These are initiatives that have grown from the inside, from the grassroots, and they are therefore less apt to be eroded away—native grasses have deep roots.

CHAPTER 14

Making Sense

Most models, theories, and abstract concepts have a distinct viewpoint to them; they study a given problem from the perspective of economics, ecology, society, health, and so on. Good theories try to integrate two or three perspectives and show how they interact, but most attempts at a truly holistic theory fail simply because the variables become too numerous to build a scientific model on them. Decision-making models cannot take into account all different perspectives, situations, and consequences. Even if they could and the resulting model could be made understandable and applicable to the limitations of the human mind, people mostly do not follow mathematical models but are impulsive, quirky, corrupt, loyal, vengeful, empathetic—in short, "irrational" and human. No theory can therefore be used as a sufficient explanation of human behavior. Capitalism, Marxism, functionalism, or deconstructionism are useful to compare theoretically certain events and thoughts, but only as necessarily cooperative tools producing symbolic results. In this respect, theories work like categories. One can look at buffalo ranching from an economic, ecological, social, symbolic, historical, agricultural, or biological perspective, but the results are bound to be symbolic each time, in the sense that they are only meaningful for the people (and the buffalo) if they can be fit into a systemic whole and make sense of each other. Although models and theories are generalized from behavior, behavior is usually not a direct application of a theory: if it is forced to be, there are usually disastrous consequences.

227

Sustainable development projects cannot only rely on an economic, ecological, social, or any other theory to the exclusion of others. This is especially true for locally controlled and directed projects, such as tribal buffalo programs. The local frame is most often not large enough to allow for narrow ideological approaches. Rural people, like Plains Indians on rural reservations and their neighbors, are usually pragmatists—bricoleurs, amateurs—in the sense that they are not consumed by theoretical limitations. Rather than to define and examine the present relations between Lakota people and the buffalo as a "sacred symbiosis," a "continuous relationship with the 'buffalo nation' that dates back to time immemorial," as Ken Zontek does (2003:1), it seems to me that the current buffalo programs are a typical embodiment of ever-changing plains pragmatism. It is for this reason that I deem them sustainable in the long run: they do not follow a strict ideological line. To the contrary, they are constantly experimenting, trying to strike a dialectic balance between economics, ecology, religion, idealism, health issues, cultural revitalization, and politics. In other words, they are integrated into the contemporary communities.

Let me reemphasize that I think it is extremely valuable to revive some of the traditional ecological connections, and that, especially in a dominant society that is drifting toward a denial of the importance of historical or traditional meanings, the upholding of cultural and social tradition is a necessity. I see two dangers, however. First, traditional people, as valuable and necessary as their vision is, do not articulate "the Lakota," or even "the Native American" vision concerning relations to buffalo. Less traditional people hold ideas that are just as valuable and authentic. Second, the use of terms, such as "sacred" and "continuous" or "time immemorial" is misleading in the context of a dominant culture—and the context of indigenous societies that take increasingly essentialist stands—that does not always understand how these concepts incorporate pragmatism and change in their traditional meaning. To achieve an understanding of contemporary communities, in all their complexities, and to analyze buffalo programs as community projects, it is necessary to look at all relationships with the buffalo, not to focus on the historical relations, although traditions and historical events—and non-events (Fogelson 1989), which are just as important in this context—clearly shape the present.

"Land and economics are intertwined in Indian country," says Fouberg (2000:155), and I would argue that there is more to the connection than economics. The Lakota today are not only integrated directly into the dominant economic system, but they are also subjected to the hegemony of ecological approaches that are in turn influenced by that system. Because land and economy are intertwined on plains reservations, to bring back a self-sufficient economy means to reestablish and guard a sustainable ecological system. Such a system can only survive, however, on the basis and with the support of a cultural background supportive of it. To only say that land and economy are intertwined, then, leaves out the mediator between the two, which is culture, ways of life, knowledge, and wisdom. It is important to make the connection between land, economics, and culture, however, because the same factors contributed to the near extermination of both buffalo and American Indians, the loss of the American Indian land base, and the destruction of the existing ecosystem: "The premises that led to conflict between settlers and American Indians were the same as those that led to the destruction of the tall grass prairie" (Bateson and Bateson 1987:176). These premises were a desire for the land and a belief in the Manifest Destiny and notions of progress and superiority.

Contemporary premises that are leading to efforts to restore the prairie are the same as those that lead to outside efforts to restore the health of American Indian nations. The notion that diversity—biological and cultural—is relevant and important has come to the forefront of at least a growing part of the dominant society. This has led to an understanding of respect toward other people and other species and a sense of responsibility for those previously oppressed. How deeply these notions pervade the dominant society is difficult to say, but they have grown important enough to carve out some metaphorical and literal space for both buffalo and Lakota.

At the moment, the literal space, namely the land base, still resembles protective parks, and sometimes it is not clear whether the inside or the outside is supposed to be protected from the other. Responsibility for others too often includes the assumption of guardianship over others. Whether the metaphorical space can grow enough for the bison or the Lakota to carve out some real agency for themselves will be the crucial question of the future. "Because of their increasingly threatened status and their cultural distinctiveness, rural peasant and tribal groups are now perceived as an endangered human resource worth saving for the benefit of modern society," says Stanford Zent (1999:92). To be saved for the benefit of the dominant society is not what people, or the buffalo, for that matter, need or want. Only after the dominant society will give up the idea that things can only be allowed to exist if they are of a benefit for it will people and buffalo be able to live their own cultures.

One of the benefits of local sovereignty for the larger society would be that the historic land appropriation and its consequences has always stood, and is still standing, in the way of a truly democratic republic. The law of conquest is fundamentally opposed to the law of equitable distribution or democracy, and the expanding United States under Manifest Destiny and under politicians, who had much to gain from the former, had neither intention nor interest to uphold the latter two. The people who had the land taken away from them fell through the invisible hands that, indeed, never showed up, and right under the wheels of capitalism. For the new settlers to be able to claim the land as theirs, rightfully theirs, previous owners had not just to give it up: they had to disappear. As Raymond Craib says (2000:10), "'imperial history' assigns meaning retrospectively and from without, rejecting context, locality, and specificity." Locality was rejected by the grids and parcellization, and context and specificity lay in the hands of the national media and government supporting westward expansion. Having already been erased from public memory, the remaining context and specificity was, and is, the physical existence of the previous owners, who would just not disappear as they were supposed to.

It was not only the land that had to change hands to fulfill a destiny that was manifest for its believers; indigenous cultures and French or Spanish cultures, in a somewhat lesser sense, were seen to be at best an obstacle to "civilization." On the steps of the unilinear evolution in which the dominant society believed, the next step for American Indians was agriculture. Even those who honestly tried to help the Plains Indians were convinced that "agriculture was essential for their assimilation; to sow and to reap was the true route to permanent prosperity and good character, to civilization" (Limerick 1987:124). After all, the favorite ideology of the day was social evolution, a theory that conveniently legitimized industrial capitalism as the highest form of achievable culture—if one was an industrial capitalist, of course. In the eyes of the elite, by bringing people civilization, they were taught rational thinking and resource management, which in turn freed up land for Americans. This was what Bernard Sheehan calls "the symmetry of the process": "the ultimate good of the native demanded the adoption of civilization; the end could not be achieved lest he surrendered the land; and the white man stood ready to accept it from him" (1973:169). The aesthetic seduction of that ideology was too great to be resisted.

This symmetry is not the only aesthetic part of the process, and American Indian peoples were not the only ones that were subjected to it. "Indian residents were not the only complication; once the United States acquired land that had been in the possession of France and Spain, prior land claims under the laws of other empires added to the legal wilderness" (Limerick 1987:60). Following the argument of aestheticism, I am tempted to read Patricia Nelson Limerick's "legal wilderness" not metaphorically, but literally: "prior land claims under the laws of other empires added to the legal *wilderness*."

The conception of wilderness in the West can be seen as a strategy of evasion from prior land claims. Wilderness describes a region that has seen none or only minimal, intermittent human presence. To declare land as legal wilderness—in both senses—is therefore a direct response (and denial) of any former claims to it. No older forms of land tenure exist, and therefore the new forms can be imposed on the land at will, or in some religious perspectives have to be imposed on the land. Frederic Jameson sees customary forms of collective land tenure, which are stamped out by the process of modernization, to be the bases of "religious or, anthropological concepts of 'the sacred'" (1998:67). And indeed, many people in the United States think of wilderness lands as sacred lands, to be saved from the onslaught of modernity and Western ideology.

The idea of wilderness is something specific to settler societies; the conception of land as it is being played out in the United States is thus not so much European or Western as a marker of a culture in the process of expansion. Although there is always a contrast between nature and culture, played out in the immediate living quarters and their environment, the idea of wilderness is the transformation of that contrast to the total environment. Some parts of the environment, the concept says, are not in the realm of human habitation or humanity, and they are therefore, in the eye of the various beholders, more impure or more pure. The fact that wilderness has become pure in the postmodern environmental movement is a remarkable reversal of the traditional nature/culture dichotomy, one of the central dichotomies that the Puritans and most settlers held. In contrast to this possible subjection of the total environment to the distinction between pure and impure, however the meanings are associated, Claude Lévi-Strauss points out that Europe is "unacquainted with virgin nature since our landscape is manifestly subservient to man" (1992:93).

Edmund Leach thinks that the "contrast between human Culture and Nature is very striking. Visible, wild, Nature is a jumble of random curves;

it contains no straight lines and few regular geometrical shapes of any kind. But the tamed, man-made world of Culture is full of straight lines, rectangles, triangles, circles and so on" (1976:51). This is true in the abstract, when we consider our distinction between the two concepts: it is also true for conscious efforts to impose abstract culture on nature, such as the grid lines and section lines imposed on the U.S. landscape. Leach says that "Whenever human beings construct a dwelling or lay out a settlement they do so in a geometrically ordered way" (51). I agree with Leach, although settlements in nonsettler societies are not so much following mathematically correct orders as the organic geometry of the land, rivers, or roads (which in turn follow natural contours). It is obvious to the native beholder that the landscape in these societies is deeply affected by human activities. Lévi-Strauss can thus say that, "even the most rugged landscapes of Europe have a kind of order" (1992:93). The resulting "sublime harmony" of the environment, which is sometimes "taken as representing the authentic wildness of the landscape," however, "far from being a spontaneous manifestation of nature, is the result of agreements painstakingly evolved during a long collaboration between man and the landscape" (93–94). It is only through the conscious imposition on the total landscape of the abstract distinctions of culture/nature, pure/impure, civilized/primitive, human/inhuman, and inhabited/uninhabited that wilderness was created, by relegating the original inhabitants and collaborators to the realm of nature. What is called wilderness is the evidence of this sublime harmony that can still be seen; not wilderness, then, but in fact the opposite, an order created in perhaps unconscious collaboration, but collaboration, nonetheless. U.S. landscapes must have shown a similar sublime harmony before the impact of people who disregarded social agreements—like rigorous zoning laws, for example—in the favor of individual economic progress:

> In the inhabited regions of America . . . there are only two alternatives: either nature has been so ruthlessly mastered that it has been turned into an open-air factory rather than a rural area . . . , or . . . the territory has been sufficiently inhabited by man for him to have had time to lay it waste but not long enough for slow and continuous cohabitation to have raised it to the dignity of a landscape (Lévi-Strauss 1992:94).

One does not have to follow Jameson's economic argument to see that the sacred is bound to aspects of a nonalienated culture and has no place in a homogenized environment. The sacred is nothing more than the revelation of an extremely pragmatic sublime harmony. It is this harmony that leads to sustainability.

Sustainability has always been an issue on the plains, like it has been in all areas of the world where resources are rare. In fact, from a local perspective, the history of the region can be seen as one big experiment in sustainability. Paleoindians, the horse cultures, early farmers and ranchers, modern agriculture, and American Indian reservations all have to deal primarily with issues of sustainability, and it would be foolish to assume that the people who live in this environment do not know that or do not care. Although the Buffalo Commons proposal springs from the tenet that the current use of the land is not sustainable, I see the resistance to the proposal more as a reaction to a perceived outside idealism than as a rejection of the basic tenet. People who live in a complex environment—and by that I do not mean complex institutional structures, but complex, hard to control interactions— know that idealistic solutions often fail because they leave no room for pragmatism. The constant local rejection of the idealistic principles simultaneously with an ongoing change to an actual buffalo commons shows how pragmatism works. True sustainability, then, comes directly from and out of local communities, whose members, in their daily lives, deal with holistic complexities, not with ideological or idealistic categories.

As Dean Howard Smith points out (1994:187), there has been, in the last fifteen years, a realization that "although tribal enterprises and entrepreneurial activity must be competitive in the global or local marketplace, the goals of those activities need not be the same as those of non-Indian businesses." The management practices and profit orientation of non-Indian companies are not necessarily compatible to the Indian social environment, but reservations have to be competitive so they can actually contribute to reaching those noneconomic goals. Sustainability does have an economic component, after all. The process can perhaps be described as the restoration of a "Middle Ground" (White 1991:50–93).

Michael Harkin says that "[Middle grounds] represent a stage in the power relations between ethnic groups at which no one side can dominate," and concludes that, from an historical perspective, "Middle grounds are a moment in the larger, fundamentally asymmetrical relationship between Indian and European—certainly not a useful way of understanding this relationship as a whole" (1997:155). This analysis rests on the axiom that the relationship is "fundamentally asymmetrical," and this has obviously been the case throughout the general history of the settlement and colonization of America. To understand this history, and the present, in terms of the middle ground, is thus certainly not fruitful, but I suggest that an understanding of the relations in terms of absences of middle ground can be rewarding, especially because these absences are rooted in the structural and functional bases of the dominant society.

If sustainability is hampered by dependency because outside forces have divergent, often extractive, interests from locals, then a middle ground between locals and outsiders, or at least between local and outside values, has to be reached to attain sustainability. Thus, sustainability can be reached if, and only if, a balanced relationship can be invented and maintained, despite the concerted and continuous efforts this will take from both sides. This relationship does not have to show exact symmetry in all aspects, either, only an overall balance. Such a middle ground has to incorporate continuous change; it therefore cannot be based on an ideological or legal fixation of its terms but needs to thrive on the willingness of all sides to seek mutual understandings and compromises. The possibility to achieve this is what the buffalo have brought to American Indian reservations and to a wide ranching community beyond them.

Tribal efforts at building buffalo ranches are probably reaching more people outside the reservations than the Buffalo Commons proposal reached on the reservations. Many non-Indian ranchers are adopting ecological and social concepts from tribal efforts. In terms of middle grounds, I see a possibility of plains communities breaching political and cultural differences and becoming a social, cultural, and even political plains community. This is made possible by the neglect the federal government and the national society show not only toward American Indian reservations, but toward rural plains society at large (Davidson 1990; Edmondson 2003). Although some groups on both sides are trying to exploit the conditions for political conflicts and zero-sum economic games, this is also a time when people can become aware of their common plight. Not unlike the situation of the French settlers during the historical era that gave rise to the middle ground, at least on a local and perhaps even regional level, the reservations and their neighboring communities and states are approaching a power balance and are increasingly finding themselves dependent on one another.

As Richard White says (1991:486), "Dependency is an economic, political, and social relationship, but it can also be an environmental relationship." This is especially true in locations such as the plains, where the land is the basis for everything else. Pte Hca Ka's decision to postpone placing the VE Ranch land in the hands of the tribe, for example, was an attempt to reach environmental sovereignty from the dominant society; it was also conceived by the tribal government as a move toward political and economic sovereignty vis-à-vis the tribe. The complex triangular relations between federal and state governments, tribal governments, and individual efforts on reservations make development efforts invariably an essay in pragmatics and compromises. They are, therefore, dependent on people to "have ears" (see DeMallie 1993); active cultural understanding, listening, and cooperation have always been the key to successful communities. It is the only way to build something akin to sublime harmony, or the sacred.

As this book enters production in late summer 2007, the bison corporation has been closed. Pte Hca Ka, Inc. is no longer in operation and exists only in history and memories. The slaughter and processing facility sits idle. The buffalo herd—in 2001 the largest tribally owned herd with over 3,500 animals—has been reduced to 220 bison. The large number of slaughtered animals beginning in 2004 was not locally sustainable; however, it was not supposed to be. The buffalo were slaughtered and sold off to bring in revenue desperately needed to pay off some of the $6 million in debt the corporation had incurred. These simple facts could be interpreted in many ways, and indeed I have heard many explanations and rumors. I will not repeat them here, but I would like to offer a few words on the closing of Pte Hca Ka, which suddenly rendered this contemporary ethnography a historic case study.

I have no doubt that some people will see Pte Hca Ka as simply another failed project on a reservation. They will point to a long list of other economic development, cultural revitalization, and ecological restoration projects on American Indian reservations that have, in their eyes, born no fruition. From this perspective, it might seem that Fred DuBray's notion in spring 2002 that the buffalo herd was large enough that it could not physically be eliminated was wrong. Others will contend that the entire project got off to a bad start because it focused on cultural revitalization instead of economics, amassed debts, and therefore could not be saved. Still others will blame the economic approach and insist that Pte Hca Ka would have found a way to survive if only the tribe had not intervened. I think all of these simplistic analyses fall short, however. That type of approach to issues on American Indian reservations—emphasizing the negative often to the point of defeatism—was what led me to write Pte Hca Ka's story in the first place.

Economically, the corporation was a disaster. The Game, Fish, and Parks Department is burdened by debt, and the tribe is still working to buy the VE land for itself. This will probably be followed by a lengthy and expensive attempt to turn it into trust land. Many people who worked for Pte Hca Ka have lost their jobs. In an economy where every job is a direly needed improvement, the loss of these jobs has extremely negative consequences.

Having said this, one of the argumentative centerpieces of this book is that indigenous economic development projects have their own standards of success and failure. Pte Hca Ka was not built with a primarily economic purpose in mind, and once it was reorganized, its structure and infrastructure was already in place, hindering the transformation to such an approach. A primarily economic evaluation is a perspective not necessarily in accordance with the cultural, social, and economic expectations and realities of the community. A long-term strategy for building sustainability, on which tribes have to operate, clearly needs to be evaluated according to criteria different from a short-term economic gains scheme already departing from available funds. The economic realities of operating on grants and loans without standing appropriation budgets leaves tribal programs no choice but to build what they can while the money lasts, then try to pay back the loans, and hope that they have at least built some usable assets. Although it is highly improbable that the corporation will be rebuilt along the same lines that it existed, the herd can be regrown given the political will and new funds. The dependence of tribal programs on external funds and the uncertainty that results is also demonstrated by the Prairie Management Program, whose work with black-footed ferrets came to a halt in 2007 when funds ran out. There is some hope that new grants can be secured in 2008 so that this important work can continue.

While the economic failure of the corporation is heartbreaking, the social and cultural impact of Pte Hca Ka should not be underestimated. For a time, the corporation was one of the most successful development projects in Indian Country. It certainly showed the possibilities of locally controlled community development. Many good people were drawn in by the corporation, voluntarily and involuntarily, and the community on the Cheyenne

River Sioux Reservation became engaged with, formulated ideas on, and applied policies to this development project. If economic, cultural, social, and political "development" must follow a comprehensive approach of liberation theology as I wrote in the beginning, and if this process must build something we can call the sacred as I tried to describe it, then Pte Hca Ka went a long way in achieving this process.

The economic, social, cultural, and political realities I describe defy any simplistic romantic notions of buffalo ranching and human-animal relationships. Those romantic notions are a product of wishful projection by the dominant society. But the story of Pte Hca Ka also shows vision, creativity, hard work, and a commitment to community that is not often seen. When I first came to Cheyenne River, I asked Michael Collins how my research could help the community. He told me that we never know what consequences our actions might have. All we can do is be honest and do our best. The people who worked for the buffalo have done exactly that.

References

Allan, George. 2000. Contexts without Absolutes. In *Being and Dialectic. Metaphysics as a Cultural Presence.* Ed. William Desmond and Joseph Grange, 101–23. Albany: State University of New York Press.

Allen, Joel A. 1876. *The American Bisons, Living and Extinct.* IV, no. 10. Cambridge, Mass.: Memoirs of the Museum of Comparative Zoology.

American Bison Association (ABA). 1993. *Bison Breeder's Handbook.* 3rd ed. Pierre: S. Dak.: American Bison Association.

American Indian Policy Review Committee (AIPRC). 1976. *Report on Reservation and Resource Development and Protection. Task Force Seven: Reservation and Resource Development and Protection. Final Report to the American Indian Policy Review Committee.* Washington, D.C.: U.S. Government Printing Office.

Amiotte, Arthur. 1987. The Lakota Sun Dance. Historical and Contemporary Perspectives. In *Sioux Indian Religion.* Ed. Raymond J. DeMallie and Douglas R. Parks, 75–89. Norman: University of Oklahoma Press.

Anakak, Buell. 1999. Magic Maker. In *Alaska Native Writers, Storytellers and Orators.* Exp. ed., 226–27. Anchorage: University of Alaska.

Anderson, Benedict. 1991. *Imagined Communities. Reflections on the Origin and Spread of Nationalism.* Rev. ed. New York: Verso.

Anderson Vern, Steve Metzger, and Dennis Sexhus. 1997. Commercial Bison Production in the Northern Plains. Carrington Research Extension Center, Beef and Bison Field Day 1997. www.ag.ndsu.nodak.edu/carringt/97beef/art8.htm.

Around Lakota Country. 2001. South Dakota Forum radio program. South Dakota Public Radio. July 19.

Askren, Mary Gales. 2002. Conservationist Reverses Effects of Poor Decisions. *Capital Journal.* June 28.

Balesi, Charles J. 1992. *The Time of the French in the Heart of North America, 1673–1818*. Chicago: Alliance Française Chicago.

Bamforth, Douglas B. 1988. *Ecology and Human Organization on the Great Plains*. New York: Plenum Press.

Barnhill, David Landis, and Roger S. Gottlieb, eds. 2001. *Deep Ecology and World Religions. New Essays on Sacred Ground*. Albany: State University of New York Press.

Basso, Keith H. 1996. *Wisdom Sits in Places. Landscape and Language among the Western Apaches*. Albuquerque: University of New Mexico Press.

Bateman, Rebecca B. 1996. Talking with the Plow: Agricultural Policy and Indian Farming in the Canadian and U.S. Prairies. *The Canadian Journal of Native Studies* 16(2):211–28.

Bateson, Gregory. 2000. *Steps to an Ecology of Mind*. Chicago: University of Chicago Press.

Bateson, Gregory, and Mary Catherine Bateson. 1987. *Angels Fear. Towards an Epistemology of the Sacred*. New York: Bantam.

Baydack, Richard K., James H. Patterson, Clayton D. Rubec, Allen J. Tyrchniewicz, and Ted W. Weins. 1996. Management Challenges for Prairie Grasslands in the Twenty-First Century. In *Prairie Conservation. Preserving North America's Most Endangered Ecosystem*. Ed. Fred B. Samson and Fritz L. Knopf, 249–59. Washington, D.C.: Island Press.

Beach, Hugh. 1981. *Reindeer-Herd Management in Transition. The Case of Tuorpon Saameby in Northern Sweden*. Uppsala Studies in Cultural Anthropology 3. Uppsala, Sweden: Acta Universitatis Upsaliensis.

Beatley, Timothy. 2004. *Native to Nowhere. Sustaining Home and Community in a Global Age*. Washington, D.C.: Island Press.

Beheler, John. 2001. Northern Plains Bison Education Network. Introduction to NPBEN. In *Bison Education Resource Guide*, 3–6. Unpublished document, Northern Plains Bison Education Network.

Bell, Ian. 2002. Co-op Forced to Delay Members' Payments. *The Western Producer*. May 2.

Bell Gease, Heidi. 2003. Lakota Man Credits Traditional Diet for Diabetes Control. *Rapid City Journal*. January 12. www.rapidcityjournal.com/articles/2003/01/12/news/local/news04.prt.

Belsky, A. J., A. Matzke, and S. Uselman. 1999. Survey of Livestock Influences on Stream and Riparian Ecosystems in the Western United States. *Journal of Soil and Water Conservation* 54:419–31.

Benedict, Russell A., Patricia W. Freeman, and Hugh H. Genoways. 1996. Prairie Legacies—Mammals. In *Prairie Conservation. Preserving North America's Most Endangered Ecosystem*. Ed. Fred B. Samson and Fritz L. Knopf, 149–66. Washington, D.C.: Island Press.

Bennett, John W. 1968. Reciprocal Economic Exchanges among North American Agricultural Operators. *Southwestern Journal of Anthropology* 24:276–307.

———. 1969. *Northern Plainsmen. Adaptive Strategy and Agrarian Life*. Arlington Heights, Ill.: AHM Publishing Corporation.

———. 1996. *Human Ecology as Human Behavior. Essays in Environmental and Development Anthropology*. New Brunswick, N.J.: Transaction Publishers.

Berger, Joel, and Carol Cunningham. 1994. *Bison. Mating and Conservation in Small Populations*. Methods and Cases in Conservation Science. New York: Columbia University Press.

Berkes, Fikret. 1999. *Sacred Ecology. Traditional Ecological Knowledge and Resource Management*. Philadelphia: Taylor and Francis.

Biegler, Martin. 1994. The First People. In *Timber Lake and Area, 1910–1985*. Pierre, S. Dak.: Timber Lake and Area Historical Society.

Bitterli, Urs. 1982. *Die 'Wilden' und die 'Zivilisierten'. Grundzüge einer Geistes- und Kulturgeschichte der europäisch-überseeischen Begegnung*. München, Germany: Beck.

Bland, David. 1994. Third World Islands in a Sea of Relative Prosperity. Minneapolis Fed Joins Effort to Capitalize Indian Reservations. *The Region*. www.mineeapolisfed .org/pubs/region/94–06/reg946b.cfm.

Boff, Leonard. 1997. *Cry of the Earth, Cry of the Poor*. Maryknoll, N.Y.: Orbis Books.

Bordewich, Fergus M. 1996. *Killing the White Man's Indian*. New York: Doubleday.

Bourland, Gregg. 2002. Where Do We Go from Here—Bourland on Referendum Election. *Eagle Butte News*. April 24.

Bragg, Thomas B., and Allen A. Steuter. 1996. Prairie Ecology—The Mixed Prairie. In *Prairie Conservation. Preserving North America's Most Endangered Ecosystem*. Ed. Fred B. Samson and Fritz L. Knopf, 53–65. Washington, D.C.: Island Press.

Braroe, Niels Winther. 1975. *Indian and White. Self-Image and Interaction in a Canadian Plains Community*. Stanford, Calif.: Stanford University Press.

Brasher, Philip. 1999. Footing a Buffalo Bill, U.S. Irks Cattlemen. *The Washington Post*. May 27.

Braun, Sebastian F. 1998. Ceremonies of Contact: Warfare and Exchange in Traditional North America. *Société Suisse des Américanistes Bulletin* 62:29–33.

———. 2002. 9–11-2001: History and Lakota Reactions. *Social Science Research Commitee, GSC Quarterly Newsletter*, No. 5, Summer. www.ssrc.org/programs/gsc/ gsc_quarterly/newsletter5/content/braun.page.

———. 2005. The United States. In *The Indigenous World 2005. Yearbook, International Work Group for Indigenous Affairs (IWGIA)*. Ed. Diana Vinding and Sille Stidsen, 84–92. Somerset, N.J.: Transaction Publishers.

———. 2007. Ecological and Un-Ecological Indians: The (Non)Portrayal of Plains Indians in the 'Buffalo Commons' Literature. In *Native Americans and the Environment: Perspectives on the Ecological Indian*. Ed. Michael E. Harkin and David Rich Lewis, 192–210. Lincoln: University of Nebraska Press.

"Bringing Back the Buffalo." 1995. *Newsweek*. May 29.

Brogden, Mette J., and James B. Greenberg. 2003. The Fight for the West: A Political Ecology of Land Use Conflicts in Arizona. *Human Organization* 62(3):289–98.

Brosius, Peter. 1999. Analyses and Interventions. Anthropological Engagements with Environmentalism. *Current Anthropology* 40(3):277–309.

———. 2001. Local Knowledges, Global Claims: On the Significance of Indigenous Ecologies in Sarawak, East Malaysia. In *Indigenous Traditions and Ecology. The Interbeing of Cosmology and Community.* Ed. John A. Grim, 125–57. Cambridge, Mass.: Harvard University Press.

Brown, Joseph Epes. 1997. *Animals of the Soul. Sacred Animals of the Oglala Sioux.* Rockport, Mass.: Element.

———. 1998. *The Spiritual Legacy of the American Indian.* New York: Crossroad.

Brown, Timothy. 2005. *The Relationship between Ethnic Identity and Cultural Perspective in the Struggle for Tribal Management of the National Bison Range.* Draft copy of paper, in possession of author.

Bucko, Raymond A. 1998. *The Lakota Ritual of the Sweat Lodge. History and Contemporary Practice.* Lincoln: University of Nebraska Press.

Bureau of Indian Affairs (BIA). 1957. *Progress Report on Individual and Tribal Rehabilitation Programs of Cheyenne River Sioux People to December 31, 1956.* Billings, Mont.: Bureau of Indian Affairs, Missouri River Basin Investigation Project.

———. 1958. *Present Status and Projected Future Needs of the Cheyenne River Rehabilitation Program as of April 15, 1958.* Billings, Mont.: Bureau of Indian Affairs, Missouri River Investigation Project, Central, Area and Agency Offices cooperating.

———. 1968. *Evaluation of Livestock Phase, Cheyenne River Rehabilitation Program, South Dakota.* Billings, Mont.: Bureau of Indian Affairs, Missouri River Basin Investigations Project.

———. 1994. *Draft Environmental Impact Statement for Livestock Grazing and Prairie Dog Management for the Rosebud and Cheyenne River Sioux Reservations.* Vols. I and II. Aberdeen, S. Dak.: Bureau of Indian Affairs.

———. 1999. *Indian Labor Force Report 1999.* Washington, D.C.: Bureau of Indian Affairs.

Bush, George W. 2001. *Address to a Joint Session of Congress and the American People.* Office of the Press Secretary of the White House, September 20.

Callenbach, Ernest. 1996. *Bring Back the Buffalo! A Sustainable Future for America's Great Plains.* Berkeley: University of California Press.

Cameron, Mindy. 2002. Muscular Metaphors for the Northern Plains. *Seattle Times.* April 22. http://seattletimes.nwsource.com/cgi-bin/PrintStory.pl?document_id=1344408113&slug-mindy22&date=20020422.

Carlin, Peter Ames, Margaret Nelson, Vickie Bane, and Sandra McElwaine. 1997. Buffalo Soldier. *People.* April 21.

Chasing Hawk, Robert. 2000. Chasing Hawk Responds to Runs After Letter. *Eagle Butte News.* November 7.

Cheyenne River Sioux Tribe (CRST). 1992. *Prairie Management Plan for the Cheyenne River Sioux Reservation.* Unpublished document in possession of author.

Christofferson, April. 2004. *Buffalo Medicine.* New York: Tor Books.

Churchill, Ward. 1997. *A Little Matter of Genocide.* San Francisco: City Lights.

Conley, Karen. 2000a. Status of the Bison Industry. *Bison World* January: 136–39.

———. 2000b. Future of the Bison Industry. *Bison World* January: 156–58.

Cook, Peggy J. 1999. Recent Indicators send Mixed Signals about Rural Economic Performance. *Rural Conditions and Trends* 9(2):4–7.

Cook, Tom Kanatakeniate. 2003. Mitakuye Oyasin: A Response to the Looking Horse Proclamation, *Indian Country Today*. April 30.

Cornell, Stephen. 2000. Enhancing Rural Leadership and Institutions. Paper presented at Beyond Agriculture: New Policies for Rural America. Rural Conference, Kansas City, Mo.

Cornell, Stephen, and Joseph P. Kalt. 1990. Pathways from Poverty: Economic Development and Institution-Building on American Indian Reservations. *American Indian Culture and Research Journal* 14(1):89–125.

———. 1992. Reloading the Dice: Improving the Chances for Economic Development on American Indian Reservations. In *What Can Tribes Do? Strategies and Institutions in American Indian Development*. American Indian Manual and Handbook Series No. 4. Los Angeles: American Indian Studies Center.

Craib, Raymond B. 2000. Cartography and Power in the Conquest and Creation of New Spain. *Latin American Research Review* 35(1):7–36.

Crosby, Alfred W. 1986. *Ecological Imperialism. The Biological Expansion of Europe, 900–1900*. Cambridge: Cambridge University Press.

"CRST Bails Out Buffalo Corp—Again." 2002. *Eagle Butte News*. November 28.

Crum, Robert. 1997. Healing the Spirit. *Wildlife Conservation* March/April: 36–43.

Cudmore, Ginny. 1984. The Annexation of Armstrong County. In *Timber Lake and Area, 1910–1985*, 113–14. Pierre, S. Dak.: Timber Lake and Area Historical Society.

Cunfer, Geoff. 2005. *On the Great Plains. Agriculture and Environment*. College Station: Texas A & M University Press.

Cushman, Frances, and Gordon Macgregor. 1948. *Harnessing the Big Muddy*. United States Indian Service, Lawrence, Kans.: Haskell Institute Print Shop.

Custer State Park. 2001. The Bison! *Tatanka* 22.

Danbom, David B. 1997. Why Americans Value Rural Life. *Rural Development Perspectives* 12(1):15–18.

Danz, Harold P. 1997. *Of Bison and Man*. Niwot: University Press of Colorado.

Dary, David A. 1989. *The Buffalo Book. The Full Saga of the American Animal*. Athens, Ohio: Swallow Press/Ohio University Press.

Davidson, Osha Gray. 1990. *Broken Heartland. The Rise of America's Rural Ghetto*. New York: Doubleday.

Davis, Lawrence J. 1944. *The Socio-Cultural Change in the Cheyenne River Sioux Indians as a Result of Contact with White Civilization*. Master's Thesis, University of Southern California.

Davis, Thomas. 2000. *Sustaining the Forest, the People, and the Spirit*. Albany: State University of New York Press.

Dawson, Bruce. 2002. 'Better Than a Few Squirrels': The Greater Production Campaign on the First Nations Reserves of the Canadian Plains. In *Plain Speaking. Essays on*

Aboriginal Peoples and the Prairie. Ed. Patrick Douaud and Bruce Dawson, 11–21. Regina, Saskatchewan: Canadian Plains Research Center.

Deloria, Ella. 1944. *Speaking of Indians*. New York: Friendship Press.

Deloria, Vine, Jr. 1991. 'Buffalo Commons' Misunderstood," *Rocky Mountain News*. May 4.

——. 1997. Anthros, Indians, and Planetary Realities. In *Indians and Anthropologists*. Ed Thomas Biolsi and Larry J. Zimmerman, 209–21. Tucson: University of Arizona Press.

DeMallie, Raymond J. 1978. Pine Ridge Economy: Cultural and Historical Perspectives. In *American Indian Economic Development*. Ed. Sam Stanley, 237–312. The Hague: Mouton Publishers.

——, ed. 1984. *The Sixth Grandfather. Black Elk's Teachings Given to John G. Neihardt*. Lincoln: University of Nebraska Press.

——. 1987. Lakota Belief and Ritual in the Nineteenth Century. In *Sioux Indian Religion. Tradition and Innovation*. Ed. Raymond J. DeMallie and Douglas R. Parks, 25–43. Norman: University of Oklahoma Press.

——. 1993. 'These Have no Ears': Narrative and the Ethnohistorical Method. *Ethnohistory* 40(4):515–38.

Densmore, Frances. 1992. *Teton Sioux Music and Culture*. Lincoln: University of Nebraska Press.

Devlin, Sherry. 2003. Debate on the Range. *Missoulian*. May 16. www.missoulian.com/articles/2003/05/16news/top/news01.txt.

Donahue, Debra L. 1999. *The Western Range Revisited. Removing Livestock from Public Lands to Conserve Native Biodiversity*. Norman: University of Oklahoma Press.

Donovan, Lauren. 2001. Could N.D. Empty Out and Become a Lawless Frontier? *Bismarck Tribune*. September 16. www.bismarcktribune.com/articles/2001/09/16/139-nws-4.txt.

Downs, James. 1973. Comments on Plains Indian Cultural Development. In *Cultural Ecology. Readings on the Canadian Indians and Eskimos*. Ed. Bruce A. Cox, 171–73. Toronto: McClelland and Stewart.

Driskell, Judy A., Martin J. Marchello, David W. Giraud, and Ahmad Sulaeman. 2004. Vitamin and Selenium Content of Ribeye Cuts from Grass- and Grain-Finished Bison from the Same Herd. *Journal of Food Quality* 27:388–98.

DuBray, Fred. 1993. Ethno-Ecological Considerations in Bison Management. In *Proceedings, North American Public Bison Herds Symposium*, Lacrosse, Wis.: 392–98. Unpublished document in possession of author.

——. 2000. DuBray Defends Practices of Pte Hca Ka. *Eagle Butte News*. October 19.

Duchéneaux, Frank. 1956. The Cheyenne River Sioux," *The American Indian* VII(3): 20–30.

Duchéneaux, Wayne L. 2001. Former Chairman Wayne Ducheneaux Refutes *TIME* Magazine Story. *Eagle Butte News*. July 5.

Dumond, Don E. 1980. A Chronology of Native Alaskan Subsistence Systems. *Senri Ethnological Studies* No. 4:23–47.

Dupree, Calvin. 1982. Fred and Mary Dupuis. In *South Dakota's Ziebach County. History of the Prairie*, 345–47. Pierre, S. Dak.: Ziebach County Historical Society.

Duraiappah, Anantha. 1996. *Poverty and Environmental Degradation: A Literature Review and Analysis*. CREED Working Paper Series No 8. London: Collaborative Research in the Economics of Environment and Development.

Dussel, Enrique. 1998. Beyond Eurocentrism. The World-System and the Limits of Modernity. In *The Cultures of Globalization*. Ed. F. Jameson and M. Miyoshi, 3–31. Durham, N.C.: Duke University Press.

Eagleton, Terry. 1997. *The Ideology of the Aesthetic*. Oxford, U.K.: Blackwell.

Economic Research Service (ERS). 2002a. *County-Level Poverty Rates for South Dakota*. February 10. www.ers.usda.gov/data/povertyrates/PovListpct.asp?st=SD.

——. 2002b. *County-Level Unemployment and Median Household Income for South Dakota*. February 10. www.ers.usda.gov/data/unemployment/RDList2.asp?ST=SD.

——. 2006. *Profiles of America: Demographic Data and Graphics Builder*. December 30. http://maps.ers.usda.gov/Profiles/index.aspx.

Edgcomb, Elaine L., and Tamra Thetford. 2004. *The Informal Economy. Making it in Rural America*. Washington, D.C.: The Aspen Institute.

Edgerton, Robert B. 1992. *Sick Societies. The Myth of Primitive Harmony*. New York: Free Press.

Editorial Cartoon. 2003. *Indian Country Today*. April 25. http://indiancountry.com/pix/105128924_small.gif.

Edmondson, Jacqueline. 2003. *Prairie Town. Redefining Rural Life in the Age of Globalization*. Lanham, Md.: Rowman and Littlefield Publishers.

Edwards, John. 1996. Symbolic Ethnicity and Language. In *Ethnicity*. Ed. John Hutchinson and Anthony D. Smith, 227–29. Oxford: Oxford University Press.

Edwards, Peter J., and Cyrus Abivardi. 1997. Ecological Engineering and Sustainable Development. In *Restoration Ecology and Sustainable Development*. Ed. Krystyn M. Urbanska, Nigel R. Webb and Peter J. Edwards, 325–52. Cambridge: Cambridge University Press.

Egan, Dave, and Bill Whitney. 1994. Buffalo Commons: Model or Metaphor? *Forum for Applied Research and Public Policy* 9(4):109–13.

Ellen, Roy F. 1986. What Black Elk Left Unsaid. On the Illusionary Images of Green Primitivism. *Anthropology Today* 2(6):8–12.

Ellingson, Ter. 2001. *The Myth of the Noble Savage*. Berkeley: University of California Press.

Enterline, James Robert. 2002. *Erikson, Eskimos and Columbus. Medieval European Knowledge of America*. Baltimore: The Johns Hopkins University Press.

Erikson, Patricia Pierce, with Elma Ward and Kirk Wachendorf. 2002. *Voices of a Thousand People. The Makah Cultural and Research Center*. Lincoln: University of Nebraska Press.

Escobar, Arturo. 1995. *Encountering Development. The Making and Unmaking of the Third World*. Princeton, N.J.: Princeton University Press.

Ewers, John C. 1955. *The Horse in Blackfoot Indian Culture*. Bureau of American Ethnology, No. 159. Washington, D.C.: U.S. Government Printing Office.

Fabrikant, Geraldine, and Stephanie Strom. 2003. Bison Burgers, for Humanity's Sake. *New York Times*. October 5.

Fadler, Ted. 1995. Dimensions of the Human-Animal Bond. *The IHS Provider* 20(11):145–49.

Feraca, Stephen E. 1998. *Wakinyan. Lakota Religion in the Twentieth Century*. Lincoln: University of Nebraska Press.

Ferguson, James. 1994. *The Anti-Politics Machine. "Development," Depoliticization, and Bureaucratic Power in Lesotho*. Minneapolis: University of Minnesota Press.

Ferreira, Mariana Leal, and Gretchen Chesley Lang, eds. 2006. *Indigenous Peoples and Diabetes. Community Empowerment and Wellness*. Durham, N.C.: Carolina Academic Press.

Fertig, Fred. 1970. Child of Nature. The American Indian as an Ecologist. *Sierra Club Bulletin* 55(8): 4–7.

Field, Tom. 2001. Homegrown Talent. The Eagles Take Flight, and the CEO's Hopes Soar with Them. *CIO Magazine*. October 1. www.crstlti.com/pages/talent.html.

Flores, Dan L. 1996. A Long Love Affair with an Uncommon Country: Environmental History and the Great Plains. In *Prairie Conservation. Preserving North America's Most Endangered Ecosystem*. Ed. Fred B. Samson and Fritz L. Knopf, 3–17. Washington, D.C.: Island Press.

Fogarty, Mark. 2002. Four Bands Community Fund Steps Up Pace of Loans. *Indian Country Today*. March 6.

Fogarty, Mark, and Robert Taylor. 2002. Micro Loans Open Doors for Small Business. *Indian Country Today*. February 14. www.indiancountry.com/content.cfm?id= 1013632185.

Fogelson, Raymond D. 1989. The Ethnohistory of Events and Nonevents. *Ethnohistory* 36(2):133–47.

Foreman, Dave. 2004. *Rewilding North America. A Vision for Conservation in the 21st Century*. Washington, D.C.: Island Press.

Foster, John Bellamy. 2000. *Marx's Ecology. Materialism and Nature*. New York: Monthly Review Press.

Fouberg, Erin Hogan. 2000. *Tribal Territory, Sovereignty, and Governance. A Study of the Cheyenne River and Lake Traverse Indian Reservations*. New York: Garland Press.

Fowler, Loretta. 1987. *Shared Symbols, Contested Meanings. Gros Ventre Culture and History, 1778–1984*. Ithaca, N.Y.: Cornell University Press.

Franscell, Ron. 2002. Indians' Aim: Better Diet. *Denver Post*. November 8.

Freeman, Milton M. R., Marc G. Stevenson, Richard A. Caulfied, Igor I. Krupnik, and Ingmar Egede. 1998. *Inuit, Whaling, and Sustainability*. Walnut Creek, Calif.: Alta Mira Press.

Game, Fish and Parks Department (GFPD). 1999. *Terrestrial Wildlife Habitat Restoration Plan for Oahe Reservoir on the Cheyenne River Sioux Reservation*. Cheyenne River Sioux Reservation: Game, Fish and Parks Department.

Gardner, Katy, and David Lewis. 1996. *Anthropology, Development and the Post-Modern Challenge*. London: Pluto Press.

Garroutte, Eva Marie. 2003. *Real Indians. Identity and the Survival of Native America*. Berkeley: University of California Press.

Gauthier, David A. 1994. The Buffalo Commons on Canada's Plains. *Forum for Applied Research and Public Policy* 9(4):118–20.

Geist, Valerius. 1991. Phantom Subspecies: The Wood Bison *Bison bison* "athabascae" Rhaods 1897 is Not a Valid Taxon, but an Ecotype. *Arctic* 44(4):283–300.

———. 1996. *Buffalo Nation. History and Legend of the North American Bison*. Stillwater, Okla.: Voyager Press.

Gilbert, Luke. 1941. Brief History of the Cheyenne River Indian Reservation. In *50th Anniversary, Establishment of the Cheyenne River Indian Agency, August 16, 1891 at Cheyenne Agency, S. Dak*. Unpublished document in possession of author.

Gilkey, Langdon. 1993. *Nature, Reality, and the Sacred. The Nexus of Science and Religion*. Minneapolis, Minn.: Fortress Press.

Glassie, Herny. 2006. *The Stars of Ballymenone*. Bloomington: Indiana University Press.

Goodstein, Carol. 1995. Buffalo Comeback. Native Americans Try Restoring a Spiritual Economy Based on Bison. *The Amicus Journal* Spring: 34–37.

Gottfried, Herbert. 1997. Corridors of value. Rural Land in Rural Life. *Rural Development Perspectives* 12(1):11–14.

Graham, Judith. 2002. For Tribes, Bringing Back Buffalo a Labor of Love. *Chicago Tribune*. November 3.

Grandin, Temple. 2001. Buffalo Handling Requirements. In *Bison Education Resource Guide*, 289–92. Northern Plains Bison Education Network, unpublished document in possession of author.

Gray, Gary G. 1993. *Wildlife and People. The Human Dimensions of Wildlife Ecology*. Urbana: University of Illinois Press.

Grim, John A. 2001. Indigenous Traditions and Deep Ecology. In *Deep Ecology and World Religions. New Essays on Sacred Ground*. Ed. David L. Barnhill and Roger S. Gottlieb, 35–57. Albany: State University of New York Press.

Haines, Francis. 1995. *The Buffalo. The Story of American Bison and Their Hunters from Prehistoric Times to the Present*. Norman: University of Oklahoma Press.

Hall, Derek, and Greg Richards, eds. 2000. *Tourism and Sustainable Community Development*. London: Routledge.

Harkin, Michael E. 1997. *The Heiltsuks. Dialogues of Culture and History on the Northwest Coast*. Lincoln: University of Nebraska Press.

Harkin, Michael E., and David Rich Lewis, eds. 2007. *Native Americans and the Environment. Perspectives on the Ecological Indian*. Lincoln: University of Nebraska Press.

Harlan, Bill. 2001. Buffalo Commons: Professor Believes Its Time Has Come. *Rapid City Journal*. August 25. www.rapidcityjournal.com/articles/2001/08/25/news01.txt.

Harries-Jones, Peter. 1995. *A Recursive Vision. Ecological Understanding and Gregory Bateson*. Toronto: University of Toronto Press.

Harriman, Peter. 2006. State's Ranchers Market Meat to Rejuvenate their Herds. *Argus Leader*. February 3.

Harrison, Faye V., ed. 1991. *Decolonizing Anthropology. Moving Further toward an Anthropology of Liberation*. Arlington, Va.: American Anthropological Association.

Harrod, Howard L. 2000. *The Animals Came Dancing. Native American Sacred Ecology and Animal Kinship*. Tucson: University of Arizona Press.

Harvard Project on American Indian Economic Development (HPAIED). 1999. *Honoring Nations. Tribal Governance Success Stories, 1999*. Cambridge, Mass.: Harvard University, John F. Kennedy School of Government.

Hastorf, Christine A., and Sissel Johannessen. 1994. Becoming Corn Eaters in Prehistoric America. In *Corn and Culture in the Prehistoric New World*. Ed. Sissel Johannessen and Christine A. Hastorf, 427–43. Boulder, Colo.: Westview Press.

Hilbert, Robert. 1987. Contemporary Catholic Mission Work among the Sioux. In *Sioux Indian Religion. Tradition and Innovation*. Ed. Raymond J. DeMallie and Douglas R. Parks, 139–47. Norman: University of Oklahoma Press.

Holder, Preston. 1970. *The Hoe and the Horse on the Plains*. Lincoln: University of Nebraska Press.

Hone, Emily. 1992. Tribal Buffalo Herd Attracts Tourists, Marketed at Tribal Enterprises. *News from Indian Country*. August 31.

Hoover, Michael T. 1992. *Wildlife on the Cheyenne River and Lower Brule Sioux Reservations: A History of Use and Jurisdiction*. Vermillion: University of South Dakota Press.

Horkheimer, Max, and Theodor Adorno. 1994. The Concept of Enlightenment. In *Ecology. Key Concepts in Critical Theory*. Ed. Carolyn Merchant, 44–50. Amherst, N.Y.: Humanities Press International.

Hornaday, William Temple. 2002. *The Extermination of the American Bison*. Washington, D.C.: Smithsonian Institution Press.

Howarth, William. 1997. The Value of Real Life in American Culture. *Rural Development Perspectives* 12(1):5–10.

Hudson, Robert J. 1998. From Prairie to Paddock: Shifting Paradigms in Bison Management. In *International Symposium on Bison Ecology and Management in North America*. Ed. Lynn R. Irby and James E. Knight, 233–37. Bozeman: Montana State University.

Huffstetter, Stephen. 1998. *Lakota Grieving*. Chamberlain, S. Dak.: Tipi Press.

Humphrey, Kay. 2001a. Cheyenne River Residents get Help Seeking Help. *Indian Country Today*. August 15.

———. 2001b. Native American Populations Show Strong Community Ties. *Indian Country Today*. October 24. www.indiancountry.com/content.cfm?id=2734.

———. 2001c. Tribal College Bailout plan Part of a Proposed $30 Million Bond Issue. *Indian Country Today*. December 5. www.indiancountry.com/content.cfm?id=1007153947.

Hunhoff, Bernie. 1993. When the Buffalo Roamed. *South Dakota Magazine* March/April: 12–16.

Huntington, Henry P. 1992. *Wildlife Management and Subsistence Hunting in Alaska.* London: Belhaven Press.

Indian Health Service (IHS). 2002. *Demographic Statistics Section of Regional Differences in Indian Health 2000–2001. Tables Only. Issued: July 2, 2002.* Rockville, Md.: Indian Health Service.

Indigenous Diabetes Education Alliance (IDEA). 2003. *Indigenous Diabetes Education Alliance.* April 9. www.geocities.com/aaninin/IDEA_info.html.

Ingold, Tim. 1980. *Hunters, Pastoralists and Ranchers. Reindeer Economies and Their Transformations.* Cambridge: Cambridge University Press.

——. 1987. *The Appropriation of Nature. Essays on Human Ecology and Social Relations.* Iowa City: University of Iowa Press.

Interagency Working Group on Environmental Justice (IWGEJ). 2003a. *Interagency Working Group on Environmental Justice Revitalization Projects.* January 2. www.epa.gov/compliance/resources/publications/ej/interagency/iwg_demo_projects _intro.pdf.

——. 2003b. *New Revitalization Demonstration Projects(15).* January 2. www.epa.gov/ compliance/resources/publications/ej/interagency/iwg_2003_demo_projects.pdf.

InterTribal Bison Cooperative (ITBC). 1996. *Gifts of the Buffalo Nation. An Educational Coloring Book.* Rapid City, S. Dak.: Spizzirri Press.

——. 1998. *ITBC Annual Report 1996–1997. Restoring a Lifestyle.* Rapid City, S. Dak.: ITBC.

Isenberg, Andrew C. 2001. *The Destruction of the Bison: An Environmental History, 1750–1920.* Cambridge: Cambridge University Press.

Iverson, Peter. 1994. *When Indians Became Cowboys. Native Peoples and Cattle Ranching in the American West.* Norman: University of Oklahoma Press.

——. 1998. *"We Are Still Here." American Indians in the Twentieth Century.* Wheeling, Ill.: Harlan Davidson.

Iverson, Peter, and Linda MacCannell. 1999. *Riders of the West. Portraits from Indian Rodeo.* Seattle: University of Washington Press.

Jackson, Bob. 2001a. Practical Applications for Natural Systems Bison Production. In *Bison Education Resource Guide,* 44–49. Northern Plains Bison Education Network, unpublished document in possession of the author.

——. 2001b. Yellowstone Bison and an Iowa Experiment. In *Bison Education Resource Guide,* 59–68. Northern Plains Bison Education Network, unpublished document in possession of the author.

——. 2002. Building Family Social Order for More Efficient Grazing, Better Breeding and Reduced Inputs. *Native Herds* January: 32.

Jameson, Fredric. 1997. *Postmodernism or, The Cultural Logic of Late Capitalism.* Durham, N.C.: Duke University Press.

——. 1998. *The Cultural Turn. Selected Writings on the Postmodern, 1983–1998.* London: Verso.

Jocks, Christopher. 1998. Living Words and Cartoon Translations: Longhouse 'Texts' and the Limitations of English. In *Endangered Languages. Language Loss and*

Community Response. Ed. Lenore A. Grenoble and Lindsay J. Whaley, 217–33. Cambridge: Cambridge University Press.

Jones, Lisa, and Linda Platts. 1995. Land-Grant Professor Offers Navajo Herders a Helping Hand. In *High Country News* 27(8):11.

Kalstad, Johan Klemet. 1998. Pastoralism and Management of Common Land in Saami Districts. In *Commons in a Cold Climate. Coastal Fisheries and Reindeer Pastoralism in North Norway: The Co-Management Approach*. Ed. Svein Jentoft, 235–46. Man and the Biosphere Series Vol. 22. Paris: United Nations Educational, Scientific and Cultural Organization.

Kansas Center for Community Economic Development (KCCED). 2004. *Economic Trends Report: Cheyenne River Counties*. Policy Research Institute Technical Report Series. Report No. 74. The University of Kansas, Kansas Center for Community Economic Development.

Katz, Eric. 2000. Against the Inevitability of Anthropocentrism. In *Beneath the Surface. Critical Essays in the Philosophy of Deep Ecology*. Ed. Eric Katz, Andrew Light, and David Rothenberg, 17–42. Cambridge: MIT Press.

Kelley, Matt. 1993. Indians Work to Restore Buffalo on Tribal Lands. *Huron Plainsman*. January 3.

Kidwell, Clara Sue. 1973. Science and Ethnoscience. *The Indian Historian* 6(4):43–54.

King, Frank John, III. 2001. Poverty Is Our Greatest Addiction. *Indian Country Today*. December 5. www.indiancountry.com/content.cfm?id=1007154562.

Klose, Nelson. 1964. *A Concise Study Guide to the American Frontier*. Lincoln: University of Nebraska Press.

Knowles, Craig J., Carl D. Mitchell, and Mike Fox. 1998. Trends in Bison Management: What It Means for the Species. In *International Symposium on Bison Ecology and Management in North America*. Ed. Lynn R. Irby and James E. Knight, 244–50. Bozeman: Montana State University.

Kougl, Alfred, and Ginny Cudmore. 1984. Early Day Ranching. In *Timber Lake and Area, 1910–1985*, 34–40. Pierre, S. Dak.: Timber Lake and Area Historical Society.

Kozlowicz, John. 2001. Bison to Stay. Legislators Reconsider Shutting down Muscoda Farm. February 7. www.muscodabison.com/Bison/Articles/bison_to_stay.htm.

Krech, Shepard, III. 1999. *The Ecological Indian. Myth and History*. New York: W. W. Norton.

Krist, John. 2002. Tourists Could Swamp Montana, Other States. *Rocky Mountain News*. January 27.

Kroeber, A. L. 1939. *Cultural and Natural Areas of Native North America*. University of California Publications in American Archaeology and Ethnology, Volume 38. Berkeley: University of California Press.

Krupnik, Igor. 1993. *Arctic Adaptations. Native Whalers and Reindeer Herders of Northern Eurasia*. Hanover: University Press of New England.

Kurkiala, Mikael. 1997. *"Building the Nation Back Up." The Politics of Identity on the Pine Ridge Reservation*. Uppsala Studies in Cultural Anthropology 22. Uppsala, Sweden: Acta Universitatis Upsaliensis.

Kurz, Rudolph Friederich. 2005. *On the Upper Missouri. The Journal of Rudolph Friederich Kurz*. Ed. and abridged Carla Kelly. Norman: University of Oklahoma Press.

Lanier, Jennifer L., and Temple Grandin. 2001. The Calming of American Bison (*Bison bison*) during Routine Handling. In *Bison Education Resource Guide*, 284–88. Northern Plains Bison Education Network, unpublished document in possession of author.

Lansing, J. Stephen. 1991. *Priests and Programmers. Technologies of Power in the Engineered Landscape of Bali*. Princeton, N.J.: Princeton University Press.

Lawson, Michael L. 1982. *Dammed Indians. The Pick-Sloan Plan and the Missouri River Sioux, 1944–1980*. Norman: University of Oklahoma Press.

Leach, Edmund. 1976. *Culture and Communication. The Logic by which Symbols Are Connected*. Cambridge: Cambridge University Press.

LeMay, Konnie. 1993. DuBray Reserved about Buffalo Slaughterhouse. *Indian Country Today*. January 14.

Leopold, Aldo. 1991a. Pioneers and Gullies [1924]. In *The River of the Mother of God and Other Essays by Aldo Leopold*. Ed. Susan L. Flader and J. Baird Callicott, 106–13. Madison: University of Wisconsin Press.

———. 1991b. Wilderness as a Form of Land Use [1925]. In *The River of the Mother of God and Other Essays by Aldo Leopold*. Ed. Susan L. Flader and J. Baird Callicott, 134–42. Madison: University of Wisconsin Press.

———. 1991c. The Farmer as a Conservationist [1939]. In *The River of the Mother of God and Other Essays by Aldo Leopold*. Ed. Susan L. Flader and J. Baird Callicott, 255–65. Madison: University of Wisconsin Press.

Lévi-Strauss, Claude. 1963. *Structural Anthropology*. New York: Basic Books.

———. 1966. *The Savage Mind*. Chicago: University of Chicago Press.

———. 1992. *Tristes Tropiques*. New York: Penguin.

Licht, Daniel S. 1994. The Great Plains. America's Best Chance for Ecosystem Restoration, Part 1 and 2. *Wild Earth* Summer: 47–53 and Fall: 31–36.

———. 1997. *Ecology and Economics of the Great Plains*. Lincoln: University of Nebraska Press.

Limerick, Patricia Nelson. 1987. *The Legacy of Conquest. The Unbroken Past of the American West*. New York: W.W. Norton & Co.

Loayza, Don Roman. 2000. The Struggle for Local Independence and Self-Determination. *Mountain Research and Development* 20(1):16–19.

Looking Horse, Arvol. 2003. Further Thoughts on the Protection of Ceremonies. *Indian Country Today*. July 9.

Lopez Community Land Trust (LCLT). 2002. *Mobile Meat Processing Unit*. May 23. www.lopezclt.org/sard/mpu.html.

Lott, Dale F. 1998. Impact of Domestication on Bison Behavior. In *International Symposium on Bison Ecology and Management in North America*. Ed. Lynn R. Irby and James E. Knight, 103–106. Bozeman: Montana State University.

MacGregor, Gordon. 1946. *Warriors without Weapons. A Study of the Society and Personality Development of the Pine Ridge Sioux.* Chicago: University of Chicago Press.

Malinowski, Bronislaw. 1992. *Argonauts of the Western Pacific. An Account of Native Enterprise and Adventure in the Archipelagoes of Melanesian New Guinea.* London: Routledge.

Manning, Richard. 1997. *Grassland. The History, Biology, Politics, and Promise of the American Prairie.* New York: Penguin.

Mapes, Lynda V. 2001. San Juan Farmers' Plan Is a Cut Above. *Seattle Times.* November 26. http://seattletimes.nwsource.com/cgi-bin/PrintStory.pl?document_id=134371066&slug=26m&date=20011126.

Marchello, Martin J. n.d. *Palatability and Nutrient Composition of Grass-Finished Bison.* Manuscript in possession of author.

Marchello, Martin J., and Judy A. Driskell. 2001. Nutrient Composition of Grass- and Grain-Finished Bison. *Great Plains Research* 11(1):65–82.

Marshall, Joseph M., III. 2001. *The Lakota Way.* New York: Penguin.

Marshall, Robert. 1937. Ecology and the Indians. *Ecology* 18(1):159–61.

Martin, Glen. 2001. Where the Buffalo Roam, Again. Humans Are Disappearing from Great Plains as Bison and other Wildlife Return. *San Francisco Chronicle.* April 22.

Martinez, Dennis. 1994. Traditional Environmental Knowledge Connects Land and Culture: American Indians Serve as the Link. *Winds of Change* Autumn: 89–94.

Marx, Karl, and Friedrich Engels. 1990. Manifest der Kommunistischen Partei (1848). In *Karl Marx, Friedrich Engels, Studienausgabe, Band III, Geschichte und Politik 1.* Ed. Iring Fetscher, 59–87. Frankfurt, Germany: Fischer.

Matthews, Anne. 1992. *Where the Buffalo Roam. The Storm over the Revolutionary Plan to Restore America's Great Plains.* New York: Grove Weidenfeld.

McHugh, Tom. 1972. *The Time of the Buffalo.* Lincoln: University of Nebraska Press.

McNeal, Lyle G. 1997. *A Condensed History of Navajo Sheep Production.* Sheepdex G-9. Logan, Utah: The Navajo Sheep Project.

Medicine, Beatrice. 1987. Indian Women and the Renaissance of Traditional Religion. In *Sioux Indian Religion. Tradition and Innovation.* Ed. Raymond J. DeMallie and Douglas R. Parks, 159–71. Norman: University of Oklahoma Press.

———. 2007. *Drinking and Sobriety among the Lakota Sioux.* Lanham, Md.: Alta Mira Press.

Melmer, David. 1997. Cheyenne River Residents Survivors. *Indian Country Today.* February 10.

———. 2001a. Crow Creek Lawsuit Freezes Missouri River Land Transfer. *Indian Country Today.* December 29. www.indiancountry.com/content.cfm?id=1009572270.

———. 2001b. Bison Distribution Favors American Indian Tribes. *Indian Country Today.* December 18. www.indiancountry.com/content.cfm?id=1008719737.

———. 2002a. Oglala Sue Army Corps Over Land Issue. *Indian Country Today.* January 18. www.indiancountry.com/content.cfm?id=1011375064.

———. 2002b. Land Issue Goes to Appeals Court. *Indian Country Today.* March 27.

Mignolo, Walter D. 1998. Globalization, Civilization Processes, and the Relocation of Languages and Cultures. In *The Cultures of Globalization.* Ed. Frederic Jameson and Masao Miyoshi, 32–53. Durham, N.C.: Duke University Press.

Milton, Kay. 1999. *Environmentalism and Cultural Theory. Exploring the Role of Anthropology in Environmental Discourse.* London: Routledge.

Mintz, Sidney W. 2003. *Devouring Objects of Study: Food and Fieldwork.* The David Skomp Distinguished Lectures in Anthropology. Bloomington: Indiana University.

Mizrach, Steven. 1999. *Natives on the Electronic Frontier: Technology and Cultural Change on the Cheyenne River Sioux Reservation.* Ph.D. Dissertation, University of Florida.

Müller, Werner. 1970. *Glauben und Denken der Sioux. Zur Gestalt archaischer Weltbilder.* Berlin: Dietrich Reimer Verlag.

Murg, Wilhelm. 2003. Is the Bison Industry Buffaloed? *Indian Country Today.* September 10.

Murray, Joanna. 2003. *Cheyenne River Sioux Reservation, South Dakota. Preliminary Community Mini-Plan.* Rural Community Planning SOC 640/650. http://sdrurallife .sdstate.edu/Rural_Planning_&_Development/Community_Planning_Projects/Che yenne_River_Sioux_Tribe.pdf.

National Buffalo Association (NBA). 1990. *Buffalo Producer's Guide to Management and Marketing.* National Buffalo Association.

National Park Service (NPS). 2000. *Bison Management for the State of Montana and Yellowstone National Park. Comments on the Draft Environmental Impact Statement.* vol. 3. Washington, D.C.: U.S. Department of the Interior.

National Wildlife Federation (NWF). 2001. *Restoring the Prairie. Mending the Sacred Hoop. Prairie Conservation and Restoration on the Cheyenne River Reservation.* www.nwf.org/wildlife/pdfs/RestoringPrairie.pdf.

Native America Calling. 2001. Saving the Wild Horses. *Native America Calling.* November 1.

Navajo Tradition. 1993. Navajo Tradition. Linking "Ag" with "Culture." *Deseret News.* September 4.

Nederveen Pieterse, Ian. 2004. *Globalization and Culture. Global Mélange.* Lanham, Md.: Rowman and Littlefield Publishers.

Nobles, Gregory H. 1997. *American Frontiers. Cultural Encounters and Continental Conquest.* New York: Hill and Wang.

North American Bison Journal (NABJ). 2001. Bison Co-op Cuts Prices to Regain Financial Footing. *North American Bison Journal* October: 9, 12.

Northern Great Plains Rural Development Commission (NGPRDC). 1997a. *Northern Great Plains Rural Development Commission Narrative.* February 10. www.ngplains .org/NGP_Commission.pdf.

———. 1997b. *Civic and Social Capacity Work Group Final Report.* February 10. www.ngplains.org/CivicandSocial.pdf.

O'Brien, Dan. 2001. *Buffalo for the Broken Heart. Restoring Life to a Black Hills Ranch.* New York: Random House.

O'Brien, Sharon. 1989. *American Indian Tribal Governments.* Norman: University of Oklahoma Press.

O'Nell, Theresa DeLeane. 1996. *Disciplined Hearts. History, Identity, and Depression in an American Indian Community.* Berkeley: University of California Press.

Paper, Jordan. 2001. 'Daoism' and 'Deep Ecology': Fantasy and Potentiality. In *Daosim and Ecology. Ways within a Cosmic Landscape.* Ed. N. J. Girardot, James Miller, and Liu Xiaogan, 3–21. Cambridge: Harvard University Press.

Parman, Donald L. 1994. *Indians and the American West in the Twentieth Century.* Bloomington: Indiana University Press.

Patterson, Marshall. 2001a. Preparation of Bison for Public Sales Venues. *SaskBISONews* September: 5–6.

——. 2001b. Bison Behavioral Management and Handling Facilities Design. *SaskBISO News* December: 5–7.

——. 2002a. Bison Behavioral Management and Handling Facilities Design. *SaskBISO News* June: 2–3.

——. 2002b. Bison Behavioral Management and Handling Facilities Design. *SaskBISO News* October: 6–7.

Perez, Jennifer. 2003. Tribal Meat Packing Plant near Malta to Open Aug. 4. *Great Falls Tribune.* July 24.

Peterson, Richard. 2001. Bi'Shee. *National Museum of the American Indian* 2(3):12–15.

Pickering, Kathleen Ann. 2000. *Lakota Culture, World Economy.* Lincoln: University of Nebraska Press.

——. 2004. Decolonizing Time Regimes: Lakota Conceptions of Work, Economy, and Society. *American Anthropologist* 106(1):85–97.

Pickering, Kathleen, and David Mushinski. 2001. Making the Case for Culture in Economic Development: A Cross-Section Analysis of Western Tribes. *American Indian Culture and Research Journal* 25(1):45–64.

Pickering, Robert B. 1997. *Seeing the White Buffalo.* Denver: Denver Museum of Natural History Press.

Pike, Bill. 1974. My Philosophy of Indian Education. In *An Indian Philosophy of Education.* Ed. John F. Bryde. Vermillion: Institute of Indian Studies, University of South Dakota.

Plumb, Glenn E., and Jerrold L. Dodd. 1993. Foraging Ecology of Bison and Cattle on a Mixed Prairie: Implications for Natural Area Management. *Ecological Applications* 3(4):631–43.

Plumwood, Val. 2000. Deep Ecology, Deep Pockets, and Deep Problems: A Feminist Ecosocialist Analysis. In *Beneath the Surface. Critical Essays in the Philosophy of Deep Ecology.* Ed. Eric Katz, Andrew Light, and David Rothenberg, 59–84. Cambridge: MIT Press.

Poole, D. C. 1881. *Among the Sioux of Dakota. Eighteen Months Experience as an Indian Agent.* New York: D. van Nostrand.

Pooley, Julie Ann, and Moira O'Connor. 2000. Environmental Education and Attitudes. Emotions and Beliefs Are What Is Needed. *Environment and Behavior* 32(5):711–23.

Popper, Deborah E., and Frank Popper. 1987. The Great Plains: From Dust to Dust. *Planning* December: 12–18.

———. 1994. Great Plains: Checkered Past, Hopeful Future. *Forum for Applied Research and Public Policy* 9(4):89–100.

———. 1999. The Buffalo Commons: Metaphor as Method. *Geographical Review* 89(4):491–510.

Popper, Frank. 1986. The Strange Case of the Contemporary American Frontier. *Yale Review* 76(1):101–21.

Porterfield, K. Marie. 1995. Bison Herds Thrive as Tribes Rebuild Heritage. *Indian Country Today*. November 9.

Powers, William K. 1982. *Oglala Religion*. Lincoln: University of Nebraska Press.

Prairie Management Program (PMP). 1999. *Prairie Management Plan Phase II for the Cheyenne River Sioux Tribe*, unpublished report in possession of author.

Public Law 106–53. 1999. Title VI-Cheyenne River Sioux Tribe, Lower Brule Sioux Tribe, and State of South Dakota Terrestrial Wildlife Habitat Restoration. PL 106–53, 106th Congress. 113 Stat. 385.

Public Law 106–511. 2000. Title I-Cheyenne River Sioux Tribe Equitable Compensation. PL 106–511, 106th Congress. 114 Stat. 2635.

Ramenstorfer, Bibiane. 1997. Cultural Survival, Cultural Revitalisation: Tribally Controlled Schooling or 'Reality Hits Back'. *Journal de la Société des Américanistes* 83:300–9.

Rappaport, Roy A. 1968. *Pigs for the Ancestors*. New Haven, Conn.: Yale University Press.

Rasmussen, Larry. 2000. Global Eco-Justice: The Church's Mission in Urban Society. In *Christianity and Ecology. Seeking the Well-Being of Earth and Humans*. Ed. Dieter T. Hessel and Rosemary Radford Ruether, 515–29. Cambridge, Mass.: Harvard University Press.

Rathge, Richard, and Paula Highman. 1998. Population Change in the Great Plains. A History of Prolonged Decline. *Rural Development Perspectives* 13(1):19–26.

Reimer, Bill, and Chris Tott, with Cheryl Croxen, Martin Hayes, Jennifer Perzow, Anna Woodrow. 1997. *Economic Integration and Isolation of First Nations Communities. Report I: An Exploratory Review*. Montreal: The Canadian Rural Restructuring Foundation, Concordia University.

Renfrew, Colin. 1993. Trade beyond the Material. In *Trade and Exchange in Prehistoric Europe*. Ed. Christopher Scarre and Frances Healy, 5–16. Oxbow Monograph 33.

Rice, Julian. 1994. *Ella Deloria's The Buffalo People*. Albuquerque: University of New Mexico Press.

Robert McLaughlin Co. 1994. *Analysis of Economic Loss Resulting from Lands Taken from the Cheyenne River Sioux Tribe for the Oahe Dam*, unpublished document in possession of author.

Rocky Mountain News. 1991. 'Buffalo Commons': Romantic Fantasy from the East. *Rocky Mountain News.* April 18.

Rodenberg, Hans-Peter. 1994. *Der imaginierte Indianer. Zur Dynamik von Kulturkonflikt und Vergesellschaftung des Fremden.* Frankfurt, Germany: Suhrkamp.

Roe, Frank Gilbert. 1951. *The North American Buffalo. A Critical Study of the Species in Its Wild State.* Toronto: University of Toronto Press.

——. 1955. *The Indian and the Horse.* Norman: University of Oklahoma Press.

Rorabacher, J. Albert. 1970. *The American Buffalo in Transition. An Historical and Economic Survey of the Bison in America.* Saint Cloud, Minn.: North Star Press.

Rowley, Thomas D. 1998. Sustaining the Great Plains. *Rural Development Perspectives* 13(1):2–6.

Rudner, Ruth. 2000. *A Chorus of Buffalo. Reflections on Wildlife Politics and an American Icon.* Short Hills, N. J.: Burford Books.

Russell, Sharman Apt. 1993. *Kill the Cowboy. A Battle of Mythology in the New West.* Lincoln: University of Nebraska Press.

Sahlins, Marshall. 1972. *Stone Age Economics.* New York: Aldine de Gruyter.

——. 1995. *"How Natives Think." About Captain Cook, For Example.* Chicago: University of Chicago Press.

Sandoz, Mary. 1954. *The Buffalo Hunters: The Story of the Hide Hunters.* New York: Hastings House.

Schreiber, Dorothee. 2002. Our Wealth Sits on the Table. Food, Resistance, and Salmon Farming in Two First Nation Communities. *American Indian Quarterly* 26(3):360–77.

Scott, Robert B. 1998. Wild Bison Restoration: The Suitability of Montana's Big Open. In *International Symposium on Bison Ecology and Management in North America.* Ed. Lynn R. Irby and James E. Knight, 360–73. Bozeman: Montana State University.

Selden, Ron. 2003. Fort Belknap opens promising meat packing venture. *Indian Country Today.* October 15.

Sell, Randall S., Dean A. Bangsund, and F. Larry Leistritz. 2000. *Contribution of the Bison Industry to the North Dakota Economy.* Agricultural Economics Report No. 442. Fargo: Department of Agricultural Economics, North Dakota State University.

Sellars, Richard West. 1997. *Preserving Nature in the National Parks. A History.* New Haven, Conn.: Yale University Press.

Sexsmith, Pamela. 2000. Traditional Foods Prevent Illness, Says Elder. *Saskatchewan Sage* 5(2):8.

Sheaff, Katharine. 2001, October. The 2000 Census and Growth Patterns in Rural America. *The Main Street Economist* October.

Sheehan, Bernard W. 1973. *Seeds of Extinction. Jeffersonian Philanthropy and the American Indian.* New York: W.W. Norton & Co.

Shell, Hanna Rose. 2002. Introduction. Finding the Soul in the Skin. In *The Extermination of the American Bison.* Ed. William Temple Hornaday, viii–xxiii. Washington, D.C.: Smithsonian Institution Press.

Shepard, John C. 1994. Grassroots Response from the Great Plains. *Forum for Applied Research and Public Policy* 9(4):101–105.

Shouse, Ben. 2005. Tribe Finds Profit in Buffalo Business. *Argus Leader*. April 13.

Smith, Dean Howard. 1994. The Issue of Compatibility between Cultural Integrity and Economic Development among Native American Tribes. *American Indian Culture and Research Journal* 18(2):177–205.

Smith-Morris, Carolyn M. 2004. Reducing Diabetes in Indian Country: Lessons from the Three Domains Influencing Pima Diabetes. *Human Organization* 63(1):34–46.

South Dakota Advisory Committee to the U.S. Commission on Civil Rights (SDAC). 2000. *Native Americans in South Dakota: An Erosion of Confidence in the Justice System*. Denver, Colo.: U.S. Commission on Civil Rights.

South Dakota Department of Tourism. n.d. *2001–2002 Guide to Indian Reservations and Art*. Pierre, S. Dak.: South Dakota Department of Tourism.

Stark, Mike. 2004. As Tribal Bison Herd gets Larger, Food Supply Dwindles. *Billings Gazette* January 24.

St. Pierre, Mark. 1991. *Madonna Swan. A Lakota Woman's Story*. Norman: University of Oklahoma Press.

St. Pierre, Mark, and Tilda Long Soldier. 1995. *Walking in the Sacred Manner. Healers, Dreamers, and Pipe Carriers—Medicine Women of the Plains Indians*. New York: Simon and Schuster.

Steinmetz, Paul B. 1998. *Pipe, Bible, and Peyote among the Oglala Lakota. A Study in Religious Identity*. Syracuse, N.Y.: Syracuse University Press.

Stevens, Stan, ed. 1997. *Conservation through Cultural Survival. Indigenous Peoples and Protected Areas*. Washington, D.C.: Island Press.

Strang, Veronica. 1997. *Uncommon Ground. Cultural Landscapes and Environmental Values*. Oxford: Berg.

Sullivan, Robert. 2000. *A Whale Hunt. How a Native American Village Did What No One Thought It Could*. New York: Simon and Schuster.

Suzuki, Peter T. 1999. The Bison Project of the Winnebago Tribe of Nebraska and Ethnic-enterprise Theory. *Journal of the Indian Anthropological Society* 34:139–48.

Swisher, Jay. 1994. South Dakotans Dig In, Seek to Stay on Plains. *Forum for Applied Research and Public Policy* 9(4):106–108.

Terkildsen, Monica. 2002. *The Lakota Connection. Sunka Wakan (horse) and the Lakota Oyate (people)*. February 28. www.ispmb.com/lakota.html.

Thorne, Christopher. 2001. Local Bison Cooperative Likely Winner of Contract. *Rapid City Journal*. December 3. www.rapidcityjournal.com/articles/2001/12/03/state03.txt.

Tinker, George E. 2004. *Spirit and Resistance: Political Theology and American Indian Liberation*. Minneapolis, Minn.: Fortress Press.

Torbit, Stephen C., and Louis LaRose. 2001. A Commentary on Bison and Cultural Restoration: Partnership between the National Wildlife Federation and the InterTribal Bison Cooperative. *Great Plains Research* 11(1):175–82.

Tribal Cup Charity Polo Match. 2002. January 24. http://horses.about.com/cs/news/a/eqpolo1120.html.

"Tribe Seeks $25 Million Bond Issue." 2002. *Eagle Butte News*. February 7.

Truett, Joe C., Michael Phillips, and Kyran Kunkel. 2001. Managing Bison to Restore Biodiversity. *Great Plains Research* 11(1):123–44.

Tsai, Chih Chung. 1994. *Zen Speaks. Shouts of Nothingness*. New York: Doubleday.

Tuhiwai Smith, Linda. 1999. *Decolonizing Methodologies. Research and Indigenous Peoples*. New York: Zed Books.

Tyndall, Margaret. 2000. Economic Development in Indian Country: Lessons Learned by The Lakota Fund. *Community Dividend* 2:6–11.

United Nations Educational, Scientific and Cultural Organization (UNESCO). 1977. *Development of Arid and Semi-Arid Lands: Obstacles and Prospects*. Man and the Biosphere (MAB) Technical Notes 6. Paris, France: UNESCO.

U.S. Census. 2002a. U.S. Census Bureau. State and County QuickFacts. *Dewey County, South Dakota*. February 10. http://quickfacts.census.gov/qfd/states/46/46041.html.

———. 2002b. U.S. Census Bureau. State and County QuickFacts. *Ziebach County, South Dakota*. February 10. http://quickfacts.census.gov/qfd/states/46/46137.html.

U.S. Department of Agriculture (USDA). 2002. *Livestock Slaughter, 2001 Summary*. USDA, National Agricultural Statistics Service. February 10. http://usda.mannlib .cornell.edu/reports/nassr/livestock/pls-bban/lsan0302.pdf.

Utley, Robert M. 1963. *The Last Days of the Sioux Nation*. New Haven, Conn.: Yale University Press.

Vaage, Leif E. 1997. Introduction. In *Subversive Scriptures. Revolutionary Readings of the Christian Bible in Latin America*. Ed. Leif E. Vaage, 1–23. Valley Forge, Penn.: Trinity Press International.

Vazeille, Danielle. 1977. *Le cercle et le calumet*. Toulouse, France: Privat.

Velarde Tiller, Veronica E. 1995. *American Indian Reservations and Indian Trust Areas*. Washington, D.C.: U.S. Department of Commerce, Economic Development Administration.

Vinje, David L. 1982. Cultural Values and Economic Development: U.S. Indian Reservations. *The Social Science Journal* 19(3):87–100.

Wagoner, Paula L. 2002. *"They Treated Us Just Like Indians." The Worlds of Bennett County, South Dakota*. Lincoln: University of Nebraska Press.

Walker, James R. 1983. *Lakota Myth*. Ed. Elaine A. Jahner. Lincoln: University of Nebraska Press.

———. 1991. *Lakota Belief and Ritual*. Ed. Raymond J. DeMallie and Elaine A. Jahner. Lincoln: University of Nebraska Press.

———. 1992. *Lakota Society*. Ed. Raymond J. DeMallie. Lincoln: University of Nebraska Press.

Weaver, T., Elizabeth M. Payson, and Daniel L. Gustafson. 1996. Prairie Ecology— The Shortgrass Prairie. In *Prairie Conservation. Preserving North America's Most Endangered Ecosystem*. Ed. Fred B. Samson and Fritz L. Knopf, 67–75. Washington, D.C.: Island Press.

Webb, Pauline. 2002. CRST Vote Forestalls Foreclosure. VE Ranch Safe for Now. *Eagle Butte News*. May 16.

Webb, Walter Prescott. 1981. *The Great Plains*. Lincoln: University of Nebraska Press.

Wernitznig, Dagmar. 2003. *Going Native or Going Naive? White Shamanism and the Neo-Noble Savage*. Lanham, Md.: University Press of America.

Whealdon, Bon I. and Robert Bigart. 2002. *"I Will Be Meat for my Salish." The Montana Writers Project and the Buffalo of the Flathead Indian Reservation*. Helena: Salish Kootenai College Press and Montana Historical Society Press.

Wheeler, Richard S. 1998. *The Buffalo Commons*. New York: Forge.

White, Richard. 1991. *The Middle Ground. Indians, Empires, and Republics in the Great Lakes Region, 1650–1815*. Cambridge: Cambridge University Press.

White Face, Charmaine. 2002. A Mouse Has Roared on the Missouri River. *Indian Country Today*. January 5. www.indiancountry.com/content.cfm?id=1010249880.

Wiebers, David O. 1995. Animals as Health Care Issues. *The IHS Provider* 20(11):137–40.

Williams, Florence. 2001. Plains Sense. Frank and Deborah Poppper's 'Buffalo Commons' is Creeping Toward Reality. *High Country News* 33(1). www.hcn.org/servlets/hcn.Article?article_id=10194.

Williams, Jeffrey R., and Penelope L. Diebel. 1996. The Economic Value of the Prairie. In *Prairie Conservation. Preserving North America's Most Endangered Ecosystem*. Ed. Fred B. Samson and Fritz L. Knopf, 19–35. Washington, D.C.: Island Press.

Wilson, T. A., R. J. Nicolosi, M. J. Marchello, and D. Kritchevsky. 2000. Consumption of Ground Bison Does Not Increase Early Atherosclerosis Development in Hypercholesterolemic Hamsters. *Nutrition Research* 20(5):707–19.

Wood, Judi. 2001. General Observations. In *Bison Education Resource Guide*, 72–80. Northern Plains Bison Education Network, unpublished document in possession of author.

Worster, Donald. 1977. *Nature's Economy. A History of Ecological Ideas*. Cambridge: Cambridge University Press.

Woster, Kevin. 2002a. Tribes' Lawsuits Delaying Transfer of River Rec Land. *Argus Leader*. January 2.

———. 2002b. Prairie Dog at Heart of Grasslands Debate. *Argus Leader*. January 21.

Wuerthner, George. 1998. Are Cows Just Domestic Bison? Behavioral and Habitat Use Differences between Cattle and Bison. In *International Symposium on Bison Ecology and Management in North America*. Ed. Lynn R. Irby and James E. Knight, 374–83. Bozeman: Montana State University.

Wuttunee, Wanda. 2004. *Living Rhythms. Lessons in Aboriginal Economic Resilience and Vision*. Montreal: McGill-Queen's University Press.

Yellow Horse Brave Heart, Maria, and Lemyra M. DeBruyn. 1998. The American Indian Holocaust: Healing Historical Unresolved Grief. *The Journal of the National Center on American Indian and Alaska Native Health Research* 8(2):60–82.

Young, Elspeth. 1995. *Third World in the First. Development and Indigenous Peoples*. London: Routledge.

Youth, Howard. 2000. Watching vs. Taking. *World Watch* May/June: 12–23.

Zent, Stanford. 1999. The Quandary of Conserving Ethnoecological Knowledge. A Piaroa Example. In *Ethnoecology. Knowledge, Resources, and Rights*. Ed. Ted L. Gragson and Ben G. Blount, 90–124. Athens: University of Georgia Press.

Ziebach County Historical Society (ZCHS). 1982. *South Dakota's Ziebach County. History of the Prairie*. Pierre, S. Dak.: State Publishing Co.

Zontek, Ken. 2003. *Sacred Symbiosis. The Native American Effort to Restore the Buffalo Nation*. Ph.D. Dissertation: University of Idaho.

Index

In this index the terms buffalo *and* bison *are used interchangeably as in the book. References to illustrations are in italic type.*